HELMSLEY
ARCHAEOLOGICAL SOCIETY

This book is lent on the understanding that it will be returned at the next meeting.
If this is not possible, please contact the librarian -
Pat Donnor..... Tel.

The cover is part of the enclosure plan for Snaith, Cowick and Rawcliffe made c.1754 by John Read, and now in Humberside County Council Record Office. The owners, Messrs R.A. and C.P. Heptonstall, of 11-13 Gladstone Terrace, Goole, have kindly given permission to make a copy of the plan. The photograph from which the cover was made was taken by Alan Marshall, photographer to the University of Hull, and the cover was printed by Clifford Ward of Bridlington. The cost of printing the cover was subsidised by Humberside County Council, through the Humberside County Record Office.

YORKSHIRE

ENCLOSURE AWARDS

BARBARA ENGLISH

Studies in Regional and Local History No. 5
University of Hull
Hull 1985

©Barbara English 1985

ISBN 0-85958-095-4

Written on an Apple II computer
with the word processing system ScreenWriter II

Printed in the University of Hull

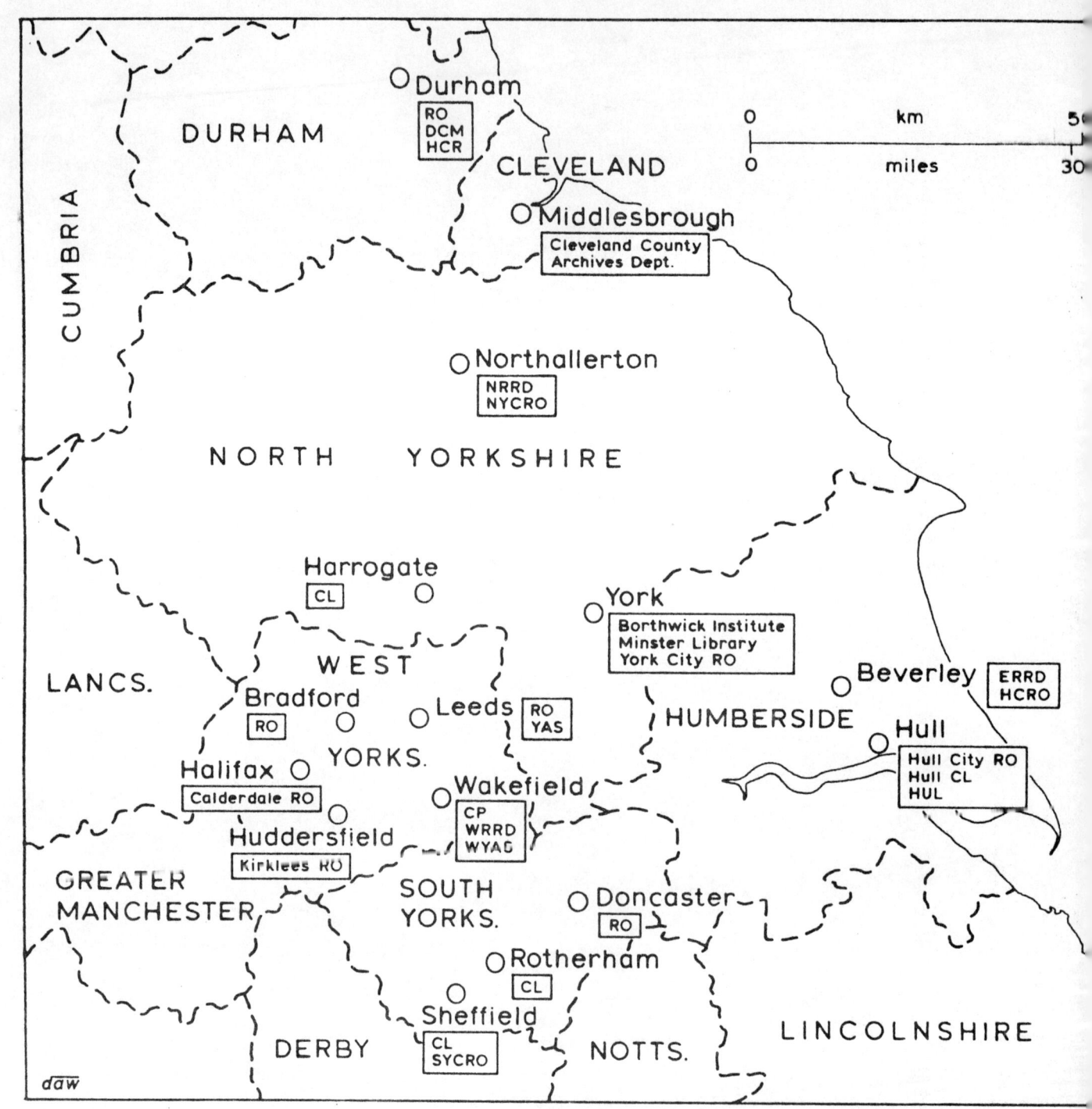

PRINCIPAL LOCATIONS OF YORKSHIRE ENCLOSURE AWARDS
(The abbreviations are explained on the following pages)

ABBREVIATIONS

Borthwick Institute York	The Borthwick Institute of Historical Research (University of York) St Anthony's Hall York YO1 2PW Tel: York 59861 ext.274
Bradford RO	West Yorkshire Archive Service Bradford, Central Library Prince's Way, Bradford BD1 1NN Tel: Bradford 753683
Calderdale RO	West Yorkshire Archive Service Calderdale, Central Library Northgate House, Halifax HX1 1UN Tel: Halifax 57257 ext.2636
Cleveland County Archives Dept	Cleveland County Archives Dept Exchange House, 6 Marton Road Middlesbrough TS1 1DB Tel: Middlesbrough 248321
CP Wakefield	Archives formerly in the custody of the Clerk of the Peace at Wakefield West Yorkshire Archive Service Newstead Road, Wakefield WF1 2DE Tel: Wakefield 367111 ext.2352
Doncaster RO	Archives Dept Doncaster MBC King Edward Road Balby, Doncaster DN4 0NA Tel: Doncaster 859811
Durham DCM	Durham Dean & Chapter Muniments The Prior's Kitchen The College, Durham DH1 3EQ Tel: Durham 64561 (see next entry)
Durham HCR	Durham Halmote Court Records 5 The College Durham DH1 3EQ Tel: Durham 61478 Both the Halmote Court Records and the Dean and Chapter muniments are administered by the Department of Palaeography & Diplomatic, University of Durham

Durham RO	Durham County Record Office, County Hall, Durham DH1 5UL Tel: Durham 64411 ext.2683
ERRD	East Riding Registry of Deeds Humberside County Record Office County Hall, Beverley HU17 9BA Tel: Hull 867131 ext.394
Guildhall London RO	Corporation of London Records Office PO Box 270, Guildhall London EC2 P2E Tel: 01 606 3030 ext.2251
HCRO	Humberside County Record Office County Hall, Beverley HU17 9BA Tel: Hull 867131 ext.394
HUL	Hull University Brynmor Jones Library Cottingham Road, Hull HU6 7RX Tel: Hull 497265
Hull City RO	Kingston upon Hull City Record Office, 70 Lowgate Kingston upon Hull HU1 2AA Tel: Hull 222015
Hull CL	Hull Central Library Albion Street, Hull HU1 3TF Tel: Hull 224040
Kirklees RO	West Yorkshire Archive Service Kirklees, Central Library Princess Alexandra Walk Huddersfield HD2 2SU Tel: Huddersfield 513808 ext.207
Lancs RO	Lancashire Record Office, Bow Lane, Preston PR1 8ND Tel: Preston 54868
Leeds RO	West Yorkshire Archive Service Leeds, Chapeltown Road Sheepscar, Leeds LS7 3AP Tel: Leeds 628339
Lincs AO	Lincolnshire Archives Office The Castle, Lincoln LN1 3AB Tel: Lincoln 25158

Notts RO	Nottinghamshire Record Office County House, High Pavement Nottingham NG1 1HR Tel: Nottingham 504524
Notts Univ. Lib.	Nottingham University Library (Manuscripts Department) University Park, Nottingham NG7 2RD Tel: Nottingham 506101 ext.3440
NRRD	North Riding Registry of Deeds County Hall Northallerton DL7 8A Tel: Northallerton 3123
NYCRO	North Yorkshire County Record Office, County Hall Northallerton DL7 8AD Tel: Northallerton 3123 ext.455
PRO (Chancery Lane)	Public Record Office Chancery Lane London WC2 A1L Tel: 01 405 0741
PRO (Kew)	Public Record Office Kew, Richmond TW9 4DU Tel: 01 876 3444
Rotherham CL	Rotherham Brian O'Malley Central Library Rotherham S65 1JH Tel: Rotherham 2121 ext.3119
Sheffield CL	Sheffield City Libraries Central Library, Surrey St Sheffield S1 1XZ Tel: Sheffield 734711
SYCRO	South Yorkshire County Record Office Cultural Activities Centre Ellin Street, Sheffield S1 4PL Tel: Sheffield 29191 ext.33
WRRD	West Riding Registry of Deeds West Yorkshire Archive Service Newstead Rd, Wakefield WF1 2DE Tel: Wakefield 367111 ext.2352
WYAS	West Yorkshire Archive Service Headquarters Newstead Rd, Wakefield WF1 2DE Tel: Wakefield 367111 ext.2352

YAS	Yorkshire Archaeological Society Claremont, Clarendon Road Leeds LS2 9NZ Tel: Leeds 456362
York City RO	York City Archives Art Gallery Building, Exhibition Square, York YO1 2EW Tel: York 51533
York Minster Library	York Minster Library Dean's Park, York YO1 2JD Tel: York 25308

YORKSHIRE ENCLOSURE AWARDS

Historians have long been aware of the importance of enclosure in many aspects of English history. Over centuries the open fields characteristic of many English shires, and the commons and moors that were once widespread, have been converted into the hedged or walled fields, of regular shape, that form the landscape of the twentieth century. This conversion took place piece by piece, at different times in different places, and it is not yet clear in which century most enclosure took place. Early enclosure (before c.1700) was not well recorded, but the age of Parliamentary enclosure, which in Yorkshire was from approximately the middle of the eighteenth century to the middle of the nineteenth century, resulted in the creation of detailed records of a landscape that was being altered. The chronology of enclosure may be uncertain; what is not in doubt is that the great majority of surviving records of the enclosure process come from the age of Parliamentary enclosure, c.1750 - c.1850, and these records form the basis of this list.

Enclosure by private agreement between landowners was often difficult to achieve, and in the eighteenth century increasing use was made of the process of the private act of Parliament. The first Yorkshire award made by private act was at Fangfoss cum Spittal with Scagglethorpe in the East Riding, the act being passed in 1726, followed by Thurnscoe, in the West Riding, in 1729. Hundreds more private enclosure acts followed; from 1836 the process was made easier by the passing of Public General Acts. The awards made recorded the enclosure and reallotment of either open fields where the open field strip system of agriculture had prevailed, or open meadow, or commons and wastes : in many cases all these types of land were enclosed together. Often the awards dealt in addition with roads, paths, and sometimes with tithes. The plan that normally accompanied the enclosure award is usually the earliest plan of that place that can be found. Enclosure awards and plan are one of the most useful types of topographic and economic record available to regional and local historians, and they still retain in addition administrative and legal importance.

Until April 1974 the county of Yorkshire was divided into three Ridings, East, North and West. Twenty years ago the present editor compiled a handlist of West Riding enclosure awards for the National Register of Archives. In 1971 Vanessa Neave produced a similar list for the East Riding: no separate list for the North Riding was ever made, but this gap was filled in 1978 by the publication of W.E. Tate's _A_ _Domesday_ _of_ _English_ _enclosure_ _acts_ _and_ _awards_, edited by M.E. Turner (the Library, University of Reading). The list that follows is not restricted absolutely to Parliamentary awards: it seemed perverse to ignore awards made by other means (most commonly agreement between the parties) if they were found in the course of searching. The relationship between agreement, act and award is not always a straightforward one, as some enclosures by agreement led to a Parliamentary award, and other agreements themselves encompassed the award. It is hoped that the list that follows includes all Yorkshire Parliamentary enclosures, but no attempt has been made to seek out and record all non-Parliamentary enclosure.

Before 1974 Yorkshire was a huge county, and the records of enclosure were divided between many different authorities and their record offices or libraries. After local government reorganisation, the same geographical area still contained as many record offices and libraries, but the situation was now made even more complicated by the movement of archives (particularly parish records) to the county record offices of the new units. The difficulty of locating enclosure awards and plans is the principal reason for the issue of a new list for the whole of the historic county of Yorkshire. At the same time the old East Riding and West Riding lists were revised, with the generous and whole-hearted co-operation of the principal record offices. Entries about awards in the old North Riding were the most difficult to compile; the basis of those that are recorded below is M.E. Turner's edition of W.E. Tate's Domesday of English enclosure acts and awards, supplemented by searches in the microfilmed volumes of the North Riding Registry of Deeds at Northallerton, catalogues of North Yorkshire archives available in some record offices, and information from the Public Record Office, the National Register of Archives and from annual accession lists. No access to original documents or office lists was permitted by the North Yorkshire County Record Office; fortunately in almost every case information about the awards could be found elsewhere.

The editor wishes to record her gratitude to the many people whose co-operation was essential to the compilation of the list. Vanessa Neave has very kindly allowed me to make use of her East Riding list (now unfortunately long out of print) which has provided, almost unaltered, the East Riding entries. Michael Turner, my colleague at the University of Hull, and the Librarian of the University of Reading, owner of the copyright, have most generously allowed me to abstract North Riding material from Michael Turner's edition of W.E. Tate's Domesday of English enclosure acts and awards. That volume is still in print, and will remain the standard catalogue for the whole country for decades to come; the present handlist is in no way a substitute for it, but is intended to serve as a finding list for Yorkshire historians. My inquiries have been

readily answered by the staff of Cleveland County Archives
Department; Cumbria Record Office; Doncaster MBC Archives
Department; Durham County Record Office;the University of
Durham, Department of Palaeography and Diplomatic; Hull
Central Library; Hull City Record Office; Hull University
Library; Humberside County Record Office; Lancashire Record
Office; Lincolnshire Archives Office; Nottinghamshire
Record Office; Nottingham University Library, Manuscripts
Department; the Brian O'Malley Central Library, Rotherham;
Sheffield City Libraries; South Yorkshire County Record
Office; the West Yorkshire Archives Service and its offices
at Wakefield, Bradford, Calderdale, Kirklees and Leeds; York
City Archives; the Dean and Chapter Library at York; the
Borthwick Institute of Historical Research at York; the
Yorkshire Archaeological Society and the Public Record
Office. To all those archivists and librarians who helped
me by allowing me to see enclosure papers and lists, and who
sent me copies of their lists, and amendments to earlier
lists I express my gratitude. Without their assistance this
list would not have been made. I have been greatly helped
by Jan Crowther, who has also contributed the index of
commissioners and surveyors and a bibliography. My
colleague David Neave has provided, as always, constructive
advice and encouragement.

The illustration on the cover comes from a plan
deposited in Humberside County Record Office by Messrs R.A.
and C.P. Heptonstall of Goole, who generously allowed it to
be reproduced. The cost of the cover was subsidised by
Humberside County Council.

NOTES ON THE ENTRIES

PLACE-NAMES have been cited in the form used in the index of
place-names in the 1971 Census published by HM Stationery
Office, supplemented where necessary by the Yorkshire
volumes of the English Place-Name Society.

COUNTIES are shown in brackets after the place-name, the
former county (ER, NR or WR, representing East Riding, West
Riding or North Riding of Yorkshire) followed by the county
in which the place was situated in 1985 (generally H, NY, SY
or WY, representing Humberside, North Yorkshire, South
Yorkshire or West Yorkshire). Some places formerly in one
of the Ridings of Yorkshire are now in Cleveland, Cumbria,
Durham, Lancashire, Greater Manchester or Nottinghamshire.

DATES represent the date of the act, (or sometimes the
agreement) followed by the date of the award. In the case
of an award under a General Act, the date of the order is
given.

AREA ENCLOSED. The second line of the entry gives the name or nature of the lands to be enclosed as described in the act or award. The acreage is included where possible, either estimated (from the act) or awarded (from the award). Many of the acreages have been taken from W.E. Tate, <u>A Domesday of English Acts and Awards</u>, edited by M.E.Turner (The Library, Reading, 1978)

COMMISSIONERS are named in most cases (if they are not named in the list, it is either because they were not named in the award, or because the information was not available). An index to the commissioners and surveyors is printed below, p.164.

AWARDS. Two or more sealed documents recording the award were usually made under each act, and often the act stated where these sealed documents were to be kept: the parish chest or the archives of a great landowner often housed awards, and there was normally a copy with the Clerk of the Peace of the County, or in the Registry of Deeds (see below). These awards are described and numbered, i,ii etc. Copies and photographs of awards and plans are also included: an exception to this rule is the collection of photographs of awards and plans in the North Yorkshire Record Office at Northallerton, of which no list was made available. An explanation of the list of abbreviations which denote places where enclosure awards and plans could be found in 1985, is printed above.

REGISTRIES OF DEEDS. All three Ridings of Yorkshire possessed offices in which deeds of title were registered from the early eighteenth century until the 1970s. Most Yorkshire enclosure awards were enrolled in the registry and sometimes in addition sealed copies of the awards were deposited there. The registries are represented by the abbreviations ERRD (East Riding Registry of Deeds), NRRD (North Riding Registry of Deeds) and WRRD (West Riding Registry of Deeds). The registries are now annexed to the County Record Offices of Humberside at Beverley, of North Yorkshire at Northallerton, and of West Yorkshire at Wakefield.

PLANS. Where a plan has been found and details of it are available, these are given in brackets after the entry "plan" as follows: any date given is that of the plan, followed by the name of the surveyor, if known. If there are buildings on the plan this is mentioned. Sometimes the whole of the parish or township was shown (not just the area enclosed) and this is recorded. If there are open field features or open field names on the plan, these are mentioned. The scale of the plan, if noted, is given.

1   ABBOTSIDE, HIGH AND LOW (NR-NY)   1824 : 1837
        Common stinted pasture, moors, commons and waste : 930
        acres estimated
        Commissioners Jeremiah Coulton, Thomas Bradley
    i   NRRD GM no.11 p28, GM no.12 p43 two enrolled awards and
        three plans (not dated, not signed, 8 ch=1"; not dated,
        not signed, buildings, 8 ch=1"; 1835, not signed, 25
        ch=1")

2   ABBOTSIDE, HIGH (NR-NY)   1840 : 1851
        Pasture : 128 acres awarded
        Commissioner Richard Garth
    i   NYCRO QDD(D) Bk 5 p169 enrolled award and plan (1851,
        surveyor Richard Garth, 3 ch=1")
    ii NYCRO QDD(I) no.3 original award

3   ABBOTSIDE, HIGH AND LOW (NR-NY)   1880 : 1881
        Common : 9701 acres awarded
        Commissioner Thomas Firbank King
    i   NYCRO QDD(I) no.1 enrolled award and plan (Ordnance
        Survey, 6" = 1 mile).   Margaret King signed plan
    ii PRO (MAF 1 531) award

    ABERFORD (WR-WY) see Becca; Lotherton

4   ACKLAM (ER-NY)   1769 : 1776
        Common fields, pasture : 796 acres awarded
        Commissioners John Graves, John Cleaver, John Dickinson
        Surveyor Joseph Dickinson
    i   ERRD AT/308/33 enrolled award

5   ACKLAM (ER-NY)   1852 : 1854
        Wold, waste : 310 acres estimated
        Commissioner and surveyor Edward Donkin
    i   HRCO IA award and plan (1854, 2 ch=1")
    ii PRO (MAF 1 393) award

6   ACKTON (WR-WY)   1812 : 1816
        Stinted pasture called Ackton Pasture and waste : 60
        acres estimated
        Commissioners Jonathan Teal (died), John Bower, Henry
        Teal
    i   WRRD B32 p177 enrolled award
    ii Featherstone UDC award and plan (surveyor William
        Pilkington)
    iii PRO DL/45/8/4 enrolled extract of award

7   ACKWORTH (WR-WY)   1772 : 1774
        Open fields, commons, waste, a stinted pasture called
        the Cow Pasture: 652 acres awarded
        Commissioners William Hill, Henson Kirkby, John Law
    i   WRRD B10 p34 enrolled award
    ii YAS MSS 933, 1064 extracts of award and copy of part of
        plan of 1774 (not signed, no scale) made 20 cent. from
        originals with the vicar of Ackworth
    iii WYAS D77/84 award and Z45 copy plan
    iv Sheffield CL NBC 64 draft award

8   ACOMB AND HOLGATE (WR-NY)   1774 : 1776
        Open fields, pasture, ings, common and waste : 1581
        acres awarded
        Commissioners Robert Bewlay, John Outram, Richard Cross
    i   York City RO Vol G enrolled award and 19 cent. copy of
        plan (not dated, surveyor Miles Dawson, buildings, 8
        ch=1")
    ii York City RO TC DP/1/1 sealed original award and 2
        copies of plan. Also Acc.51 typescript copy award
    iii Borthwick Institute York PR/AC/56 extracts from award

9   ADDINGHAM (WR-WY)   1865 : 1873
        High Moor, Middle Moor, Low Moor : 735 acres awarded
        Commissioner Joseph Smith
    i   CP Wakefield A75 sealed original award and plan (1872,
        surveyor J.C. Giles, buildings, 3 ch=1")
    ii Addingham parish council sealed original award and plan
    iii PRO (MAF 1 410 and 1074) award

    ADEL (WR-WY) see Arthington

10 ADLINGFLEET (WR-H)   1843 : 1847
        By agreement   Commissioner Christopher Paver
        Turf Moors, Winsgate Moors : 1051 acres awarded
    i   WRRD B52 p75 enrolled award and plan Vol 4/20 (not
        dated, signed by commissioner, buildings, 6 ch=1")
    ii Whitgift church award and plan

11 ADLINGFLEET, FOCKERBY and HALDENBY (WR-H)   1767 : 1769
        Certain lands, grounds, commons
        Commissioners Edward Forster (refused), John Cleaver,
        John Raines, John Dickinson
    i   WRRD B7 p220 enrolled award and plan Vol 1/2 (not dated,
        unsigned, buildings, no scale stated)
    ii Whitgift church award and plan
    iii York Dean and Chapter Library BB 33, 18 cent. copy of
        award, no plan

12 ADWICK LE STREET (WR-SY)   1760 : 1761
        Open and common fields, meadows, commons and waste :
        1000 acres awarded
        Commissioners Richard Frank, William Simpson, Edward
        Forster
    i   WRRD B3 p148 enrolled award
    ii Doncaster RO Enc.1 award

AIKE (ER-H) see Lockington

13 AIRTON (WR-NY) 1801 : 1802
       By agreement. Green and open fields
       Commissioners Thomas Ingilby, John Preston, Thomas Hudson
    i   NRA Raistrick MSS agreement and draft award

14 AIRTON (WR-NY) 1860 : 1861
       Highside Pasture : 600 acres awarded
       Commissioner Joseph Smith
    i   CP Wakefield A41 sealed original award and plan (not dated, unsigned, 3 ch =1")
    ii PRO (MAF 1 567) award

15 AISKEW (NR-NY) 1804 : 1807
       By agreement
       Moor and waste : 194 acres awarded
       Commissioner William Whitelock
    i   NRRD DB no.83 p164 enrolled award with plan (1805, surveyor William Whitelock, buildings, scale not stated)
    ii NYCRO PR/BED 5/1/3 original award and plan

16 AISLABY, CROPTON, MIDDLETON, WRELTON AND HARTOFT (NR-NY)
                                                        1765 : 1766
       Act confirms agreement : 9074 acres awarded
       Commissioners Matthew Peirson, Mark Haines jun, Joseph Foord, John Foord, George Coates
    i   NYRD AT no.1 p1 enrolled award
    ii NYCRO ZPC 1/9 bound copy award no plan

17 AISLABY (near Whitby) (NR-NY) 1829 : 1830
       Deed of covenant
       Moors, commons and waste : 199 acres
       Commissioner George Peirson
    i   NRRD GA no.80 p155 enrolled award with plan (not dated, unsigned, buildings, 8ch=1")

18 ALDBOROUGH (WR-NY) 1808 : 1809
       Four open fields, pasture, ings or meadow, common, waste : 989 acres awarded
       Commissioner William Dawson
    i   WRRD B27 p96 enrolled award and plan Vol 1/1 (1808, surveyor William Shipton, whole township, buildings, open field names, 6 ch=1")
    ii Aldborough church sealed original award and plan

19 ALDBROUGH (ER-H) 1764 : 1766
       Open fields, pasture, meadow : 1630 acres estimated
       Commissioners John Dickinson, John Outram, John Raines
    i   ERRD AH/1/1/ enrolled award
    ii   HCRO DDPK/29/2 award in bound volume
    iii HCRO DDPK/8/2 copy award made c 1851
    iv   HCRO DDCC/142/11 draft award
    v   HCRO IA plan (1764, buildings, 8 ch=1")

20 ALLERSTON (NR-NY)   1809 : 1818
        Commons and waste : 9174 acres awarded
        Commissioner Arthur Strickland
    i   NRRD 3D enrolled award and plan (1810 surveyor John
         Hall, buildings, 24 ch=1")
    ii   NYCRO ZJQ3 original award and plan
    iii PRO DL/45 enrolled abstract of award
    iv   NYCRO ZJQ 2 another plan, surveyor Margaret King, 12
         ch=1")

21 ALLERTON (Bradford) (WR-WY)   1840 : 1850
        Commons or waste : 170 acres estimated
        Commissioners John Benjamin Ingle (died), Thomas William
        Rawson
    i   CP Wakefield A6 sealed original in volume with 4 plans
         (1841, surveyor John Benjamin Ingle (died), G.T. Lister,
         the plans being (1) Fairweather Green; (2) Allerton Ley;
         (3) Moorhouse Moor and Guide Moor; (4) Harrop Edge, Peat
         Dyke and Pikeley Upper Green, all show buildings, 3
         ch=1")
    ii   YAS MD 290/7 draft award signed and witnessed, no plan
    0   Sealed original award to be deposited in Bradford parish
         church under the act. Not found

22 ALLERTON BYWATER (WR-WY)   1803 : 1810
        Common fields, ings, commons and waste : 471 acres
        awarded
        Commissioner William Shipton
    i   CP Wakefield C p21 enrolled award with plan A54 (1805,
         surveyor W.S, whole township, buildings, open field
         names, 6 ch=1")
    ii   Leeds RO sealed original award with plan
    iii Leeds RO copy plan
    iv   PRO DL/45/8/10 enrolled extract of award

    ALLERTON MAULEVERER (WR-NY) see Clareton

    ALMONDBURY (WR-WY) see North Crosland

23 ALNE (NR-NY)   1807 : 1811
        Open fields, ings and waste : 680 acres awarded
        Commissioners John Tuke, Thomas Scott
    i   NRRD DO no.1 p1 enrolled award and plan (not dated,
         surveyor J. Humphries, buildings, 4 ch=1")
    ii   NYCRO PR/ALN 11/1 original award and plan

24 ALTOFTS (WR-WY)   1809 : 1811
        Open fields, ings, commons and waste : 756 acres awarded
        Commissioners William Whitelock (died), Thomas Gee
    i   WRRD B29 p1 enrolled award
    ii   Normanton UDC award and plan (1810, surveyor Thomas Gee)
    iii Leeds RO copy award and plan
    iv   Leeds CL plan (1810)
    v   Leeds CL DB/M 339 plan

    ALVERTHORPE (WR-WY) see Wakefield

25 AMOTHERBY (NR-NY)   1776 : 1777
        Common fields, commons and waste : acreage not stated
        Commissioners John Outram, William Richardson, Isaac
        Leatham
        Surveyor John Kendall
    i   NRRD BE no.26 p223 enrolled award
    ii YAS DD 132 award

26 AMPLEFORTH AND OSWALDKIRK (NR-NY)   1804 : 1810
        Amending act of 1806. Commons and wastes : 812 acres
        awarded
        Commissioners Edward Cleaver, William Dawson; William
        Dawson alone for amended award
    i   NRRD DA no.70 p172 enrolled award and plan (1809,
        unsigned, buildings, 6 ch=1")
    ii NYCRO PR/AMP original award and plan

    ANLABY (ER-H) see Hessle

    ANSTON (WR-WY) see North Anston

27 APPLETON-LE-MOORS (NR-NY)   1767 : 1767
        By agreement. The Rigg : 55 acres awarded
        Commissioners Thomas Hudson, John Dodsworth, Mark
        Staines jun, John Foord
    i   NRRD AT no.2 p142 enrolled award no plan

28 APPLETON-LE-MOORS (NR-NY)   1767 : 1767
        By agreement. Hambley : 160 acres awarded
        Commissioners Thomas Hudson, John Dodsworth, Mark
        Staines, John Foord
    i   NRRD AT no.3 p149 enrolled award no plan

    APPLETON ROEBUCK (WR-NY) see Bolton Percy

29 APPLETREEWICK (WR-NY)   1815 : ?
        Two stinted pastures called Ruska and the Great Pasture
        and Appletreewick Common: 6330 acres estimated
        Commissioners John Humphries, Alexander Calvert
    i   NRA report Yorke MSS late 19 cent. copy of award, no
        plan (surveyor Samuel Swire)
    ii Appletreewick parish council award (in bank) and plan
    iii Leeds RO several plans

30 ARDSLEY (Barnsley) (WR-SY)   1760 : 1763
        Commons or waste called Ardsley Common : 300 acres
        awarded
        Commissioners John Spencer, Edward Oates, George Walker,
        James Wright, Samuel Turner, Henry Wilkinson (died),
        George Marsh (refused)
    i   WRRD B4 p45 enrolled award
    ii Sheffield CL NBC 56 sealed original award and plan
        (1762, surveyor Joseph Colbeck, commons only, 3 ch=1")
        Related papers NBC 491; enclosure agreement, 1788,
        Ph.c.357

ARDSLEY (WR-WY) see West Ardsley or Woodkirk and East Ardsley

31 ARKENDALE (WR-NY)   1773 : 1774
        Open fields, stinted pasture, commons and waste : 673
        acres awarded
        Commissioners William Hill, Miles Dawson, John Flintoff
        jun.
    i   WRRD B10 p202 enrolled award
    ii NYCRO PR/ARD 11 sealed original award no plan (surveyor
        John Flintoff jun.)

32 ARKLESIDE (NR-NY)   1882 : 1884
        Common : 450 acres awarded
        Commissioner James Rutherford
    i   NYCRO QDD(I) no.2 enrolled award and plan (not dated,
        unsigned, 3 ch=1")
    ii NYCRO PR/COV original award
    iii PRO (MAF 1 453)

ARKSEY (WR-SY) see Bentley with Arksey

33 ARMLEY (Leeds) (WR-WY)   1793 : 1799
        Commons and waste land : 158 acres awarded
        Commissioner William Whitelock
    i   WRRD B20 p256 enrolled award
    ii Leeds RO sealed original award and plan (not dated,
        surveyor William Whitelock, buildings, 6 ch=1")
    iii Leeds Civic Hall modern copy of award and plan
    iv YAS MS 1156 copy plan

34 ARMTHORPE (WR-SY)   1773 : 1774
        Open fields, open arable lands, commons and waste : 1146
        acres awarded
        Commissioners Miles Dawson, George Kelk, Joseph Colbeck
    i   WRRD B10 p163 enrolled award
    ii Doncaster RO Enc.2 plan (1774, surveyor William Kelk,
        whole village shown, buildings, 8 ch =1")
    iii Wakefield County Hall award and plan
    iv Wakefield CP A101 modern copy of award and plan
    v   SYCRO 375/Z copy plan

35 ARNCLIFFE (WR-NY)   1766 : 1766
        Stinted pastures called Cow Close, West Moor and Clowder
        or Clowther : 3000 acres estimated
        Commissioners Peter Wilson Overend, William Reynard,
        Henry Waddington
    i   WRRD B6 p1 enrolled award
    ii NYCRO PR/ARN 9/1 sealed original award and plan
    iii NRA Raistrick MSS copy award

36 ARNCLIFFE (WR-NY)   1846 : 1848
        Fawcett Moor : 500 acres awarded
        Commissioner Richard Clapham
    i   CP Wakefield sealed original award and plan A39
    ii NYCRO PR/ARN 9/4 sealed original award and plan
    iii PRO (MAF 1 655) award
    iv Leeds RO photocopy award and plan

ARNCLIFFE (WR-NY) (Kirkgilll Pasture) see Buckden

ARNOLD (ER-H) see Long Riston

37   ARTHINGTON, ADEL and ECCUP (WR-WY)   1807 : 1839
Commons and waste grounds called Blackhill, Eccup Moor, Adel Moor and East Banks and others : 560 acres awarded
Commissioner William Dawson (died), Jonathan Taylor (died), Thomas Newman
- i   WRRD B45 p192 enrolled award and plan Vol 1/4 (not dated, surveyor Jonathan Taylor (died), buildings, no scale stated)
- ii   Leeds Civic Hall certified copy
- iii   Adel parish church award and plan
- iv   Leeds RO photocopy plan

ASKERN (WR-SY) see Campsall

38   ASKHAM BRYAN (WR-NY)   1811 : 1813
Open fields, common and waste : 686 acres awarded
Commissioner William Dawson
Surveyor Daniel Tuke
- i   York City RO TC DP/1/2 sealed original award and plan (separate) (not dated, not signed, whole township shown, buildings, open field names, 8 ch=1")
- ii   Askham Bryan parish council sealed original award and plan

39   ASKHAM RICHARD (WR-NY)   1813 : 1821
Open fields, balks, uninclosed land : 258 acres awarded
Commissioners William Dawson (died), John Tuke
- i   York City RO sealed original award in Vol E with plan annexed (1821, surveyor Jonathan Tuke, whole township shown, buildings, open field names, 5 ch=1")
- 0   Sealed original award to be deposited in the parish church under the act. Not found

40   ASKRIGG (NR-NY)   1763 : 1763
By agreement. Woodhall Pasture
Commissioners Henry Waddington, William Bradley, William Brown, George Dinsdale, Michael Spence, Alexander Fothergill
- i   NRRD AO no.3 p.19 enrolled award, no plan

41   ASKRIGG (NR-NY)   1816 : 1819
Pasture, moor and waste : 2800 acres estimated
Commissioner John Bower
- i   NYCRO DC/AY original award and plan (not dated, surveyors Thomas Halliday and Thomas Bradley, 8 ch=1")
- ii   PRO (Chancery Lane) CRES 6/145 extract from plan

42   ASKRIGG (NR-NY)   1818 : 1821
Woodhall moor or common : 430 acres estimated
Commissioner Thomas Bradley
- i   NYCRO ZIF 2478 draft award

43   ASKWITH (WR-NY)   1779 : 1782
        Commons and waste called Askwith Moor and Snowden Moor,
        and inclosed lands : 1342 acres awarded
        Commissioners John Lund sen, John Outram (died), John
        Dunnington, Joseph Dickinson
    i   WRRD sealed original award only (no plan) in Map Vol 2/1
        (surveyor John Lund jun)
    ii Leeds RO award and plan

44   ASSELBY (ER-H)   1836 : 1840
        Open arable fields, common pastures : 945 acres awarded
        Commissioner and surveyor John George Weddall
    i   HCRO QDB 8 enrolled award
    ii HCRO IA two original plans (1840, J.G. Weddall,
        buildings, 6 ch=1")

45   ASTON CUM AUGHTON AND WALES (WR-SY)   1766 : 1768
        Open fields, commons or waste : 830 acres estimated
        Commissioners Edward Oates, George Jackson, Henson
        Kirkby, William Simpson (died), Thomas Smith (died)
    i   WRRD B6 p242 enrolled award
    ii Wales parish council has 1897 copy of award (no plan)
    iii Rector of Wales, award and plan
    iv Sheffield CL MD 5716 copy award and plan for Wales

46   ATTERCLIFFE AND DARNALL (WR-SY)   1810 : 1820
        Commons, waste, open fields : 239 acres awarded
        Commissioners Joseph Bishop, Josiah Fairbank
    i   Wakefield CP E p67 enrolled award and 4 plans A65 (1817,
        surveyors William and Josiah Fairbank (1) Attercliffe,
        whole township, buildings, 10 ch=1"; (2) larger plan of
        part of Attercliffe, buildings, no scale stated; (3)
        Darnall, whole township, buildings, no scale stated; (4)
        larger plan of part of Darnall, buildings, no scale
        stated, some open field features)
    ii Sheffield CL CA 364 sealed original award and plans

47   ATWICK (ER-H)   1769 : 1772
        Open fields, meadow, pasture, moor : 1436 acres awarded
        Commissioners John Raines, Peter Nevill
        Surveyor Peter Nevill
    i   ERRD AQ/221/20 enrolled award
    ii HCRO PC 14/1 sealed original award and plan (1769,
        buildings, 8 ch-1")
    iii HCRO PE 32/34 copy award
    iv HCRO DDX/154/5 copy award

     AUCKLEY (WR-SY) see Blaxton Auckley

     AUGHTON (WR-SY) see Aston

48   AUSTERFIELD (WR-SY)   1765 : 1767
        High and Low Commons, open fields : 1200 acres estimated
        Commissioners Henson Kirkby, Thomas Smith, Joseph
        Pursglove
   i   WRRD B5 p110 enrolled award
   ii   CP Wakefield A97 award and plan (not dated, unsigned,
        buildings, whole township shown, open field names, 6
        ch=1")
   iii Lincs AO 2T.G.3/B/2/1 agreement

        AUSTONLEY (WR-WY) see Wooldale

49   AUSTWICK (WR-NY)   1809 : 1814
        Commons and waste : 2154 acres awarded
        Commissioner Thomas Buttle
   i   WRRD sealed original award with plan in Vol 2/2 (not
        dated, signed by commissioner, 12 ch=1")
   ii   Clapham church award and plan
   iii Ingleborough estate office copy of award

50   AYSGARTH (NR-NY)   1771 : 1778
        Pasture, common : 681 acres awarded
        Commissioners William Brown, Henry Waddington, Ingram
        Gill
   i   NRRD BL no.3 p5 enrolled award
   ii   NYCRO PR/AYS original award

        AYTON (NR-NY) see East Ayton; West Ayton

51   BADSWORTH (WR-WY)   1810 : 1813
          Open fields, mesne inclosures, commons and waste : 250
          acres awarded
          Commissioner Thomas Gee
      i   WRRD B30 p195 enrolled award
      ii Sheffield CL NBC 65 draft award
      0   Sealed original award to be kept by the steward of the
          Lord of the Manor (Earl Fitzwilliam) under the act. Not
          found

52   BAGBY (NR-NY)   1788: 1794
          Moor : 109 acres awarded
          Commissioners John Flintoff, Edward Cleaver
      i   NRRD no.27 enrolled award and plan (not dated, unsigned,
          4 ch=1")

53   BAGBY AND BALK (NR-NY)   1793 : 1803
          Awards of 1796, 1797, 1799 and 1803 : moor
          Commissioner John Flintoff
      i   NRRD enrolled awards nos.23,26 and plan (1796, not
          dated, surveyor not named, scale not stated)

54   BAINBRIDGE (NR-NY)   1762 : 1762
          By agreement.   Pasture
          Commissioners
      i   NRRD AL no.52 p181 (illegible microfilm, original not
          available)

55   BAINBRIDGE (NR-NY)   1805 : 1816
          By agreement. Pasture : 14,991 acres awarded
          Commissioner Alexander Calvert
      i   NYCRO QDD(D) Bk P p1 enrolled award
      11 Barclays Bank Hawes original award and 12 plans of 1807

56   BAINBRIDGE (NR-NY)   1807 : 1810
          By agreement. Pasture
          Commissioner Alexander Calvert
      i   NYCRO ZPG 9/3/1 copy award made 1879 and 2 plans
      ii Barclays Bank Hawes original award and 2 plans (not
          dated, unsigned, 4 ch=1", 8 ch=1")

57   BAINBRIDGE (NR-NY)   1840 : 1844
          Meadow, Stalling Busk : 441 acres awarded
          Commissioner Thomas Bradley
      i   NYCRO QDD(D) Bk S p146 enrolled award and plan (1837,
          surveyor Thomas Bradley, 2 ch=1", copy made 1846
      ii NYCRO QDD(I) no.9 award

58   BAINBRIDGE (NR-NY)   1849 : 1850
            Common, Cragg
            Commissioner Richard Garth
     i   NYCRO QDD(I) no.4 sealed original award with plan (1849,
            unsigned, buildings, 3 ch=1")
     ii   PRO (MAF 1 502)

59   BAINBRIDGE (NR-NY)   1850 : 1859
            Pasture : 853 acres awarded
            Commissioner Edward Broderick
     i   NYCRO QDD(I) no.6 certified original award and plan (3
            plans on 1 sheet) (1851, 1855, undated, surveyor Edward
            Broderick, 3 ch, 8 ch and 2 ch=1")
     ii   PRO (MAF 1 843) award

60   BAINTON (ER-H)   1774 : 1775
            Open fields, meadow, pasture and moor : 2764 acres
            awarded
            Commissioners Joseph Butler, John Outram, William Hill
     i   ERRD AT/334/34 enrolled award
     ii   HCRO PE/5/34 copy award
     iii   HCRO IA plan (177?, buildings, 8 ch=1")

BALBY (WR-SY) see Hexthorpe

BALNE (WR-NY) see Pollington

61   BARKISLAND (WR-WY)   1814 : 1817
            Commons, moors and waste : 750 acres awarded
            Commissioners Thomas Gee, Jonathan Taylor (refused),
            Nicholas Brown
            Surveyors Joseph Young and Thomas Dinsley
     i   WRRD B33 p1 enrolled award
     ii   Ripponden UDC copy award copy plan
     0   Sealed original award to be kept in Halifax parish
            church under act. Not found

BARKSTON ASH (WR-NY) see Sherburn in Elmet

62   BARLBY (ER-NY)   1836 : 1846
            Common arable fields, pasture : 216 acres awarded
            Commissioner and surveyor George Alderson
     i   HCRO QDB 7 p188

63   BARLBY (ER-NY)   1854 : 1858
            Waste : 85 acres awarded
            Commissioner and surveyor George Alderson
     i   HCRO IA original award and plan (1858, buildings, shows
            village and common, scale not stated)
     ii   PRO (MAF 1 795) award

64   BARLOW (WR-NY)   1838 : 1839
            By agreement. Uninclosed land
            Commissioner John Bell
     i   WRRD B39 p383 enrolled award and plan Vol 2/3 (1839,
            unsigned, 8 ch=1")

65   BARMBY MOOR (ER-H)   1771 : 1783
           Common fields, pastures, ings, waste : 2309 acres
           awarded
           Commissioners Richard Cross, Miles Dawson, John Outram
           (died), Edward Watterson (replacement)
           Surveyors Edward Watterson, Peter Nevill
      i   York Minster Library X 1 sealed original award and plan
           (not dated, scale not stated)
      ii   HCRO 20 cent copy award and plan

66   BARMBY ON THE MARSH (ER-H)   1847 : 1853
           Marsh, open fields : 1030 acres estimated
           Commissioner and surveyor John George Weddall
      i   ERRD sealed original award with plan (not dated,
           buildings, 3 ch=1")
      ii   HCRO DDTR/806 tracing of plan
      iii PRO (MAF 1 193) award

67   BARMSTON (ER-H)   1757 : 1758
           By agreement. Two open cornfields, pasture : 25 and a
           half oxgangs awarded
           Commissioners John Outram, John Fox
           Surveyor Thomas Lazenby
      i   HUL DDWB/2/33 sealed original award (DDWB/2/31 and 32
           agreement)

68   BARMSTON (ER-H) AND WINKTON (LOST)   1819 : 1820
           Open field, common pasture, waste : 237 acres awarded
           Commissioners Thomas Scott (refused), Thomas Scott jun.
           Surveyor Edward Page
      i   ERRD DA/318/59 enrolled award and (F1) plan (1819,
           buildings, 5 ch=1")
      ii   HCRO PE/6/11 sealed original award and plan
      iii HUL DDWB/2/35 award
      iv   HUL DDCV/7/1 award and plan

69   BARNBURGH CUM HARLINGTON (WR-SY)   1819 : 1822
           Open fields, commons and wastes : 1074 acres awarded
           Commissioner Joseph Whitaker
      i   WRRD B36 p129 enrolled award and plan Vol 1/15 (not
           dated, surveyor William Bingley, buildings, open field
           names, 6 ch=1")
      ii   Barnburgh parish council award and plan
      iii SYCRO 392/Z copy award and plan

70   BARNBY DUN, THORPE IN BALNE, KIRK SANDALL (WR-SY)   1766 : 1768
           Open common or waste called Thorpe Marsh common to the 3
           townships and a piece of unclosed land called Grumble
           Hirst : 560 acres awarded
           Commissioners William Simpson (died), Edward Forster,
           Joseph Pursglove, Edward Oates
      i   WRRD B6 p186 enrolled award
      ii   Doncaster RO PR.Bar award, no plan
      0   Sealed original award to be kept by the Lord of the
           Manor of Thorpe under the act : not found

71   BARNBY DUN (WR-SY)   1803 : 1807
              Common and waste, open fields, meadows, ings, pasture :
              1332 acres awarded
              Commissioners William Whitelock, William Shipton,
              William Dawson
       i   WRRD B26 p1 enrolled award and plan Vol 1/10 (1805,
              surveyor Joseph Haywood, buildings, whole township
              shown, 8 ch=1")
       ii   Doncaster RO PR.Bar award and plan

72   BARNINGHAM (NR-Durham)   1803 : 1807
              Stinted pasture : 321 acres awarded
       i   NRRD DA no.41 p129
       ii   NRRD ZQAI 4/1 award
       iii   Church vestry award and plan

       BARNINGHAM (NR-Durham) see Little Newsham

73   BARNOLDSWICK AND SALTERFORTH (WR-NY and Lancs)   1814 : 1829
              Commons, moors and waste called White Moor and other
              common and waste : 1500 acres awarded
              Commissioner Thomas Buttle
       i   WRRD B48 sealed original award and plans (4 plans on 3
              sheets, not dated, surveyor Thomas Buttle, buildings.
              (1) Barnoldswick, 6 ch=1"; (2) encroachments, 3 ch=1";
              (3) Salterforth Lane encroachments, 3 ch=1"); (4)
              Salterforth Drainage including part of Kelbrook and
              Earby, parish of Thornton, 6 ch=1")
       ii   Lancs CRO P82 photocopy plans
       0   Until c.1942 original award was in the possession of the
              vicar of Barnoldswick. Not found

74   BARNSLEY (WR-SY)   1777 : 1779
              Commons, moors or waste, 5 open fields : 782 acres
              awarded
              Commissioners William Hill, John Hardy, John Birks
       i   WRRD bound vol containing award and plan marked B13
              (1779, surveyor William Fairbank, whole township shown,
              open field names and features, 6 ch=1")
       ii   Sheffield CL Sil 132 draft plan
       iii   Sheffield CL EM 1090 copy award
       iv   Sheffield CL NBC 68-70,388 copy award and plan
       0   Sealed original award to be kept by the steward of the
              manor courts of Barnsley under the act. Not found

       BARNSLEY (WR-SY) see Ardsley; Monk Bretton

       BARUGH (WR-SY) see Darton

75   BARWICK IN ELMET (WR-WY)   1796 : 1804
           Amending act 1809
           Open fields, ings, common and waste : 2563 acres awarded
           Commissioners William Dawson, John Crowder, John Sharp
           (died), William Whitelock
       i   WRRD sealed original award Roll 2
       ii Leeds RO sealed original award
       iii PRO DL/45/7/6 enrolled extract of award; also DL/41/70
           enclosure papers
       iv Leeds Civic Hall extracts award

       BASHALL EAVES (WR-LANCS) see Grindleton

76   BATLEY (WR-WY)   1803 : 1809
           Open common, moors and waste, a field : 250 acres
           estimated
           Commissioner Nicholas Brown
       i   WRRD B28 p32 enrolled award
       ii YAS MS 700 draft award
       iii Kirklees RO original plan (undated, unsigned, buildings,
           3 ch=1"); also typed copy award

77   BEADLAM (NR-NY)   1817 : 1819
           Beadlam Rigg : 673 acres awarded
       i   NRRD no. 16 enrolled award and plan
       ii NYCRO ZEW V 2/4 original award

78   BEAL, KELLINGTON AND KELLINGLEY (WR-NY)   1791 : 1793
           Open fields, meadows, ings or pasture : 745 acres
           awarded
           Commissioners John Beighton, Thomas Mould
       i   WRRD B19 p51 enrolled award and plan Vol 1/6 (1793,
           surveyor Jonathan Teal, buildings, whole township shown,
           open field names, 6 ch=1")
       ii Beal parish council award and plan
       iii HCRO DDCL/242, 18 cent copy of award and plan (*HCRO)?
       iv CP Wakefield A27 first part of award

79   BEAMSLEY (WR-NY)   1881 : 1883
           Beamsley Moor : 699 acres estimated
           Commissioner Joseph Smith
       i   CP Wakefield A81 sealed original award and plan
           (Ordnance Survey)
       ii PRO (MAF 1 1038) award

80   BECCA AND ABERFORD (WR-WY)   1825 : 1828
           Commons or moors, Becca Little Moor, Aberford or Bramham
           Moor and other waste : 460 acres awarded
           Commissioner John Bower
       i   WRRD B38 p212 enrolled award and plan Vol 1/18 (1828,
           surveyor William Porter, buildings, 6 ch=1")
       ii Aberford parish council award and plan

       BECKWITHSHAW see Knaresborough, Forest of

81   BEEFORD (ER-H)   1766 : 1768
         Common fields, pastures, common, waste : 3200 acres
         awarded
         Commissioners John Outram, John Dickinson, John Raines
         Surveyor Peter Nevill
     i   ERRD AK/57/6 enrolled award and plan (IA) (not dated,
         buildings, 10 ch=1")
     ii HCRO PE/114/111 copy award made 1769

     BELLASIZE (ER-H) see Eastrington

82   BELLERBY (NR-NY)   1770 : 1772
         Pasture, moor : 1867 acres estimated
         Commissioners Christopher Pickering, Richard Richardson,
         George Jackson, Christopher Watson
     i   NRRD BB no.20 p28 arbitration, award and plan (1773,
         G.J. of Richmond, buildings, 6 ch=1")
     ii NYCRO PC/BEL original award and plan

83   BEMPTON (ER-H)   1765 : 1767
         Open fields, pastures, meadow : 1410 acres estimated
         Commissioners John Dickinson, John Outram, John Lund
         Surveyor Peter Nevill
     i   ERRD AK/2/2 enrolled award
     ii HCRO DDX/154/16 copy award

84   BENTHAM (WR-NY)   1767 : 1768
         Common or waste called Bentham Moor : 3000 acres
         estimated
         Commissioners John Moore, Thomas Hawkshead, Robert Lang,
         Thomas Goss, Henry Ellershaw, Richard Clapham, John
         Forster
     i   WRRD B8A sealed original award and plan (not dated,
         unsigned, buildings, 16 poles =1")
     ii WRRD B8 p1 enrolled award
     iii Messrs Clark, Oglethorpe & Sons, solicitors, Bentham,
         sealed original award and plan

85   BENTLEY WITH ARKSEY (WR-SY)   1759 : 1759
         Commons and waste : 958 acres awarded
         Commissioners William Simpson, Edward Forster, William
         Lamplugh
     i   WRRD B3 p42 enrolled award
     ii Doncaster RO Enc.8 sealed original award
     0   Sealed original awards to be kept by the Lord of the
         Manor under the act. Not found

86   BENTLEY WITH ARKSEY (WR-SY)   1827 : 1830
         Open fields, intermixed inclosures, ings, meadows,
         pastures, commons, wastes, commonable lands : 1555 acres
         awarded
         Commissioner Joseph Whitaker
     i   WRRD B39 p116 enrolled award and plan Vol 1/20 (1830,
         surveyor James Alexander, buildings, whole township
         shown, open field names, 9 ch=1")
     ii Doncaster RO Enc.9 award and plan

     BESSACARR (WR-SY) see Cantley

87   BESSINGBY (ER-H)   1766 : 1768
            Open fields, wastes : 1080 acres estimated
            Commissioners John Dickinson, John Outram, John Raines
            Surveyor Joseph Dickinson
        i   ERRD AK/35/4 enrolled award
        ii HCRO DDX/154/12,17 copies of awards
        iii Bridlington public library, certified copy made 1768 and
            20 cent typescript copy
        iv HUL DDCV/13/1 copy plan (1769, buildings, 5 ch=1")

        BEVERLEY (ER-H) see Woodmansey; Molescroft

88   BEWERLEY AND HARDCASTLE (WR-NR)   1850 : 1858
            Moors : 3020 acres awarded
            Commissioner James Powell
        i   CP Wakefield A15 sealed original award and plan
            (undated, unsigned, buildings, 3 ch=1")
        ii NYCRO PC/BEW award and plan
        iii PRO (MAF 1 258) award

89   BEWHOLME (ER-H)   1740 : 1740
            Open cornfields, common, pasture : 1042 acres awarded
            Commissioners Samuel Neck, Richard North, John Conyers,
            Samuel Hellard, William Peirson
        i   ERRD B/131/41 enrolled award

90   BIELBY (ER-H)   1814 : 1817
            Open fields, pasture, common, carr, waste : 1694 acres
            awarded
            Commissioners John Hall, Richard Crabtree (refused),
            Thomas Scott
            Surveyor Robert Plummer Weddall
            Umpire Thomas Scott (refused), Peter Jackson
        i   ERRD DA/90/4 enrolled award and plan C2 (1817,
            buildings, 6 ch=1")
        ii HCRO IA plan
        iii Hull CL commissioners minutes and papers 1811-1817 bound
            with act

        BIGGIN (WR-NY) see Sherburn in Elmet

91   BILLINGLEY (WR-SY)   1822 : 1831
            By agreement. Commons and waste
        i   Sheffield CL NBC 57 award and plan (commons only, 3
            ch=1")

92   BILTON (near Wetherby) (WR-NY)   1776 : 1782
            Three open fields, pasture, common and waste : 794 acres
            awarded
            Commissioners John Outram (died), Richard Cross, Miles
            Dawson
      i   York City RO Vol G enrolled award
      ii   Bilton church no award plan only (not dated, surveyor
            William Dawson, buildings including the village, nearly
            all township shown, open field names, scale not stated)

      BILTON (Harrogate) (WR-NY) see Knaresborough, Forest of

      BINGLEY (WR-WY) see Gilstead; Hainworth; Riddlesden

93   BINNINGTON, POTTER BROMPTON AND GANTON (ER-NY)   1803 : 1804
            Open fields, pastures, carrs : 3339 acres awarded
            Commissioner Joseph Dickinson
      i   ERRD CA/320/43 enrolled award

94   BIRDSALL (ER-NY)   1691 : 1692
            By agreement. Uninclosed lands
      i   Leeds RO TN/BL/A14, B2 and C, agreement, award and
            papers

95   BIRKIN (WR-NY)   1809 : 1815
            Common called Birkin Little Common, other land, and part
            of Maspin Moor : 60 acres awarded
            Commissioners William Whitelock (died), William
            Pilkington
      i   WRRD B32 p85 enrolled award and plan Vol 1/12 (1815,
            surveyor William Pilkington, buildings, whole township
            shown, 8 ch=1")
      0   Sealed original award to be enrolled and deposited in
            the parish church or elsewhere as the commissioners
            should direct. Not found

      BIRSTWITH (WR-NY) see Knaresborough, Forest of

96   BISHOP BURTON (ER-H)   1767 : 1772
            Open fields : 3000 acres awarded
            Commissioners John Dickinson, John Outram, Robert Bewlay
            jun.
            Surveyors Peter Nevill, Charles Tate
      i   ERRD AQ/1/1
      ii   HCRO IA sealed original award
      iii   HUL DDGE/3/2 sealed original plan (1771, signed by David
            Tate, buildings, 10 ch=1")

97   BISHOPDALE (NR-NY)   1789 : 1797
            Pasture : 178 acres awarded
            Commissioners James Coulton, William Fothergill
      i   NYCRO ZBH 244 sealed original award

      BISHOPDALE (NR-NY) see Newbiggin

98   BISHOP MONKTON (WR-NY)   1807 : 1816
           Open fields, ings, waste : 1120 acres estimated
           Commissioners Jonathan Teal (died), George Addinell, John
           Humphries
      i   NYCRO DC/RIC sealed original award with plan in volume
           (not dated, surveyor John Humphries, buildings including
           village, open field names, scale not stated)

      BISHOPSIDE (WR-NY) see High and Low Bishopside; Bishop
           Thornton

      BISHOPSOIL (ER-H) see Howden

99   BISHOP THORNTON WITH BISHOPSIDE (WR-NY)   1757 : 1758
           Open and uninclosed moor, stinted pasture or common
           called Thornton or Bishop Thornton Moor : 735 acres
           awarded
           Commissioners William Reynard, Marmaduke Hodgson,
           William Sands
      i   WRRD B5 p73 enrolled award
      ii   NRA report Ingilby MSS copy award
      iii Bradford RO award

100   BISHOPTHORPE (WR-NY)   1757 : 1760
           By agreement confirmed by act. Four common fields,
           meadow, common or waste : 650 acres estimated
           Commissioners Robert Bewlay, Thomas Mitchell, John
           Cleaver, Francis Gainford, Samuel Milbourn (last 2 did
           not join in award)
      i   York City RO Vol F enrolled award

      BISHOPTON (WR-NY) see Ripon

101   BISHOP WILTON (ER-H)   1726 : 1726
           By agreement. One open field : 432 acres awarded
           Commissioners Francis Wright, Thomas Armistead, William
           Lister
      i   Borthwick Institute York PR B/W/32 sealed original award
      ii   HUL DDSY/4/151 award
      iii HCRO typescript copy

102   BISHOP WILTON (ER-H)   1769 : 1772
           Open fields, common pastures : 3113 acres awarded
           Commissioners John Outram, Richard Cross, Robert Bewlay
           jun (refused), John Graves
           Surveyors Miles Dawson, Joseph Dickinson
      i   ERRD AN/334/24 enrolled award
      ii   HCRO IA award and 2 plans (IA) (not dated, some
           buildings, 8 ch=1")
      iii Borthwick Institute York PR B/W/33 award

103 BLACKTOFT, HIVE, GILBERDIKE AND FAXFLEET (ER-H) 1830 : 1833
    Common fields, meadows, pastures : 631 acres awarded
    Commissioner John Bell, John George Weddall
  i   ERRD DQ/261/14 enrolled award and 2 plans (Gilberdyke
      and Hive, and Blacktoft and Faxfleet, not dated,
      buildings, 5 ch=1")
  ii HCRO PR/2477 copy 1833 (original burnt)
      Related documents, Hull CL, minutes of meetings etc.
      bound with act

104 BLAXTON AND AUCKLEY WITH FINNINGLEY (NOTTS & WR, now SY)
                                                    1774 : 1778
    Open fields, meadows, pastures, commons and waste : 3321
    acres awarded
    Commissioners Thomas Tofield, Henson Kirkby (died),
    George Kelk, Isaac Milbourn
  i   WRRD B11 p253 enrolled award and Z5(L) copy plan
  ii   Notts CRO award
  iii Rector of Finningley award and plan
  iv   Blaxton parish council copy award and plan
  v   SYCRO 238/P typescript copy award and copy plan (1778)

105 BOLSTERSTONE (WR-SY)   1778 : 1782
    Commons and waste called the Nether Commons, the
    Whitwell Moor and the Upper Commons : 3000 acres
    estimated
    Commissioners John Renshaw, George Kelk (died), John
    Kay, Thomas Fletcher
  i   CP Wakefield A31 sealed original award and plan (1782,
       surveyor Joseph Renshaw, buildings, whole township
       shown, 18 ch=1")
  ii   CP Wakefield A60 duplicate award, no plan
  iii Sheffield CL CA 366 copy award and plan

106 BOLTON (Bradford) (WR-WY)   1819 : 1824
    Common or waste called Bolton Common and other waste :
    23 acres awarded
    Commissioner Joseph Fox
  i   WRRD B38 p69 enrolled award and plan Vol 1/17 (1824,
       unsigned, buildings, 4 ch=1")
  ii   PRO DL/45/9/8 enrolled abstract of award
  iii Leeds RO sealed original award

107 BOLTON PERCY AND APPLETON ROEBUCK (WR-NY)   1797 : 1804
    Open fields, ings, lands, commons and commonable places
    in Bolton Percy and Appleton Roebuck : 1850 acres
    awarded
    Commissioners Richard Clark, William Whitelock
  i   Bolton Percy parish church award and plan
  0   Enrolled award and plan should be in custody of TC York
       under the act. Not found

108   BOLTON UPON DEARNE (WR-SY)   1759 : 1761
            Open fields, meadows, commons, common pastures or waste
            : 800 acres awarded
            Commissioners Godfrey Wentworth, John Battie, William
            Simpson, Edward Forster, George Walker, Henry Wilkinson,
            James Wright
       i   WRRD B3 p172 enrolled award
       ii   Dearne UDC certified copy award

       BONDGATE (WR-NY) see Ripon

109   BORDLEY (WR-NY)   1847 : 1852
            Bordley Intake : 128 acres awarded
            Commissioner William Talbot
       i   CP Wakefield A55 sealed original award and plan (not
            dated, surveyor John Greenwood, 3 ch=1")
       ii   NYCRO I PR/RYL 4 award and plan
       iii PRO (MAF 1 853) award

110   BOROUGHBRIDGE (WR-NY)   1846 : 1857
            Common : 27 acres awarded
            Commissioner Anthony Reed
       i   CP Wakefield A57 sealed original award and plan (not
            dated, unsigned, buildings, 2 ch=1")
       ii   NYCRO DC/NID sealed original award and plan
       iii PRO (MAF 1 882) award

       BOSTON SPA (WR-WY) see Clifford

111   BOWES (NR-DURHAM)   1766 : 1772
            Also an award of 1768. Open grounds pastures, moor and
            waste
       i   NRRD BA no.1 p1; BB no.22 p71 award

112   BOWES (NR-DURHAM)   1857 : 1859
            Moor : 12,517 acres awarded
            Commissioner Crayston Webster
       i   NRRD no.7 enrolled award and plan (Ordnance Survey)
       ii   PRO (MAF 1 192) award

113   BOYNTON (ER-H)   1777 : 1783
            Common fields, pastures : 2000 acres estimated
            Commissioners John Outram (died), Robert Bewlay (died),
            Peter Nevill, Edward Watterson
       i   ERRD BB/397/52 enrolled award

114   BRACEWELL (WR-Lancs)   1766
            By agreement. An open field
            Commissioners Robert Lane, Thomas Chamberlain, Richard
            Haignton
       i   NRA Raistrick MSS agreement

115   BRADFIELD (WR-SY)   1811 : 1826
         Commons, moors, wastes, unenclosed lands, open fields,
         open or mesne wood : 13,773 acres awarded
      i   CP Wakefield F p1 enrolled award
      ii Bradfield parish council award and plans
      iii Sheffield CL ACM 573 no award, photocopies of 4 maps
          (1826, surveyor William Bingley, buildings, whole
          township shown, various scales, 2 ch, 12 ch, 24 ch=1")
      iv SYCRO 236/P microfilm of award and plans.
          Related papers Sheffield CL MD 5721 Commissioners'
          minute book

      BRADFIELD (WR-SY) see Hallam

      BRADFORD (WR-WY) see Allerton; Bolton; Eccleshill; Heaton;
          Idle; Thornton; Wibsey Slack; Wyke

116   BRADLEY, HIGH AND LOW (WR-NY)   1789 : 1791
         Ings or meadow, moors or commons : 700 acres estimated
         Commissioner Benjamin Chambers
      i   WRRD B18 p60 enrolled award and plan Vol 1/8 (not dated,
          unsigned, buildings, 10 ch=1")
      ii Kildwick parish church sealed original award
      iii Bradley parish council copy award and plan made 1896
      0   Sealed original award to be deposited with Lord George
          Cavendish under act; in 1896 with duke of Devonshire.
          Not found

      BRAITHWAITE MOOR (WR-WY) see Dacre

117   BRAITHWELL (WR-SY)   1765 : 1766
         Two common pastures, waste called Braithwell Green : 154
         acres awarded
         Commissioners Eneas Macdonald, Edward Oates, George
         Pashley
      i   WRRD B5 p53 enrolled award
      0   Sealed original award to be kept in parish chest under
          the act. Not found

118   BRAITHWELL (WR-SY)   1855 : 1858
         Open fields : 492 acres awarded
         Commissioner George Dyson Simpson
      i   CP Wakefield Vol A3 sealed original award and plan
          (1857, surveyor Henry Ellison, some buildings, open
          field names, 6 ch=1")
      ii Ravenfield parish council award and plan
      iii NRA report Lumley MSS tracing of plan and papers
      iv Sheffield CL NP 11 draft award
      v   Doncaster RO DD.YAR/E2/2 copy award

      BRAITHWELL (WR-SY) see Bramley

119 BRAMHAM (WR-WY) 1807 : 1812
   Common town fields, commons and waste : 1329 acres awarded
   Commissioners William Shipton, John Hall
   - i WRRD B29 p104 enrolled award and plan Vol 1/9 (1809, surveyors William Shipton, Daniel Tuke, buildings, whole township shown, open field names, 8 ch=1")
   - o Sealed original award to be deposited in parish church under the act. Not found

BRAMHAM (WR-WY) see Becca

120 BRAMHOPE (WR-WY) 1805 : 1809
   Commons and waste : 470 acres awarded
   Commissioners John Binns, Jonathan Teal
   - i WRRD B27 p134 enrolled award and plan Vol 1/5 (1806, surveyor Jonathan Taylor, buildings, whole township shown, open field features, 6 ch=1")
   - ii Leeds RO award and plan
   - iii Leeds RO plan (1806)

121 BRAMLEY (BRAITHWELL WITH BRAMLEY) (WR-SY) 1769 : 1770
   Four commons or moors : 400 acres estimated
   Commissioners William Hill, Henson Kirkby, John Kay
   - i WRRD B8 p240 enrolled award
   - ii Sheffield CL MD 3871 award

122 BRAMLEY (Leeds) (WR-WY) 1789 : 1799
   Commons and waste grounds : 670 acres estimated
   Commissioners Richard Richardson (died), John Bainbridge
   - i CP Wakefield A p8 enrolled award
   - ii Leeds Civic Hall certified copy award and plan (1811, surveyor Jonathan Taylor, buildings, whole township shown, 6 ch=1")
   - iii Thoresby Society Leeds photocopy award
   - iv YAS DD IJ sealed original award to be deposited in Leeds parish church under the act. Not found

BRAMLEY (Leeds) (WR-WY) see Headingley

123 BRAMPTON BIERLOW (WR-SY) 1714
   By agreement. Hoober Common
   - i SYCRO 524/Z copy agreement

124   BRAMPTON BIERLOW, WATH UPON DEARNE, SWINTON (WR-SY)
                                                                1815 : 1820
             Open fields, undivided inclosures, common or waste :
             1260 acres awarded
             Commissioner Thomas Gee
      i   WRRD B34 p264 enrolled award for Brampton Bierlow and
             Wath
      ii   WRRD B35 p157 enrolled award for Swinton
      iii   Rotherham CL award and plan
      iv   Sheffield CL NBC 58 award and 2 plans (1816, surveyor
             William Bingley, open fields, 6 ch=1")

125   BRAMPTON EN LE MORTHEN (WR-SY)   1771 : 1773
             Commons and waste : 307 acres awarded
             Commissioners Edward Oates, Henson Kirkby, John Sybury
             Roebuck
      i   WRRD B8 p300 enrolled award
      ii   Thurcroft parish council original award
      iii   Sheffield CL NBC 45 draft award

126   BRANDESBURTON (ER-H)   1844 : 1847
             Common fields, meadows, pastures, waste : 1324 acres
             awarded
             Commissioner Samuel Vessey
             Surveyor Edward Page
      i   ERRD GI/1/1 enrolled award
      ii   HUL DDCV/24/9 award and plan
      iii   HCRO IA award and plan
      iv   HCRO PE/77/54 plan (1847, 3 ch=1")
      v   Guildhall RO London Emanuel Hospital records copy award
             and plan

127   BRANDSBY (NR-NY)   1856 : 1859
             Dale and common : 98 acres awarded
             Commissioner Robert William Fenwick Mills
      i   NYCRO QDD(I) no.5 sealed original award and plan
             (1857,1858, 3 ch=1")
      ii   Brandsby parish council original award
      iii   PRO (MAF 1 856) award

128   BRANTINGHAM AND BRANTINGHAM THORPE (ER-H)   1765:1766
             Open fields, lands, meadows, pastures : 1200 acres
             estimated
             Commissioners James Bradley (died), John Raines, Edward
             Holgate, John Outram
             Surveyors Edward Johnson, Charles Tate
      i   ERRD AF/361/16 enrolled award
      ii   Durham HCR sealed original award and plan; also copy
             plan
      iii   Durham DCM sealed original award and plan
      iv   HCRO DDMT/638 copy award
      v   HUL DDCV/25/2 & 3, copy award and plan (undated,
             buildings, no scale stated)

      BRANTON (WR-SY) see Cantley

BRANTON GREEN (WR-NY) see Upper Dunsforth

129 BRAYTON, THORPE WILLOUGHBY, BURTON HALL AND GATEFORTH WITH
    LUND (WR-NY)   1799 : 1805
    Open fields, commons and waste : 2311 acres awarded
    Commissioners Richard Clark, John Tuke, Thomas Mould
  i   WRRD B22 p142 enrolled award and plan Vol 1/11 (1803,
      surveyor William Shipton, buildings, whole townships
      shown, 6 ch=1")
  ii Brayton parish church award and plan

130 BREARTON (WR-NY)   1772 : 1773
    Moors or commons, Rigg Moor and Brearton Moor : 650
    acres estimated
    Commissioners John Outram, John Flintoff, Samuel
    Brailsford
  i   WRRD B10 p1 enrolled award
  ii YAS DD 124/3 sealed original award and plan (1772,
      surveyor John Flintoff, buildings including township, 6
      ch=1")

131 BRIDLINGTON (ER-H)   1768 : 1771
    Open fields, lands, meadows, pastures, commons, waste :
    2011 acres awarded
    Commissioners Edward Cleaver, John Outram, Peter Nevill
    Surveyors Charles Tate, Joseph Dickinson
  i   ERRD AN/121/11 enrolled award and plan (IA) (not dated,
      9 ch=1")
  ii HCRO DDX/154/3-4,17 award
  iii Bridlington Public Lib. 19 cent copies award and plans

BRIDLINGTON see Speeton and Marton

132 BRIESTFIELD (FORMERLY BRIESTWISTLE) (WR-WY)
    1816 : 1849   1816 : 1849
    Commons or waste : 518 acres estimated
    Commissioners Nicholas Brown (died), John Farrer
  i   WRRD B52 p100 enrolled award
  ii WYAS D14/45 sealed original award and plans (surveyors
      Henry Teal (died), Joseph Thompson; 3 maps (1) Grange
      Moor; (2) Sowood; (3) Howroyd, Falhouse and Lower
      Whitley)
  iii Kirklees RO two copies of award; copy plan (1816,
      surveyor Henry Teal, all township)
      Related papers Kirklees RO survey book 1816

BRIESTWISTLE (WR-WY) see Briestfield

133 BRIGHAM (ER-H)   1766 : 1767
    Open fields, meadows, pastures, commons : 1019 acres
    awarded
    Commissioners John Outram, John Raines, Thomas Walker,
    James Farthing, Peter Nevill
    Surveyor Peter Nevill
  i   ERRD AK/164/9 enrolled award
  ii Hull CL draft award
  iii HCRO PC/13/2 tracing, possibly enclosure plan? (1813, unsigned,
      buildings, scale not stated)

BRIGHOUSE (WR-WY) see Clifton

134 BRIGHTSIDE (Sheffield) (WR-SY) 1788 : 1795
      Commons and waste : 107 acres awarded
      Commissioners John Kent (died), Arthur Elliot, Joseph Outram
- i   WRRD B19 p214 enrolled award
- ii Sheffield CL ACM 568 sealed original award and plan (1790, surveyor William Fairbank, buildings, whole township shown, 1 mile = 10")

135 BRINSWORTH (Rotherham) (WR-SY) 1812 : 1814
      Open meadow, mesne inclosure or stinted pasture called Bradmarsh commons : 220 acres awarded
      Commissioners Thomas Gee, Francis Raynes
- i   WRRD B29 p307 enrolled award
- ii Rotherham parish church award
- iii Rotherham CL copy award and plan (1814, surveyor W. Bingley, 4 ch=1")
- iv Sheffield CL NBC 71 copy award

136 BRODSWORTH (WR-SY) 1815 : 1830
      Open common or moor, open fields, wastes, other commonable lands : 789 acres awarded
      Commissioners Thomas Dyson, Joseph Whitaker
- i   WRRD B38 p277 enrolled award and plan Vol 1/19 (not dated, surveyor Joseph Colbeck, buildings, whole township shown, open field names and features, 6 ch=1")
- ii Doncaster RO P10 award
- iii SYCRO 168/2 microfilm of plan, 1830
- iv PRO DL/45/9/10 enrolled extract of award

137 BROMPTON AND SAWDON (NR-NY) 1758 : 1760
      Common fields, meadows, common and waste : 4629 acres awarded
      Commissioners Thomas Robinson, Timothy Foord, Richard Storr, H. Bushell, Thomas Mitchell, Samuel Milbourn
- i   NRRD AG no.11 p20 enrolled award
- ii NYCRO PC/BRO 5/1 original award
- iii D of L
- iv NYCRO PC/BRO 5/2,5/3, ZDS V 4/2 copies of award

138 BROTHERTON (WR-NY) 1793 : 1799
      Common or waste, common or stinted pasture, open fields, ings or meadow : 422 acres awarded
      Commissioners William Dawson, Richard Clark, John Sharp
- i   WRRD B20 p99 enrolled award
- ii WYAS D74 sealed original award

BROUGH (ER-H) see Elloughton

139 BROUGHTON (Ryedale) (NR-NY) 1788 : 1789
      Open field : 327 acres awarded
      Commissioners Ingram Gill, Samuel Milbourn
- i   NRRD CF no.5 p3 enrolled award

BROXA (NR-NY) see Hackness

140 BUBWITH AND HARLTHORPE (ER-H)   1832 : 1838
      Open fields, ings, meadows, pasture : 1880 acres awarded
      Commissioners John Ayer (died), William Pilkington, Makin Durham
      Surveyors Makin Durham (for Bubwith), Francis Carr (for Harlthorpe)
      Umpire Thomas Musgrave
- i   ERRD FG/1/1 enrolled award and 2 plans (1837, buildings, 6 ch=1")
- ii   HCRO IA coloured photocopy of Harlthorpe plan
- iii   HCRO DDCL/3425 draft award
- iv   York Minster Library plan

141 BUCKDEN AND STARBOTTON (WR-NY)   1816 : 1831
      Stinted pastures, common field lands, dales and waste : 2996 acres awarded
      Commissioner Alexander Calvert
- i   WRRD B42 sealed original award
- ii   NYCRO PR/HBB 11/1 sealed original award and plans
- iii   Leeds RO DB 111 award and plan of Buckden 1828

142 BUCKDEN (WR-NY)   1847 : 1850
      Kirkgill Pasture : 1000 acres awarded
      Commissioner Ralph Lodge
- i   CP Wakefield A23 sealed original award, plan (1847, unsigned, some buildings, 3 ch=1")
- ii   PRO (MAF 1 404) award

143 BUGTHORPE (ER-H)   1777 : 1779
      Open fields and pastures : 654 acres awarded
      Commissioners John Flintoff, John Outram, Miles Dawson
- i   ERRD BB/165/19 enrolled award

144 BULMER (NR-NY)   1771 : 1779
      Open fields, pastures and moor : 42 oxgangs in act
      Commissioners Richard Richardson, Samuel Milbourn, Miles Dawson
- i   NRRD BQ no.3 p153 enrolled award

145 BURGHWALLIS AND HAYWOOD (WR-SY)   1813 : 1818
      Commons and waste : 200 acres awarded
      Commissioner William Shipton
- i   WRRD B33 p106 enrolled award and plan 1/13 (1813 surveyor Joseph Colbeck sen. buildings, scale not stated)
- ii   Clerk to Burghwallis parish meeting, award and plan
- iii   YAS MD 2/8/Add award

BURLEY (Leeds) (WR-WY) see Headingley

146 BURN (near Selby) (WR-NY)   1850 : 1853
      Burn commons : 70 acres awarded
      Commissioner Christopher Paver
- i   CP Wakefield A26 sealed original award and plan (not dated, surveyor William Sisson, buildings, 3 ch=1")
- ii   PRO (MAF 1 381) award

147   BURNBY (ER-H)   1731
          By agreement.
          Commissioner and surveyor John Dickinson
      i   HCRO DDAN 239 agreement and pre-enclosure plan 1725,
          signed JD
          Related documents Lincs AO Anderson 2/5

      BURNBY (NR-NY) see Mulgrave

      BURNSALL (WR-NY) see Thorpe; Thresfield

148   BURSTWICK AND SKECKLING (ER-H)   1773 : 1777
          Open arable fields, meadow, pasture : 850 acres
          estimated
          Commissioners Robert Foster, John Outram, Edward Johnson
          Surveyor Peter Nevill
      i   ERRD AX/433/12 enrolled award
      ii   HCRO DDCK/32/9 copy award and 19 cent copy plan
           (buildings, scale not stated)
      iii HCRO PE/73/30 award
      iv   HCRO DDCC/142/15 draft award
      v   HUL DDKG/170 photograph of plan
      vi   HCRO DDCK 32/9 has schedule of ancient enclosed lands

      BURTON (NR-NY) see Newbiggin

149   BURTON FLEMING (ER-H)   1768 : 1769
          Open fields : 3652 acres estimated
          Commissioners Edward Cleaver, John Outram, John Raines
          Surveyor Joseph Dickinson
      i   ERRD AN/312/16 enrolled award
      ii   HCRO DDX/154/18-19 2 copies award

      BURTON HALL (WR-NY) see Brayton

150   BURTON LEONARD (WR-NY)   1790 : 1792
          Three open fields : 273 acres estimated
          Commissioners John Lund jun. Richard Clark
      i   WRRD B18 p100 enrolled award and plan Vol 1/7 (1790,
           surveyor Benjamin Mitchell, buildings, open field
           features, 6 ch=1")
      ii   Burton Leonard parish council award and plan (kept at
           bank)

151   BURTON PIDSEA (ER-H)   1761 : 1762
          By agreement 1760 and act 1761. Open fields, pasture,
          carr : 1800 acres estimated
          Commissioners John Dickinson, John Lund, Robert Buckels,
          William Iveson, Thomas Carter
          Surveyors Peter Nevill, Charles Tate
      i   ERRD AF/34/7
      ii   ERRD sealed original award
      iii HCRO DDCC/142/5,7 volumes containing 2 copies
      iv   HCRO DDCK/32/5 19 cent bound copy of act, award and plan
      v   HCRO PC/11/2 plan (1761, buildings, 8 ch=1")
           Related documents in HCRO PR/1633, ERRD AF/14/6, HUL
           DDKG/40-44

152 BURTON SALMON (WR-NY)   1817 : 1824
         Open fields, commons and waste : 290 acres estimated
         Commissioners William Pilkington, Henry Teal
    i   CP Wakefield E p279 enrolled award
    ii   WYAS Z42(L) copy of part of plan made 1921 (1819,
         unsigned, buildings, scale not stated)
    0   Sealed original award to be deposited in Monk Fryston
         parish church under act. Not found
    00   Sealed original award to be deposited with the Lord of
         the Manor under the act. Not found 1964

153 BUTTERWICK (ER-NY)   1771 : 1774
         Open fields, lands : 1664 acres awarded
         Commissioners John Outram, Isaac Milbourn, Joseph Butler
    i   ERRD AT/79/10 enrolled award
    ii   ERRD AT/88/11 survey 1774

154　CADEBY (WR-SY)　　　　　　　　　　　　　　　　1809 : 1813
　　　　　Open fields, common pasture, commons or waste : 620
　　　　　acres awarded
　　　　　Commissioner Thomas Dyson
　　i　　WRRD B30 p12 enrolled award and plan Vol. 1/21 (1809,
　　　　　surveyor Robert Rodgers, buildings, whole township
　　　　　shown, open field features, decorated cartouche with
　　　　　picture of large house, scale not stated)
　　0　　Sealed original award to be deposited in Sprotborough
　　　　　church under the act. Not found

155　CALDBERGH (NR-NY)　　　　　　　　　　　　　　　　1836 : 1840
　　　　　Pasture : 228 acres awarded
　　　　　Commissioner Thomas Bradley
　　i　　NYCRO QDD(D) Bk R p47 enrolled award
　　ii　 NYCRO QDD(I) no.13 original award

156　CALVERLEY (Pudsey) (WR-WY)　　　　　　　　　　　1755 : 1758
　　　　　Common or moor called Calverley Moor, Bradford Moor or
　　　　　Pudsey Moor and waste : 855 acres awarded
　　　　　Commissioners William Lamplugh, John Smyth, Samuel
　　　　　Lister
　　i　　WRRD B5 p44 enrolled award
　　ii　 Leeds RO sealed original award and plan
　　iii　YAS DD II copy award

CAMBLESFORTH (WR-NY) see Carlton by Snaith

CAMERTON (ER-H) see Ryhill

157　CAMPSALL, ASKERN AND NORTON (WR-SY)　　　　　　1814 : 1818
　　　　　Open fields, meadows, ings, pastures, commons, wastes
　　　　　and other commonable lands : 2846 acres awarded
　　　　　Commissioners Thomas Gee, Francis Raynes, William
　　　　　Shipton and William Pilkington
　　i　　WRRD B33 p147 enrolled award
　　ii　 Norton parish council sealed original award and 3 plans;
　　　　　(1) Campsall, not dated, unsigned, buildings, whole
　　　　　township shown, 6 ch=1" ; (2) Askern, not dated,
　　　　　surveyor Robert Moore, buildings, open field names, 6
　　　　　ch=1" ; (3) Norton, 1814, surveyor Joseph Colbeck,
　　　　　pre-enclosure, buildings, whole township shown, open
　　　　　field names, scale not stated
　　iii　YAS MD 225 copy plan
　　iv　 Doncaster RO Enc.10 copy award

158　CANTLEY, BRANTON, BESSACARR AND (HIGH) ELLERS (WR-SY)
　　　　　　　　　　　　　　　　　　　　　　　　　　1777 : 1779
　　　　　Open fields, meadows, pastures, commons and waste : 2856
　　　　　acres awarded
　　　　　Commissioners Isaac Milbourn, Miles Dawson, Francis
　　　　　Raynes
　　i　　WRRD B12 p211 enrolled award
　　ii　 Doncaster RO P12 award

CANTLEY (WR-SY) see Doncaster

159 CARLETON IN CRAVEN (WR-NY)   1861 : 1873
          Carleton Common and Howshaw Moor : 1135 acres awarded
          Commissioner Samuel Dickinson Martin
     i   CP Wakefield sealed original award A72 and 2 plans A72a
          (not dated, unsigned, buildings, 3 ch-1")
     ii   Clerk of parish council, award and plan
     iii PRO (MAF 1 179 and 1070) award
     iv   YAS MS 1200 and MS 1224 copy award and plan
     v   Leeds RO copy award

     CARLETON (near Pontefract) (WR-WY) see Pontefract

160 CARLTON (near Aysgarth) (WR-NY)   1772 :1776
          Moor called Carlton Moor or Common, an open field : 620
          acres awarded
          Commissioners Henry Waddington, Robert Arthington
          (refused), Miles Dawson, William Eamonson
     i   WRRD B11 p160 enrolled award
     ii   Guiseley parish church sealed original award no plan

     CARLTON (WR-wY) see Lofthouse; Rothwell

161 CARLTON BY SNAITH AND CAMBLESFORTH (WR-NY)   1800 : 1808
          Open fields, ings, marshes, common, commonable lands and
          waste : 1362 acres awarded
          Commissioners Richard Clark (refused), William Dawson,
          Joseph Dickinson, Richard Clark jun
     i   WRRD B26 p100 enrolled award and plans Vol 2/4 (1808,
          surveyor William Shipton; (1) Carlton, buildings, whole
          township shown, 6 ch=1"; (2) Camblesforth, buildings,
          whole township shown, open field features, 6 ch=1")
     ii   HCRO DDCL/242 sealed original award and plan in volumes;
          also copy award and plans
     iii HCRO award

162 CARLTON MINIOTT (NR-NY)   1793 : 1803
          Common
          Commissioners Richard Clark, John Flintoff
     i   NRRD no.29 sealed original award

163 CARPERBY (NR-NY)   1809 : 1819
          Pasture and moor : 2000 acres estimated
          Commissioner Alexander Calvert
     i   NRRD Bk R p1 enrolled award
     ii   NYCRO ZBO original award and plan (not dated, unsigned,
          buildings, 8 ch=1")
     iii NYCRO QDD(I) no.12 original award

     CARTWORTH (WR-WY) see Wooldale

     CASTLEFORD (WR-WY) see Glass Houghton

164 CASTLEY (Leathley) (Wr-WY)   1814 : 1818
          By agreement. Commons and waste
          Commissioner Jonathan Teal
     i   YAS DD 151 award and plan (1814, 3 ch=1")

165 CATTON (NR-NY) 1810 : 1812
By agreement. Moor and Greens : 253 acres awarded
Commissioner William Dawson
   i   NRRD DO no.9 p33 enrolled award

166 CATTON (HIGH AND LOW), NEWTON UPON DERWENT, FULL SUTTON AND
       WILBERFOSS (ER-H)
1760 : 1766
Open fields, meadows, commons, waste : 2200 acres awarded
Commissioners Robert Bewlay, Robert Bewlay jun, Richard Mason (died)
   i   ERRD AH/177/5 enrolled award
   ii   Petworth House Sussex archives 3175, original award
   iii Borthwick Institute York PR CATN/84 and PR F/S/14 awards

167 CATWICK (ER-H) 1731 : 1732
Open fields, pastures : 1425 acres awarded
Commissioners Ralph Brigham, Robert Smithson, John Conyers, Thomas Birkwood, Richard North, Samuel Finley
Surveyor William Brown (refused), Joseph Colbeck
   i   ERRD B/57/24 enrolled award and altered award plan (IA)
        (1780-90, buildings, 8 ch=1")

168 CAWOOD AND WISTOW (WR-NY) 1776 : 1780
Open fields, woods, average grounds, ings, marshes, carrs, commons and waste : 1846 acres awarded
Commissioners Robert Bewlay, John Graves, Joseph Butler (withdrew), Richard Clark
   i   WRRD B14 p1 enrolled award
   ii   NYCRO PC/WIS sealed original award and plan (not dated, buildings, 8 ch=1")
   iii York CL plan
   iv   NYCRO ZNQ copy award

CAWTHORNE (WR-SY) see Silkstone

169 CHAPEL ALLERTON (WR-WY) 1808 : 1813
Amending Act 1811. Moors, commons and waste : 878 acres awarded
Commissioners William Whitelock (died), John Binns (died), Jonathan Taylor
   i   WRRD B29 p158 enrolled award
   ii   Leeds parish church sealed original award and plan in volume (1812, surveyor Jonathan Taylor, buildings, 6 ch=1")
   iii Leeds Civic Hall   copy award and plan
   iv   Leeds RO copy award and 2 plans
   v   Leeds RO DB M/145 plan

170 CHAPEL HADDLESEY (WR-NY) 1759
   i   Borthwick Institute York PR C/HAD/15 post enclosure plan and survey 1759

CHAPEL HADDLESEY (WR-NY) see West Haddlesey

171 CHERRY BURTON (ER-H) 1823 : 1829
        Open fields, balks, commons, waste : 2059 acres awarded
        Commissioners John Hall, John Lee, Cornelius Collett
        Surveyors James Bulmer, Edward Page
    i   ERRD DQ/136/6 enrolled award and plan (1829, buildings, 6 ch=1")
    ii   HCRO DDX/218/2 bound original award and plan
    iii HUL DDCB/4/38 bound original award and plan; also survey of open fields 1803 DDCB/4/33
    iv   HUL DDHO/16/57 copy plan

CHURCH FENTON (WR-NY) see Sherburn in Elmet

172 CLAPHAM (NR-NY) 1758 : 1758
        Pasture : 150 cattle-gates
        Commissioners Richard Clapham jun. Henry Waddington, John Foster
    i   NYCRO ZUG 3/1 original award
    ii   Ingleborough estate office photostat of award
    iii Leeds RO copy award and plan

173 CLAPHAM CUM NEWBY (WR-NY) 1848 : 1849
        Skew and Liquorhead Pasture : 125 acres awarded
        Commissioner John Greenwood
    i   CP Wakefield sealed original award A29 and plan (1849, surveyor John Greenwood, 3 ch=1"
    ii   PRO (MAF 1 834) award

174 CLARETON (CONEYTHORPE AND CLARETON), ALLERTON MAULEVERER AND
        FLAXBY (WR-NY) 1772 : 1776
        Open fields and waste : 519 acres awarded
        Commissioners John Flintoff, Ambrose Gray
    i   WRRD B11 p118 enrolled award

CLAYTON WITH FRICKLEY (WR-SY) see Frickley

CLAYTON WEST (WR-WY) see Denby Dale

175 CLECKHEATON (WR-WY) 1795 : 1797
        Open fields, stinted pastures : 202 acres awarded
        Commissioner Richard Clark
    i   WRRD Map Vol 2/5 sealed original award and plan (not dated, surveyor John Johnson, buildings, open field names, 2 and a half ch=1")
    ii   WRRD B18 p375 enrolled award
    iii Spenborough TC copy award and plan
    iv   Leeds RO copy award and plan
    v   YAS MD 335 award

176 CLECKHEATON AND SCHOLES (WR-WY) 1802 : 1806
    Commons, moors and waste : 150 acres estimated
    Commissioner Alexander Calvert
    i   CP Wakefield sealed original award A77
    ii Kirklees RO sealed original award with plan (1803, surveyor Alexander Calvert, Hartshead Moor and Scholes Green, buildings, 3 ch=1")
    ii Kirklees RO copy award and copy plan

CLEMENTHORPE (WR-NY) see Dringhouses

CLIFFE (ER-H) see North Cliffe, South Cliffe

CLIFFE CARR (WR-WY) see Farnham

177 CLIFFE CUM LUND (NEAR SELBY) (ER-NY) 1843 : 1863
    Common fields, commons and waste : 355 acres awarded
    Commissioners Christopher Paver (died), Makin Durham, William Paver
    Umpires Henry Teal (died), Thomas Musgrave, Samuel Dickinson Martin
    i   ERRD G bound original award and plan (1863, buildings, 6 ch=1")
    ii Borthwick Institute York PR HEM/30 award and 2 plans
    iii HCRO DDCL/244 copy award

178 CLIFFORD (WR-WY) 1803 : 1806
    Open fields, commons and waste : 836 acres awarded
    Commissioner William Shipton
    i   CP Wakefield B p176 enrolled award and plan A40 (1807, unsigned, buildings, whole township including Boston Spa, open field features, 6 ch=1") The dates have been checked, and the plan is dated a year after the award
    ii Bramham parish church sealed original award and plan
    iii Leeds RO tracing of plan

179 CLIFTON AND BOOTHAM (YORK) (NR-NY) 1763 : 1764
    Common : 481 acres awarded
    Commissioners Robert Bewlay sen, Robert Bewlay jun
    i   NRRD AH No.5 p23 enrolled award
    ii York City RO TC DP/1/3 sealed original award
    iii Bedfordshire RO Lucas MSS copy award and related papers : microfilm in York City RO

180 CLIFTON (Brighouse) (WR-WY) 1778 : 1778
    Commons and waste : 177 acres awarded
    Commissioners John Sharpe, Joseph Jagger, Benjamin Patchett
    i   WRRD B11 p318 enrolled award
    ii NRA Report Kirklees records sealed original award

CLIFTON (near Doncaster) (WR-SY) see Conisbrough

CLIFTON (WITH NORWOOD) (WR-NY) see Knaresborough, Forest of

CLIFTON (NEWALL WITH CLIFTON) (WR-NY) see Otley

CLINT (WR-NY) see Knaresborough, Forest of

181 COATHAM (Kirkleatham) (NR-NY) 1759 : 1760
        Open field and common : 396 acres awarded
   i   NRRD enrolled award

182 COATHAM (Kirkleatham) (NR-Cleveland) 1847 : 1849
        East Coatham Common : 396 acres awarded
        Commissioners Michael Smith, William Richardson, John Jackson
   i   NRRD AG no.113 p14 enrolled award
   ii   Cleveland County Archives PR/KRL 3 original award and plan (1849, surveyor George Peirson, buildings, 2 ch=1")
   iii NYCRO ZK 2601-6 associated papers
   iv   PRO (MAF 1 620) award

183 COLBURN (NR-NY) 1767 : 1769
        Bonds of 1767. Pasture, moor : 291 acres awarded
        Commissioners George Jackson, Hugh Tootell
   i   NRRD BA no.4 p80 enrolled award

184 COLD KIRBY (NR-NY) 1789 : ?
        Award unexecuted. Open fields, stinted pasture, commons and waste
        Commissioners Richard Clark, Thomas Mould
        Surveyors Daniel Seaton, Ralph Burton

185 COLLINGHAM (WR-WY) 1814 : 1816
        Common or waste, open fields, inclosed lands : 500 acres estimated
        Commissioner Francis Raynes
   i   WRRD B31 p11 enrolled award and Z3(L) copy plan (1816, surveyor C. Paver, buildings, whole township shown, 6 ch=1")
   ii   Collingham parish council award and plan

COLLINGHAM (WR-WY) see Linton

CONEYTHORPE (WR-NY) see Clareton

186 CONISBROUGH (WR-SY) 1855 : 1858
        Open fields : 601 acres awarded
        Commissioner George Dyson Simpson
   i   CP Wakefield sealed original award with plans A21 (3 plans, 1857, not signed, buildings, open field names, 3 ch=1" ; (1) North Cliff Hill Field, Far and Near Underhill Fields, Skitholme, Wrangholme and Bur Croft; (2) Holywell and Kearsley Medley Field and Aberskills ; (3) High Field and Clifton Fields
   ii   Doncaster RO Enc.13a original award and 3 plans
   iii PRO (MAF 1 279) award

187 CONISBROUGH AND CLIFTON (WR-SY) 1856 : 1858
       Commons and wastes : 313 acres awarded
       Commissioner Thomas Bradley
   i   CP Wakefield sealed original award with plan A16 (1857,
       not signed, buildings, 3 ch=1" and 12 ch=1")
   ii Doncaster RO Enc.13 award

188 CONISTON (ER-H) 1789 : 1790
       Open arable fields, meadows, pasture, waste : 555 acres
       awarded
       Commissioners Peter Nevill, John Raines, John Wood
       Surveyors Joseph Dickinson (refused), John Wood jun,
       Robert Atkinson
   i   ERRD BG/291/39 enrolled award and plan IA (1789,
       buildings, 4 ch=1"; another copy Acc.1316)
   ii HCRO DDPK/29/2 copy award

     CONISTONE (WR-NY) see Kettlewell

189 CONONLEY (WR-NY) 1768 : 1769
       Common and waste called Cononley Moor : 534 acres
       awarded
       Commissioners Thomas Watkinson, Thomas Harrison, James
       Hargreaves, John Squire, Thomas Chamberlain
   i   WRRD B7 p187 enrolled award
   ii Cononley parish council (kept at village institute),
       sealed original award and plan (1768, surveyor J Teal, 2
       ch=1")

190 COPMANTHORPE (WR-NY) 1836 : 1843
       Open fields, meadow or pasture : 507 acres awarded
       Commissioner Edward Page
   i   WRRD B37 p349 enrolled award and plan Vol 1/26 (1840
       unsigned, buildings, whole township shown, oepn field
       names and features 6 ch=1")
   ii Copmanthorpe parish council award

191 COPT HEWICK (WR-NY) 1772
       By agreement? Stinted pasture and common
   i   Leeds RO award and plan with related papers

192 CORNBROUGH (NR-NY) 1858 : 1872
       Stony Hill : 25 acres awarded
       Commissioners Constantine Richard Moorsom
   i   CP Wakefield A74 award and plan (not dated, surveyor J.
       Brown, 2 ch=1"); related papers C328
   ii PRO (MAF 1 1036) award

193 COTHERSTONE (NR-Durham) 1863 : 1867
       Cotherstone Moor : 4495 stints
   i   NRRD QDD(I) no.10 sealed original award and plan
   ii Durham CRO D/HH/2/14/62-3, award

194 COTTAM (ER-H) 1846 : 1851
    Open field : 2553 acres awarded
    Commissioner and surveyor Henry Scott
- i   HCRO IA original award and plan (1851, buildings, scale not stateld)
- ii HCRO DDX/40/198 and DDX/131/3 copies of award and part of plans
- iii Borthwick Institute York CCD/C.11 plan of 1848
- iv PRO (MAF 1 130) award

Related papers HCRO DDGD/29

195 COTTINGHAM (ER-H) 1766 : 1771
    Common pastures : 3000 acres estimated
    Commissioners John Dickinson, John Outram, Peter Nevill
    Surveyors Charles Tate, Edward Johnson
- i   ERRD AN/203/14 enrolled award and plan IA (1766, Cottingham common 8 ch=1"); also typescript copy
- ii Hull CL 19 cent copy and plan

HCRO DDX/24/18 and HUL DRA/97 associated papers

196 COTTINGHAM (ER-H) 1791 : 1793
    Open fields : 1532 acres awarded
    Commissioners Robert Dunn, John Wood sen (died), Peter Nevill, Joseph Dickinson, John Wood
- i   ERRD BG/371/58 enrolled award and copy plan IA (copy made 1838, some buildings, 4 ch=1")
- ii Hull City RO modern copy award and plan

COWDEN (ER-H) see Great and Little Cowden

COWICK (WR-H) see Snaith

197 CRACOE (WR-NY) 1787 : 1788
    Three open fields, stinted pasture : 677 acres awarded
    Commissioners Thomas Chippendale, Thomas Ingleby, Henry Wrathall
- i   WRRD sealed original award with plan in map Vol 2/6 (1787, surveyor Thomas Ingleby, buildings, open field names and features, 4 ch=1"
- 0   Sealed original award to be kept by Thomas Cockson, landowner, under the act. Not found

198 CRAKEHALL (NR-NY) 1833 : 1837
    Open fields, meadows and waste : 182 acres estimated
- i   NRRD GM no.3 p9 enrolled award and plan (1837, surveyor Thomas Bradley)
- ii NYCRO tracing of plan

199 CRIDLING STUBBS (WR-NY) 1797 : 1799
    Common or waste : 180 acres awarded
    Commissioner William Lambe
- i   WRRD B20 p184 enrolled award
- 0   Sealed original award to be deposited in Womersley parish church under the act. Not found

CRIGGLESTONE (WR-WY) see Sandal Magna

200   CROOM (ER-H)   1775 : no award
          Open ground and tracts : 1263 acres estimated
          Commissioners Roger Pocklington, John Graves, Joseph
          Butler
      i   HUL DDSY/9/18 act

      CROPTON (NR-NY) see Aislaby

201   CROWLE, EASTOFT AND EALAND (Lincs and Yorks - H)   1813 : 1861
          Act amended 1816 : award made under Thorne Moor
          Improvement acts 1848 and 1861 with CP Wakefield
          Open fields, meadow, pastures, ings, carrs, moors,
          commons and waste with powers to drain land : 4286 acres
          awarded
          Commissioners Joseph Thackray, Anthony Bower, Jonathan
          Teal, Francis Raynes

202   CUDWORTH (WR-SY)   1809 : 1812
          Open fields and mesne inclosures, commons, waste and
          other commonable lands : 244 acres estimated
          Commissioner Jonathan Teal
      i   WRRD B29 p65 enrolled award and plan Vol 1/22 (1812,
          surveyor Richard Birks, scale not stated)
      ii Sheffield CL LD 1021-2 sealed original award and plan;
          also NBC 72 copy award
      iii SYCRO 365/Z microfilm of award and plan
      iv PRO DL/45/8/7 and 8 enrolled extract of award and plan

203   CULLINGWORTH (WR-WY)   1809 : 1817
          Common or moor called Cullingworth Common and other
          waste : 250 acres estimated
          Commissioners Jonathan Teal (died), Richard Clark, Henry
          Teal, Joseph Robinson (refused)
      i   WRRD B32 p348 enrolled award and plan Vol 1/25 (1816,
          surveyor Henry Teal, buildings, whole township shown, 6
          ch=1")
      ii Bradford RO sealed original award and plan

204   CUMBERWORTH (WR-WY)   1799 : 1804
          Open commons, moors and waste : 431 acres awarded
          Commissioner Richard Clark
      i   WRRD B21 p341 enrolled award
      ii Sheffield CL draft plans (6 plans, 1801, surveyor
          William Fairbank, buildings, whole township shown, scale
          not stated but very large)
      iii Leeds RO award and plan
      iv Kirklees RO four plans dated 1807 (sic) (W. & F. Fairbank)

205   DACRE (WR-NY)   1836 : 1845
            Open and stinted pasture called Dacre Pasture : 1180
            acres awarded
            Commissioner Daniel Seaton
      i   WRRD B52 p1 enrolled award and map Vol 4/19 (1844,
            surveyor James Powell, buildings, inset of Dacre Banks
            enlarged, scale otherwise 6 ch=1")
      ii   Dacre parish council contemporary copy award and plan

206   DACRE (WR-NY)   1868 : 1876
            Hayshaw and Braithwaite Moor : 1625 acres awarded
            Commissioner Constantine Richard Moorsom
      i   CP Wakefield sealed original award and plan A76a
            (buildings, 3 ch=1")
      ii   Leeds RO plan (Ordnance Survey overprinted 1876, with
            valuers' papers)
      iii   Ripon and Pateley Bridge RDC award
      iv   PRO (MAF 1 202) award

207   DALTON (near Topcliffe) (NR-NY)   1759 : 1760
            By agreement. Commons and waste
            Commissioners Thomas Mitchell, George Pinkney
      i   NYCRO ZPT 18/3/4 sealed original award

208   DALTON (Huddersfield) (WR-WY)   1799 : 1811
            Commons or waste : 194 acres awarded
            Commissioners Jonathan Teal, Elihu Dickinson, James
            Milner (died), Timothy Bainbridge
      i   WRRD B51 sealed original award with plan bound together
            (not dated, surveyor Nicholas Brown, buildings, 6 ch=1")
      ii   Huddersfield TC copy award and plan
      iii   Kirklees RO sealed original award

209   DALTON (Rotherham) (WR-SY)   1797 : 1800
            Common fields or uninclosed lands and waste : 500 acres
            awarded
            Commissioners William Whitelock, Richard Parkinson
            (died), William Rodgers
      i   WRRD B20 p300 enrolled award and plan Vol 1/28 (1798,
            surveyor Joseph Colbeck, buildings, whole township
            shown, open field names, 6 ch=1")
      ii   Rotherham CL sealed original award and plan

210   DANTHORPE (ER-H)   1735 : 1735
            By deed poll. Open fields, pasture : 587 acres
            estimated
            Commissioners John Brown, Thomas Birkwood, John Conyers
            Surveyors Alexander Parke, William Brown
      i   ERRD N/436/907 enrolled deed poll
      ii   HCRO DDCC/142/1,2

211 DARFIELD (WR-SY) 1805 : 1810
   Commons and waste : 50 acres awarded
   Commissioner William Whitelock
   i   WRRD B28 p140 enrolled award
   ii Sheffield CL LD 1071 sealed original award and plan
       (1806, surveyor William Bingley, buildings, scale not
       stated)

DARLEY (WR-NY) see Knaresborough, Forest of

DARNALL (Sheffield) (WR-SY) see Attercliffe

212 DARRINGTON AND WENTBRIDGE (WR-WY) 1812 : 1817
   Open fields, meadows, pastures, moor, commons and waste
   : 1264 acres awarded
   Commissioners John Bower, George Addinell, John Hall
   i   CP Wakefield enrolled award C p259. Plan of Darrington
       only CP Wakefield A49 (1813, surveyors William Bingley
       and William Pilkington, buildings, whole township shown,
       open field names, 8 ch=1")
   ii PRO DL/45/9/3 enrolled extract of award

213 DARTON AND BARUGH (WR-SY) 1820 : 1823
   Commons and waste lands : 259 acres awarded
   Commissioner William Bingley
   i   WRRD B36 p273 (Darton) and p322 (Barugh) enrolled award
       and two plans (1 Darton, not dated, unsigned, buildings,
       3 ch=1"; 2 Barugh 1821 unsigned, not by same hand as
       Darton plan, whole township shown, 6 ch=1")
   ii Darton parish church award and two plans

DEANHEAD (WR-WY) see Longwood

214 DENBY DALE WITH CLAYTON WEST (WR-WY) 1800 : 1804
   An open common field or mesne inclosure, commons, moors
   and waste : 270 acres awarded
   Commissioner Richard Clark
   i   WRRD B22 p1 enrolled award
   ii   WRRD Map Vol 4/22 sealed original award
   iii Kirklees RO sealed original award and plan (1802,
        surveyor Richard Birks, buildings, whole township shown,
        6 ch=1"); also 1850 copy
   iv   Leeds RO photocopy of copy of plan dated 1876
   v   WYAS Z64(L) photocopy of plan from original at Bolton
        Town Hall (Clayton West, 1802, unsigned, 6 ch=1")
   0   Sealed original awards and plans to be kept in Penistone
        church and Clayton West town chest under the act. One
        is probably (iii) above.

215 DENSHAW AND QUICK (WR-Greater Manchester)   1809 : 1813
        Common or waste called Denshaw Moor : 638 acres
            estimated
        Commissioners Ralph Fletcher, John Buckley
    i   CP Wakefield F p187 enrolled award
    ii   NRA Report Saddleworth CL typed copy award
    iii   WYAS Z78 copy plan
    iv   PRO DL/45/8/13 enrolled extract of award
    0   Sealed original award to be deposited in Saddleworth
            church under the act. Not found

216 DENT (WR-Cumbria)   1849 : 1859
        Dent Fells or Dent Commons : 20,000 acres awarded
        Commissioner John Elam
    i   CP Wakefield A18 sealed original award and plan
            (Ordnance Survey)
    ii   PRO (MAF 1 247 and 1060) award
    iii   Kendal RO award

217 DEWSBURY (WR-WY)   1803 : 1806
        Commons, moors and waste : 298 acres estimated
        Commissioner William Whitelock
    i   WRRD B25 p23 enrolled award
    ii   Messrs Chalker Mosby & Hick, solicitors, Wakefield, plan
            of Dewsbury Moor and drafts (not dated, surveyor Thomas
            Gee, buildings, 3 ch=1")
    iii   Dewsbury CL papers and plans
    iv   WYAS D9/377 original award and plan

218 DINNINGTON ST JOHN'S (WR-SY)   1778 : 1779
        Open fields, meadow, carr, common and waste : 909 acres
            awarded
        Commissioners Jonathan Bromehead, John Birks, William
            Hill
    i   WRRD B12 p54 enrolled award and plan Vol 1/27 (1778,
            surveyor George Kelk, buildings, whole township shown, 9
            ch=1")
    ii   NRA report Lumley MSS copy award
    iii   Sealed original award at the church of St Leonard's
            Dinnington in 1976
    iv   Rotherham CL photocopy of plan
    v   Sheffield CL MD 5718 copy award and plan

    DISHFORTH (NR-NY) see Hutton Conyers

219 DOLCLIFF AND MEXBOROUGH (WR-SY)   1859 : 1861
        Dolcliff Common and Banks Common
        Commissioner George Dyson Simpson
    i   CP Wakefield A45 sealed original award and plan (1861,
            surveyor James Alexander, buildings, 3 ch=1")
    ii   Doncaster RO Enc.19 award and plan
    iii   PRO (MAF 1 630) award

220 DONCASTER, CANTLEY, ROSSINGTON AND WADWORTH (WR-SY)
1765 : 1771
Pieces of land in Doncaster and Cantley, and carrs and other land in Rossington and Wadworth : 4000 acres estimated
- i WRRD B7 p265 enrolled award and photocopy of plan Z 23/1 (not dated, unsigned, building plots, 4 ch=1")

DONCASTER (WR-SY) see Hexthorpe

221 DORE (Derbyshire, WR-SY) 1809 : 1822
Includes open field : 5000 acres estimated
- i Sheffield CL CA 361 award

222 DRAUGHTON (WR-NY) 1858 : 1868
Draughton Moor : 300 acres awarded
Commissioner Samuel Dickinson Martin
- i CP Wakefield A44 sealed original award and plan (1864 surveyor W. Wrightson, 3 ch=1")
- ii PRO (MAF 1 742) award

223 DRAX (WR-NY) 1773 : 1775
Open fields : 178 acres awarded
Commissioners John Dunnington, Thomas Mould
- i WRRD B10 p276 enrolled award
- ii Sheffield CL LD 114 award
- iii Borthwick Institute York, PR DR/69 award
- iv HUL DDT 16/9 papers and plan c 1774*

224 DRIFFIELD, GREAT AND LITTLE (ER-H) 1741 : 1742
Open fields, pastures, commons : 3800 acres estimated
Commissioners John Carr, Richard North, John Conyers
- i ERRD B/153/42 enrolled award and A5 copy plan made 1856 (buildings, 8 ch=1"); also tracing
- ii HUL DP/4 volume containing copy award made 1823
- iii HUL DDKG/172 & 219 photograph and tracing of plan
- iv Borthwick Institute York CCPr 11/1 19 cent copy plan
Related papers HCRO DDX/128/9

225 DRINGHOE, UPTON AND SKIPSEA BROUGH (ER-H) 1762 : 1763
Open fields, meadow, pasture : 1420 acres estimated
Commissioners John Dickinson, John Outram, John Raines
Surveyors Peter Nevill, Thomas Lazenby
- i ERRD AC/178/9 enrolled award and (IA) plan (19 cent copy of 1762 original, buildings, 12 ch=1")
- ii HCRO DDX/154/13-14, 2 copies of award
- iii HCRO sealed original award from Borthwick Institute York

226 DRINGHOUSES (York), MIDDLETHORPE, CLEMENTHORPE (WR-NY)
1822 : 1835
Common, waste and uninclosed lands in Dringhouses, rights of stray in Half Year Lands in the named places and in Micklegate Ward : 560 acres estimated
Commissioners James Bulmer, Daniel Tuke
- i York City RO Vol H enrolled award and plan in volume

227 DUGGLEBY (ER-NY) 1765 : 1765
Common fields and pasture : 1580 acres estimated
Commissioners John Dickinson, Robert Bewlay jun, John Conyers
Surveyor Isaac Milbourn
- i ERRD AH/40/2 enrolled award

DUNGWORTH (Bradfidle) (WR-SY) see Hallam

228 DUNNINGTON (ER-NY) 1707 : 1709
By agreement. Award 1707, chancery decree 1709. Open fields, ings, intack : 1000 acres estimated
Commissioners Henry Howlett, Robert Stamper, John Winder
- i HCRO DDX/195/9-11 agreement
- ii HCRO DDGD/30 award and copy chancery decree

229 DUNNINGTON (ER-NY) 1770 : 1772
Open moor (Dunnington and Heslington) : 917 acres estimated
Commissioners John Outram, John Lund, William Smith
Surveyor Miles Dawson
- i HRCO DDGD Box 1 original award
- ii Borthwick Institute York copy award

230 DUNKESWICK AND WEETON (WR-WY) 1790 : 1793
Moors and commons called Dunkeswick Common, Huby Common, Wescoehill Common and Weeton Green : 900 acres estimated
Commissioners Richard Clark, Miles Dawson, William Dawson
- i WRRD B18 p214 enrolled award and plans Vol 1/29 (1793, surveyor Jonathan Teal (1) Dunkeswick (2) Huby, Wescoehill Common, Weeton Green, buildings, 5 ch=1")
- ii Leeds RO Harewood archives, sealed original award and plans
- iii Weeton parish clerk modern copy award

DUNSFORTH (WR-NY) see Upper Dunsforth and Lower Dunsforth

231 DUNSLEY (NEWHOLM-CUM-DUNSLEY) (NR-NY) 1793 : 1803
Moor : 782 acres awarded
Commissioners Peter Merry, Richard Scarth
Surveyor Robert King
- i NRRD ES no.31 p96 enrolled award
- ii NYCRO ZPA original award and plan
- iii NYCRO ZW plan (no scale) and paper copy

EALAND (WR-H) see Crowle

EARBY (WR-Lancs) see Barnoldswick

232 EARSWICK (NR-NY)   1770 : 1775
       Common : 600 acres estimated
       Commissioners Robert Bewlay, Miles Dawson
  i   NRRD AX no.61 p213 enrolled award
  ii Borthwick Institute York PR/HUN 10/50

233 EASINGTON (ER-H)   1770 : 1771
       Open fields, common pastures : 1200 acres estimated
       Commissioners John Graves, Joseph Butler, John Baxby,
       John Raines, James Dunn
       Surveyor Charles Tate
  i   ERRD AQ/297/27 enrolled award
  ii HCRO PC/15/1 sealed original award and PC 15/2 copy plan
     (damaged) (not dated, buildings, 8 ch=1")
  iii HCRO DDCK/32/12 copy award and DDCK/35/1d copy plan
  iv HCRO DDCC/142/14 draft award and DDCC/32/42 plan (1771,
     buildings, scale not stated)
  v   HUL DDKG/173 copy plan and photograph

234 EASINGTON (NR-CLEVELAND)   1808 : 1817
       High Moor and Low Moor : 748 acres awarded
       Commissioner John Humphries
  i   NRRD DZ no.23 p180 enrolled award
  ii NYCRO ZPO copy award and plan
  iii Cleveland County Archives PR/EAT
  iv YAS MS 1123 copy plan

235 EASINGTON (WR-LANCS)   1860 : 1864
       Halstead and Crutchenber Fells : 540 acres awarded
       Commissioner John Hartley
  i   CP Wakefield A30 sealed original award and plan (1864,
     surveyor J. Hartley, 3 ch=1")
  ii PRO (MAF 1 632) award

236 EASINGTON (WR-LANCS)   1861 : 1864
       Hasgill Fell : 370 acres awarded
       Commissioner John Hartley
  i   CP Wakefield A48 sealed original award and plan (1862,
     surveyor J. Hartley, 4 ch=1")
  ii PRO (MAF 1 972) award

237 EASINGWOLD (NR-NY)   1808 : 1812
       Open fields and waste : 566 acres awarded
       Commissioners Thomas Scott, John Tuke
  i   NRRD DO no.18 p92 enrolled award and plan (1812,
     surveyor John Humphries, buildings, 4 ch=1")
  ii NYCRO PC/EAW original award and plan

EAST ARDSLEY (WR-WY) see West Ardsley

231　EAST AYTON (NR-NY)　　　　　　　　　　　　　　　　1768 : 1769

　　　　　Open fields, meadows and commons : 1337 acres awarded
　　　　　Surveyor John Foord
　　i　　NRRD BA no.13 p119 enrolled award

EASTBURN (WR-WY) see Steeton

EASTBY (WR-NY) see Embsay

EAST COATHAM (NR-NY) see Coatham

233　EAST COTTINGWITH (ER-H)　　　　　　　　　　　　　　1773 : 1774

　　　　　Open fields, pasture, ings, commons, waste : 960 acres
　　　　　estimated
　　　　　Commissioners William Hall, John Dunnington, Richard
　　　　　Cross
　　i　　ERRD AT/121/17 enrolled award and (IA) plan (1774,
　　　　　buildings, 8 ch=1")
　　ii　　York Minster Library BB33 19 cent copy award
　　　　　Related documents HUL DDJ/34/56-61

EAST HADDLESEY (WR-NY) see West Haddlesey

EAST HARDWICK (WR-WY) see Pontefract

234　EAST HESLERTON (ER-NY)　　　　　　　　　　　　　　　1770 : 1772
　　　　　Open fields, meadows, pasture : 3084 acres awarded
　　　　　Commissioners William Iveson, Joseph Butler, John Outram
　　　　　Surveyor Peter Nevill
　　i　　ERRD AQ/156/14 and (IA) copy plan (1770, buildings, 16
　　　　　ch=1")

235　EAST KESWICK AND HAREWOOD (WR-WY)　　　　　　　　　1797 : 1803
　　　　　Open fields, meadow, pasture, moor or commons : 706
　　　　　acres awarded
　　　　　Commissioners William Dawson, Timothy Bainbridge,
　　　　　Jonathan Teal, John Sharpe (refused)
　　i　　WRRD B21 p187 Vol 2/9 enrolled award and plan (1801,
　　　　　surveyor Jonathan Teal, buildings, open field names, 8
　　　　　ch=1")
　　ii　　Leeds RO Harewood archives sealed original award and
　　　　　plan

236　EAST LUTTON and WEST LUTTON (ER-NY)　　　　　　　　1801 : 1804
　　　　　Open fields, pastures, leys, commons, waste : 2497 acres
　　　　　awarded
　　　　　Commissioners William Whitelock, Joseph Dickinson
　　　　　Surveyor Ralph Burton
　　i　　ERRD CA/356/45 enrolled award
　　ii　　HUL DDSY/70/105 award
　　iii　 NYCRO ZDS copy award

243 EAST NEWTON (ER-H) 1770 : 1772
Open fields, lands : 507 acres awarded
Commissioners John Graves, Robert Foster, Peter Nevill
Surveyor Charles Tate
- i ERRD AQ/46/6 enrolled award
- ii HCRO PE/76 original award

EASTOFT (WR-H) see Crowle

244 EASTRINGTON, BELLASIZE AND SANDHOLME (ER-H) 1813 : 1822
Open fields, meadows, pastures : 800 acres awarded
Commissioners John Hall, Robert Plummer Weddall
- i ERRD DQ/73/3 enrolled award and (IA) plan (1819, buildings, parts of townships of the named places and Newland, 10 ch=1")
- ii Durham DCM 21644 two copies plan

EASTRINGTON (ER-H) see also Howden

245 EBBERSTON (NR-NY) 1769 : 1775
Open fields, commons and waste : 9400 acres estimated
Commissioners Robert Bewlay jun, John Outram, William Willmott
- i   NRRD BE no.3 p66 enrolled award
- ii NYCRO ZJQ1 award and plan (1770, surveyor J. Foord, buildings, 12 ch=1")
- iii York City RO M20 copy award
- iv PRO DL/41/72 enclosure papers for Ebberston, Scalby and Seamer

246 ECCLESALL (Sheffield) (WR-SY) 1779 : 1788
Open commons, moors and waste : 1000 acres estimated
Commissioners William Hill, Samuel Brailsford, John Renshaw
- i   WRRD B17 p68 enrolled award
- ii Sheffield CL CA 363 award and plan
- iii Sheffield CL copy award and copies of 3 plans (1788, surveyor William Fairbank)
- iv Wentworth Woodhouse original award

247 ECCLESFIELD AND GRENO WOOD (WR-SY) 1784 : 1789
Commons and waste : 600 acres estimated
Commissioners John Kent, John Birks (died), Arthur Elliott, Joseph Outram
- i WRRD B17 p297 enrolled award
- ii Sheffield CL ACM 563 sealed original award and 4 plans (not dated, surveyor William Fairbank, buildings, whole township shown, 1 mile =10")

242 ECCLESHILL (BRADFORD) (WR-WY) 1841 : 1848
Common, moor or waste : 240 acres awarded
Commissioners John Benjamin Ingle (died), Thomas William Rawson
- i CP Wakefield A5 sealed original award with plans (2 plans 1848, unsigned; (1) township of Eccleshill, buildings, whole township shown, 6 ch=1"; (2) common, moor and waste, buildings, 3 ch=1")
- 0 Copy award to be deposited in Bradford parish church under the act. Not found

ECCUP (WR-WY) see Arthington

EDLINGTON (WR-SY) see Stainton

243 EGGBOROUGH, SHERWOOD, HUT GREEN AND TRANMORE (WR-NY) 1800 : 1803
Open fields, meadows, commons and waste : 564 acres awarded
Commissioners John Bradford, Isaac Leatham
- i WRRD B21 p212 enrolled award and plan Vol 2/16 (1802, surveyor John Tuke, buildings, whole township shown, open field names, 6 ch=1")
- ii Eggborough parish council award
- iii HCRO DDCL/245 copy award signed by commissioners and copy map

244 EGTON (NR-NY) 1848 : 1854
Commons : 7313 acres awarded
Commissioners Christopher Lonsdale Bradley
- i NYCRO QDD(i) 15 sealed original award and plans (1852, C.L. Bradley, buildings, 3 & 6 ch=1")
- ii Egton vicarage award and plan
- iii PRO (MAF 1 1130) award

245 ELLAND CUM GREETLAND (WR-WY) 1803 : 1808
Open fields or mesne inclosures, commons, moors and waste : 716 acres estimated
Commissioner Jonathan Taylor
- i WRRD B26 p209 enrolled award
- ii Halifax Town Hall sealed original award and 2 plans (1807, surveyor Jonathan Taylor; (1) Allotments on South Lane, Blackley Broad Carr, Elland Banks etc., buildings, 6 ch=1"; (2) Lindwell Bank, Copley Gren, Thick Hollin Moor, Greetland Moor and Sykehouse Green, buildings, 6 ch=1"). Also later copies of award and plan 1
- iii WYAS Z38 photocopy of plan
- iv Calderdale RO copy award

ELLERBURN (NR-NY) see Thornton Dale

252 ELLERKER (ER-H) 1765 : 1766
    Open fields : 1800 acres estimated
    Commissioners John Cleaver, John Dickinson, John Outram
    Surveyors Edward Johnson, Charles Tate
- i   ERRD AH/71/3 enrolled award and (E8 and IA) plan, 3 copies (1766, signed David Tate, buildings, 10 ch=1")
- ii HCRO DDBD/19/3 copy award
- iii Durham HCR sealed original award and plan
- iv Durham DCM sealed original award and plan; also related papers

    Related documents HCRO DDBD/19/4 survey and valuation 1771

ELLERS (WR-SY) see Cantley

253 ELLERTON (ER-H) 1802 : 1810
    Open fields, ings, meadows, pastures, commons, waste : 965 acres awarded
    Commissioners Edward Cleaver, John Hall
    Surveyor John Humphries
- i   ERRD CI/404/32
- ii HCRO DX/21/draft award
- iii Borthwick Institute York PR ELL/78 award and plan
- iv HUL DDHO/16/55 plan (1810, buildings, 12 ch=1")

254 ELLOUGHTON, BROUGH AND WAULDBY (ER-H) 1794 : 1796
    Open fields, meadow, pasture, commons, waste : 2374 acres awarded
    Commissioners Peter Nevill, Joseph Dickinson, Thomas Barrow
- i   ERRD BT/306/41 enrolled awarded and (IA) plans, two copies of each, (1 Elloughton and Brough; 2 Wauldby (not dated, unsigned, buildings, 12 ch=1")

255 ELMSWELL (ER-H) 1770 : 1771
    Open grounds : 1053 acres estimated
    Commissioners John Outram, William Hall
- i   HCRO IA award and copy at DDX/131/4

256 ELSTRONWICK (ER-H) 1806 : 1813
    Open fields, meadow, pasture : 901 acres awarded
    Commissioners John Lee, John Lockwood, John Hall
    Surveyor John Dalton
- i   ERRD CQ/218/15 enrolled award and plan A2 (not dated, buildings, 4 ch=1")
- ii HCRO DDCC/142/2,20 bound copy and bound draft award
- iii HCRO DDCK/35/1(1) copy plan
- iv HUL DKG/175 photograph of plan

    Related documents, Hull CL Commissioners' minutes with act; HCRO DDIV/4 accounts and notices

257 ELVINGTON (ER-NY)   1743 : 1743
         Moor : 600 acres awarded
         Commissioners Charles Headlam, Marmaduke Lawson, John
         Skilbeck, Richard Darley, Robert Harrison, Henry
         Yarborough, John Plaxton, William Tomlinson, Peter
         Duffield, Thomas Carr, James Cooper, Francis Gainford
         "or any 5 or more of them"
         Surveyor Robert Bewlay
    i   ERRD Bk D p37 enrolled award
    ii   YAS MS 679 award and plan

258 ELVINGTON (ER-NY)   1769 : ?
         Open fields, meadows, ings, common lands : 800 acres
         estimated; probably no award
    i   Borthwick Institute York, Elvington glebe terrier 1770,
         mentions act

259 EMLEY (WR-WY)   1817 : 1820
         Commons, moors and waste : 300 acres
         Commissioners Thomas Gee, Nicholas Brown
    i   WRRD B34 p316 enrolled award
    ii   Kirklees R O   award and plan in volume
    iii YAS MD 225 copy award with plan in volume (not dated,
         surveyor William Bingley, buildings, 3 ch=1")
    iv   Mr J. Clegg of Emley had plan in 1978
    v   Leeds RO photocopy of plan
    vi   WYAS Z29 photocopy of plan

260 EMBSAY WITH EASTBY (WR-NY)   1759

         By agreement. Embsay pasture
    i   Craven Water Board typscript copy award and tracing of
         plan

261 ETTON (ER-H)   1818 : 1820
         Open fields, commons, pastures, waste : 2855 acres
         awarded
         Commissioners William Ware, John Hall, Peter Jackson
         Surveyor Edward Page
    i   ERRD DA/266/58 enrolled award and plan (1819, buildings,
         12 ch=1")
    ii   HCRO PC/28/1 original award in bound volume with plan
    iii HUL DDSY/17/1 plan
         Related documents HCRO DX/7-8 and DDX 309

262 EVERINGHAM (ER-H)   1765 : none
         Act confirmed enclosure. Common fields, commons, waste,
         ings : 1590 acres estimated
         Commissioners : none
    i   HUL DDEV/9/116-8 and DDLA/8/1; 4 copies of act. Related
         documents in HUL DDEV/9

     EVERLEY (NR-NY) see Hackness

263 EVERTHORPE (ER-H)   1773 : 1774
         Open fields : 470 acres awarded
         Commissioners William Hall, John Wood, Richard Cross
         Surveyor Peter Nevill
    i   ERRD AT/89/13 enrolled award and (IA) plan (township and
         allotment on Wallingfen, buildings, 8 ch=1")
    ii   HCRO DDX/149/4 copy plan
         Related documents HCRO DDBD/23/6

264 EXELBY, LEEMING AND NEWTON (NR-NY)   1836 : 1840
         Four open fields : 94 acres awarded
         Commissioner Thomas Bradley
    i   NYCRO QDD(d) Bk R p59 enrolled award and plan (1840
         Thomas Bradley and son, 4 ch=1")
    ii   NYCRO ZCH 1 original award and plan

265   FACEBY (NR-NY)   1748 : 1748
            Common fields, pastures and meadows : 1027 acres awarded
            Commissioners
      i   NRRD L no.127 p210 enrolled award

266   FADMOOR (NR-NY)   1763 : 1763
            By agreement. Open fields
            Commissioners Thomas Hudson, Joseph Foord, Thomas Foord
      i   NYCRO ZEW V 2/2 sealed original award and plan ZEW M/1
            (1763, unsigned, 4 ch=1")

      FADMOOR (NR-NY) see Kirkbymoorside

267   FAIRBURN (WR-WY)   1813 : 1816
            Open fields, stinted pastures, intermixed inclosures,
            commons, waste and other commonable lands : 793 acres
            awarded
            Commissioners William Dawson (died), Thomas Dyson,
            Christopher Paver
      i   WRRD B32 p187 enrolled award and plan Vol 2/10 (1815,
            surveyor Christopher Paver, buildings, whole township
            shown, open field names, 6 ch=1")
      0   Sealed original award to be deposited in Ledsham church
            under the act. Not found

268   FALSGRAVE (NR-NY)   1773 : 1775
            Commons and waste : 368 acres awarded
            Commissioners Edward Cleaver, John Graves, William Hall
      i   NRRD BE no.2 p30 enrolled award
      ii   NYCRO QDD(I) no.48 original award

269   FANGFOSS CUM SPITTAL (ER-H)   1726 : 1724
            Agreement 1723, act 1726. Open fields, pasture : 1068
            acres estimated
            Commissioners Francis Wright, William Cordeaux, Thomas
            Bramskell, Joseph Armitage
            Surveyor James West
      i   HCRO typescript copy
      ii   Fangfoss parish church 1971 copy
            Related documents HCRO DPX/50 survey 1723 by John West

270   FARLINGTON (NR-NY)   1813 : 1815
            Open land and waste : 78 acres awarded
            Commissioner Daniel Tuke
      i   NRRD no.7 sealed original award and plan (not dated,
            Edmund Gray, buildings, 4 ch=1")

271   FARNHAM (WR-NY)   1814 : 1814
            Pasture called Cliff Carr
            Commissioner John Humphries
      i   WRRD B30 p371 enrolled award and plan B30 p373 (not
            dated, unsigned, 4 and a half ch=1")
      ii   YAS DD56/D/2 award

      FARNHAM (WR-NY) see Scriven

272 FAWDINGTON (NR-NY)   1821 : 1821
        By deed poll. Common : 220 acres awarded
        Commissioner John Bower
     i NRRD EP no.42 p88 enrolled award and plan (1821,
        surveyor John Humphries, 4 ch=1")

     FAXFLEET (ER-H) see Blacktoft

273 FEATHERSTONE (WR-WY)   1788 : 1795
        Open fields, common or waste : 680 acres estimated
        Commissioners Richard Clark, Isaac Leatham, William
        Whitelock
     i   WRRD B19 p173 enrolled award
     ii Featherstone UDC sealed original award and plan
     iii Featherstone church award and plan

274 FELIXKIRK AND SUTTON-UNDER-WHITESTONECLIFFE (NR-NY) 1794 :
        1799
        (Not open field) : acres not stated
        Commissioners Edward Watterson (deceased), Richard
        Clark, John Flintoff
     i   NRRD CS no.6 p9 enrolled award and 3 plans (1795, 1796,
         unsigned, 4 ch=1")
     ii NRRD no.4 original award and plan

     FELLISCLIFFE (WR-NY) see Knaresborough, Forest of

275 FENWICK (WR-SY)   1779 : 1780
        Common or waste : 300 acres estimated
        Commissioners John Lund jun, John Crowder, George Kelk
     i   WRRD B12 p290 enrolled award
     ii Sheffield CL BFM 72 B6 enrolled award
     0   Sealed original award to be kept in Campsall parish
         church under the act. Not found

276 FERRENSBY (WR-NY)   1808 : 1809
        By agreement. Moor, common or waste called Ferrensby
        Moor
        Commissioner William Dawson
     i   WRRD B27 p123 enrolled award
     ii NYCRO I Acc. no.1112 sealed original award with plan
         (not dated, buildings, half a ch=1")

     FERRIBY (ER-H) see North Ferriby

277 FERRYBRIDGE (WR-WY)   1831 : 1834
         Open fields, mesne inclosures, ings, common or stinted
         pasture, balks : 689 acres awarded
         Commissioner Henry Teal
     i   WRRD B37 p135 enrolled award and plan Vol 2/11 (not
         dated, surveyor James Bulmer, buildings, whole township
         shown, 3 ch=1"). The volume also contains a plan of
         Ferrybridge open fields, 1800, open field names and
         features, 3 ch=1".
     o   Sealed original award to be kept in parish chest under
         the act. Not found

FERRYBRIDGE (WR-WY) see Pontefract

278 FILEY (ER-NY)   1788 : 1791
         Open fields, meadows, pastures, commons, waste : 695
         acres awarded
         Commissioners Isaac Leatham, John Wood, John Foord
         Surveyor Joseph Dickinson, John Wings
     i   ERRD BG/310/43 enrolled award
     ii HCRO IA bound copy award and 2 plans (one bound with
         award : not dated, buildings, 4 ch=1")
     ii HCRO DDHU/3/4 copy award

FIMBER (ER-H) see Wetwang

FINNINGLEY (WR-SY) see Blaxton

FISHLAKE (WR-SY) see Hatfield

279 FLAMBOROUGH (ER-H)   1765 : 1767
         Open fields, meadows, pastures, commons, waste : 2500
         acres awarded
         Commissioners John Dickinson, John Outram, John Raines
         Surveyor Peter Nevill
     i   ERRD AH/295/6 enrolled award
     ii HCRO IA enrolled award and copy plan (not dated,
         buildings, 10 ch=1")
     iii Bridlington Public Library typescript copy award and
         plan
     iv HCRO DDX/88/1 copy plan

FLASBY WITH WINTERBURN (WR-NY) see Winterburn

FLAWITH (NR-NY) see Tholthorpe

FLAXBY (WR-NY) see Clareton

280 FLINTON (ER-H)   1751 : 1752
         By agreement. Two large open cornfields, pasture : 114
         oxgangs, 12 acres awarded
         Commissioners Joseph Thompson, Richard North, John
         Raines (died), Robert Bell
         Surveyors William Williamson, Samuel Milbourn
     i   HCRO DDCC/142/4 copy award

281   FLIXTON (ER-NY)   1802 : 1806
            Open fields, meadows, pastures, ings, carr, common,
            waste : 2441 acres awarded
            Commissioners Joseph Dickinson, John Hall, Isaac Leatham
            Surveyors Samuel Dickinson, Thomas Barrow
      i   ERRD CI/69/4 enrolled award
      ii   HCRO DDX/154/10 copy award
      iii   Flixton parish clerk award

282   FLOCKTON (WR-WY)   1775 : 1776
            By agreement. Commons and waste
            Commissioners George Stringer, Joseph Hunter
      i   WRRD B11 p146 enrolled award
      ii   Kirklees RO   1945 copy award
      iii   YAS DD70/109 award

      FLOTMANBY (ER-NY) see Folkton

      FOCKERBY (WR-H) see Adlingfleet

283   FOLKTON AND FLOTMANBY (ER-NY)   1802 : 1807
            Open fields, ings, carrs, wastes, commons : 1765 acres
            awarded
            Commissioners John Foakes, Joseph Dickinson
            Surveyors Samuel Dickinson, Ralph Burton
            Umpire John Hall
      i   ERRD CI/256/19 enrolled award and 2 plans (D1) by
            different surveyors (1) East and West Flotmanby,
            buildings, 8 ch=1"; (2) Folkton, buildings, 8 ch=1"

284   FOLLIFOOT (WR-NY)   1772 : 1774
            Open fields and waste ground called Follifoot Moor :
            1265 acres awarded
            Commissioners George Jackson, Ambrose Gray, Miles Dawson
      i   WRRD B10 p108 enrolled award
      ii   Leeds RO Harewood archives, sealed original award and
            plan (1772, surveyor William Dawson, overmarked with
            enclosure allotments, buildings, open field names, 4
            ch=1")

      FORDON (ER-H) see Hunmanby

285   FOSTON ON THE WOLDS (ER-H)   1776 : 1780
            Open fields, meadows, pastures, carrs : 1000 acres
            awarded
            Commissioners John Graves, Peter Nevill
            Surveyor John Kendall
      i   ERRD BB/212/25 enrolled award and plan (IA)
      ii   HCRO DDX/154/15 copy award
      iii   HCRO PE/136/73 sealed original award
      iv   HCRO PC/13/1 plan (1776, buildings, 6 ch=1")
      v   HCRO DX/116 plan
      vi   HUL DDKG/53 copy plan

286 FOUNTAINS EARTH (WR-NY)　　　　　　　　　　　　　　1850 : 1856
        Fountains Earth Moor : 4000 acres awarded
        Commissioner George Henry Strafford
    i   CP Wakefield A14 sealed original award and 3 plans
        (1854, 3 ch=1")
    ii PRO (MAF 1 MR 887) award

287 FOXHOLES (ER-NY)　　　　　　　　　　　　　　　　　　1836 : 1840
        Open fields : 1539 acres awarded
        Commissioners Thomas Scott, Leonard Brooks Earnshaw,
        William Richardson
        Surveyors William Rawson, Henry Scott
    i   HCRO DDX/364 sealed original award and plan (1840,
        buildings, 6 ch=1")
    ii HCRO DDX/154/10,24 award
    iii HCRO DDHU/4/1 award
    iv HCRO QDB 8 p11 enrolled award

288 FREMINGTON (NR-NY)　　　　　　　　　　　　　　　　　1777 : 1778
        Moor and waste : 1074 acres awarded
        Commissioners William Brown, George Jackson, Thomas
        Humphrey
    i   NRRD BL no.15 p99 enrolled award
    ii NYCRO PR/GR original award and plan

289 FRICKLEY WITH CLAYTON (WR-SY)　　　　　　　　　　　1814 : 1821
        Open fields, commons, wastes and other commonable lands
        and enclosed lands : 450 acres awarded
        Commissioner Thomas Gee
    i   WRRD B36 p72 enrolled award
    ii CP Wakefield A87 sealed original award and plan,
        deposited by parish council (1814, surveyor Robert
        Moore, buildings, whole parish shown, open field names,
        6 ch=1")

290 FRIDAYTHORPE (ER-H)　　　　　　　　　　　　　　　　　1810 : 1817
        Open fields, lands, common, pasture, waste : 1842 acres
        awarded
        Commissioners Joseph Dickinson, John Singleton, William
        Shipton
        Surveyor Richard Page
    i   ERRD DA/2/1 enrolled award and (IA) plan
    ii HCRO PE/49/30 sealed original award, bound with plan
        (1811, buildings, 8 ch=1")
    iii HCRO IA award and plan
    iv HCRO DX/53 draft award

    FRODINGHAM (ER-H) see North Frodingham

291 FULFORD (ER-NY)　　　　　　　　　　　　　　　　　　　1757 : 1759
        Fields, meadows, commons : 780 acres awarded
        Commissioners Robert Bewlay, Richard Mason, Samuel
        Milbourn
    i   ERRD AC/265/12 enrolled award
    ii York City RO TC DP/1/4 copy award made 1798
    iii NYCRO Sandys-Renton no.73 copy award

FULL SUTTON (ER-H) see Catton

FULSTONE (WR-WY) see Wooldale

FULWOOD (Sheffield) (WR-SY) see Hallam

292 FYLINGDALES (NR-NY) 1808 : 1810
      Open field or pasture : 220 acres estimated
      Commissioners John Humphries, William Merry
  i   NYCRO ZPA, ZW, ZNK copies of award and plan (1808, scale not stated)

GALPHAY (WR-NY) see Kirkby Malzeard

293 GAMMERSGILL (NR-NY)   1864 : 1867
         Not open field : 304 acres awarded
     i   NRRD enrolled award and plan
     ii   NYCRO original award
     iii   PRO (MAF 1 311) award

GANTON (ER-NY) see Binnington

294 GARFORTH (WR-WY)   1810 : 1815
         Open fields, a common or waste called Garforth Moor : 782 acres awarded
         Commissioner Francis Raynes
     i   CP Wakefield C p121 enrolled award and plan A53 (1813, surveyor John Humphries, buildings, whole township shown, 5 ch=1")
     ii   Leeds RO two awards and plan

295 GARTON ON THE WOLDS (ER-H)   1774 : 1775
         Open fields
         Commissioners Edward Cleaver, William Hill, Samuel Milbourn
         Surveyors Isaac Milbourn, Christopher Wilkinson
     i   ERRD AT/243/27 enrolled award
     ii   HUL DDSY/23/46 award
         Related documents HCRO DDHB/1/14

296 GARSDALE (WR-Cumbria)   1850 : 1859
         Garsdale Common : 5000 acres awarded
         Commissioners Francis Garth
     i   CP Wakefield A10 sealed original award and plan (1850, surveyor Francis Garth, buildings, 3 ch=1")
     ii   PRO (MAF 1 13) award

GATEFORTH (WR-NY) see Brayton

GATE HELMSLEY (NR-NY) see Osbaldwick

297 GAYLES (NR-NY)   1773 : 1774
         Moor : 1452 acres awarded
         Commissioners William Jopson, Thomas Humphreys, Ingram Gill
     i   NRRD AX no.54 p195 enrolled award

GILBERDYKE (ER-H) see Blacktoft

298 GILDERSOME (WR-WY)   1800
         By agreement?
     i   WYAS award and plan (1800, surveyor Samuel Gawthorp, buildings, whole township shown, 3 ch=1")

299 GILLAMOOR (NR-NY) 1770 : 1771
    By agreement. Town fields
    Commissioners Thomas Hudson, Joseph Foord
  i   NYCRO ZEW V 2/3/1 sealed original award with plan, ZEW m/2 (not dated, unsigned, scale not stated)
  ii NYCRO ZEW V 2/3/1 award

GILLAMOOR (NR-NY) see Kirkbymoorside

300 GILLING EAST (NR-NY) 1810 : 1815
    Common field, moors, commons, waste : 300 acres awarded
    Commissioner John Humphries
  i   NRRD DZ no.3 p5 and no.11 enrolled award and plan (1815, John Humphries, buildings, 6 ch=1")
  ii NYCRO ZAZ copy award

301 GILMONBY (NR-Durham) 1802 : 1802
    By agreement : 240 acres awarded
    Commissioners Alexander Calvert, Richard Clark
  i   NYCRO ZAY 35 sealed original award
    ii Durham CRO D/HH 2/14/63 and D/Wat p18 award and plan

302 GILSTEAD (WR-WY) 1858 : 1861
    Gilstead Moor and Romels Moor : 1928 acres awarded
    Commissioner Crayston, Webster
  i   CP Wakefield A11 sealed original award (printed) with plan and A78 without plan (plan of Gilstead and Romels Moors, 1861, surveyor C. Webster, buildings, 6 ch=1")
  ii   YAS printed award MD 290/7 with 2 plans
  iii Bingley UDC copy award and plan
  iv   Leeds RO copy plan
  v   Messrs Weatherhead and Butcher, Bingley, award
  vi   Sheffield Council awards and plans
  vii PRO (MAF 1) award

GIPTON (WR-WY) see Potternewton

303 GLAISDALE (WR-NY) 1768 : 1769
    By agreement. Pasture
    Commissioners Joseph Foord, William Harding, William Fordon
  i   NRRD vol AT no.29 p206 enrolled award
  ii NYCRO ZW copy award

304 GLASS HOUGHTON WITH CASTLEFORD 1816 : 1822
    Open fields, ings, commons and waste : 628 acres awarded
    Commissioners William Dawson (died), Henry Teal
  i   CP Wakefield E p181 enrolled award and plan A68 (1822, surveyor Christopher Paver, buildings, whole townships shown, open field names and features, 6 ch=1")
  ii   Wakefield Town Hall sealed original award and plan
  iii PRO DL/45/6 enrolled extract of award
  iv   WYAS Z69 typescript copy of award

305 GLUSBURN (WR-NY)   1778 : 1779
        Commons or waste called Glusburn Moor : 700 acres
        awarded
        Commissioners Thomas Whyman, George Jackson, John Asquith
        jun
    i   WRRD B12 p27 enrolled award
    ii WRRD Roll 4, sealed original award and plan (1778,
        unsigned, buildings, 6 ch=1")
    iii Kildwick parish church award

306 GOLCAR (Huddersfield) (WR-WY)   1820 : 1823
        Commons, moors and waste called Wholestone Moor, Bolster
        Moor, and other waste : 320 acres awarded
        Commissioners William Pilkington, Frederick Jones
    i   WRRD B37 p1 enrolled award
    ii Kirklees RO   sealed original award and plan in
        volume (1823, surveyor Thomas Dinsley, buildings, whole
        township shown, 6 ch=1"); also later copies of award and
        plan ; also 3 printed copies of award
    iii YAS MD 225 award and commissioners' minute book

307 GOODMANHAM (ER-H)   1775 : 1777
        Open fields, common, waste : 2852 acres awarded
        Commissioners Samuel Brailsford, John Outram, John
        Raines
    i   ERRD BB/40/9 enrolled award and E7 copy plan made 1934
    ii HCRO DDX/199/1 and DDX/131/6 copies award and copies
        plan; another copy plan IA
    iii Borthwick Institute York PR GOOD/18 sealed original
        award and plan (1775, buildings, 12 ch=1")

308 GOWDALL (WR-H)   1773 : 1775
        Open fields, meadows, pastures, commons or waste : 901
        acres awarded
        Commissioners Thomas Tofield, William Hill, John
        Fretwell
    i   WRRD B11 p99 enrolled award
    ii D of L Lib 2 p202 enrolled award and plan
    iii HCRO DDCL/243, 18 cent copy of award in volume and plan
        separate (draft, not dated, surveyor William Dawson,
        buildings, 20 ch=1")
    iv Doncaster RO P50 sealed original award

309 GOWTHORPE (in Bishop Wilton) (ER-H)   1810 : 1814
        Open fields, stinted pastures : 306 acres awarded
        Commissioners John Hall, Richard Page
    i   ERRD G sealed original award and plan (1811, buildings,
        6 ch=1")
    ii Borthwick Institute York PR B/W/36 award
        Related documents HCRO DX/54-62 and HUL DDSY/99/22

310 GRAFTON (Marton cum Grafton) (WR-NY)　　　　　　　1800 : 1803
　　　　Four open fields, common or waste, common balks or waste
　　　　in Grafton) : 439 acres awarded
　　　　Commissioners Alexander Watford (did not sign), John
　　　　Moiser, John Abbey, Benjamin Gray
　　i　WRRD B21 p244 enrolled award and plan Vol 2/12 (not
　　　　dated, unsigned, buildings, whole township shown, 6
　　　　ch=1")
　　ii　NYCRO PR/MAG 12/2 award

　　GRAFTON see Marton cum Grafton

　　GRANTLEY (WR-NY) see Skelding

311 GRASSINGTON (WR-NY)　　　　　　　　　　　　　　　　1788 : 1792
　　　　Four stinted pastures : 2262 acres awarded
　　　　Commissioners Henry Waddington, Thomas Chippendale
　　　　(died), Thomas Ingilby
　　i　WRRD B18 p121 enrolled award
　　ii　Grassington parish council sealed original award and plan
　　　　(1788, unsigned, buildings, including township, open
　　　　field features, 6 ch=1")
　　iii　NRA Raistrick MSS copy award and related papers

312 GREAT BROUGHTON (NR-NY)　　　　　　　　　　　　　　1811 : 1819
　　　　Open field, common and waste : 327 acres awarded
　　　　Commissioner John Humphries
　　i　NRRD EI no.17 p25 enrolled award and plans (3 on 1 sheet:
　　　　undated, unsigned, buildings, 2 and a half ch or 6 ch=1"
　　ii　NYCRO ZMI 23 two plans (1812, surveyor John Humphries,
　　　　buildings, 2 and a half ch and 6 ch=1")

313 GREAT COWDEN AND LITTLE COWDEN (ER-H)　　　　　　1770 : 1772
　　　　Open fields, meadows, pastures : 1100 acres estimated
　　　　Commissioners Peter Nevill, John Outram
　　　　Surveyor Joseph Dickinson
　　i　ERRD AQ/61/8 enrolled award

　　GREAT DRIFFIELD (ER-H) see Driffield

　　GREAT AND LITTLE EDSTONE (NR-NY) see Sinnington

314 GREAT GIVENDALE (ER-H)　　　　　　　　　　　　　　1833 : 1845
　　　　Open fields : 641 acres awarded
　　　　Commissioners William Ware (died), Edward Page, John
　　　　Bell (died), Robert Smith
　　　　Surveyor Richard Allen Stickney
　　　　Umpire William Stickney
　　i　ERRD FG/386/4 enrolled award
　　　　Related document HCRO DX/10 road plan

　　GREAT AND LITTLE HECK (WR-H) see Pollington

315 GREAT KELK (ER-H)   1849 : 1849
     By agreement. Open field : 886 acres estimated
     Commissioners John Young Macvicar, Samuel Vessey
     Surveyor Henry Scott
   i   ERRD HB/358/442 enrolled award
   ii   HCRO QDB 9 p1 enrolled award
   iii HUL DDLG/15/20 sealed original award, bound, with plan
        (1848, buildings, 6 ch=1")
     Related documents HCRO DX/125 plan 1789 showing strips.

     GREAT MITTON (WR-Lancs) see Mitton

316 GREAT OUSEBURN (WR-NY)   1770 : 1777
     Open fields, moor, ings, commonable ground : 968 acres
     awarded
     Commissioners William Chippendale, Joseph Butler, John
     Outram, John Lund, Richard Richardson
   i   WRRD B11 p168 enrolled award
   ii   Borthwick Institute York, parish award
        iii NYCRO PR/OUG 13/3 award

     GREEN HAMMERTON (WR-NY) see Whixley

     GREETLAND (WR-WY) see Elland

     GRENO WOOD (WR-SY) see Ecclesfield

317 GREWELTHORPE (WR-NY)   1780 : ?
     Moors, commons and waste : 1700 acres estimated
     Commissioners Richard Richardson, George Jackson,
     Richard Beckwith
   i   Parish council copy award and extract of plan
   ii   YAS DD69/66 award
   0   Sealed original award to be kept in Kirkby Malzeard
        church under the act : probably destroyed by fire at
        church 1908

318 GRINDALE (ER-H)   1836 : 1844
     Open fields : 1317 acres awarded
     Commissioners Leonard Brooks Earnshaw, Thomas Donkin,
     Edward Page
     Surveyors Henry Scott, Gregory Page
   i   HCRO QDB 8 p167 enrolled award and (IA) plan (1844,
        buildings, 8 ch=1", reduced from original)
   ii   HUL DDLG/16/137 award and DDLG/16/151 plan (1842)
   iii HUL CL plan
   iv   NYCRO DZV draft enclosure plan showing strips and new
        enclosures overlaid, 1842, 3 ch=1"

319 GRINDLETON, WEST BRADFORD, WADDINGTON AND BASHALL EAVES
       (WR-Lancs)   1812 : 1819
       Common, moor, heath and waste : 1500 acres awarded
       Commissioner William Harper
   i   WRRD B35 p1 enrolled award and 4 plans Vol 1/14 (not
       dated, unsigned, buildings, various scales)
   ii Lancs CRO PR/3031/13/1 award and plans; also DDHC1 copy
       award and plan

320 GRINTON (NR-NY)   1808 : 1809
       By deed poll. Pasture : 429 acres awarded
       Commissioner Alexander Calvert
   i   NRRD DK no.77 p100 enrolled award

321 GRINTON (NR-NY)   1812 : 1812
       By deed poll. Pastures : 242 acres awarded
       Commissioners A. Calvert, G. Dowthwaite
   ii NRRD DT no.55 p84 enrolled award and plan (not dated,
       unsigned, buildings, 4 ch=1")

322 GRINTON (NR-NY)   1825 : 1827
       By deed poll. Pasture : 140 acres estimated
       Commissioner Thomas Bradley
   i   NRRD FH no.56 p 133 enrolled award and plan (not dated,
       unsigned, buildings, 4 ch=1")

323 GUISELEY (WR-WY)   1796 : 1801
       Common called Guiseley Common and other waste : 400
       acres estimated
       Commissioners William Dawson, John Sharpe (refused),
       Jonathan Teal
   i   YAS MD 283 sealed original award and plan (1800,
       surveyor Jonathan Teal, buildings, including town, 6
       ch=1")
   ii Guiseley parish church sealed original award and plan

324 HACKNESS, SUFFIELD-CUM-EVERLEY, SILPHO AND BROXA (NR-NY)
                                                      1818 : 1821
          Moors, common and waste : 1500 acres awarded
          Commissioner John Tuke
      i   NYCRO QDD(I) no.18 enrolled award and plan (not dated,
          surveyor James Bulmer, 6 ch=1")

325 HAINWORTH AND LEES (BINGLEY AND KEIGHLEY) (WR-WY)   1851 : 1862
          Hainworth and Lees Commons : 600 acres awarded
          Award apparently not enrolled
      i   Keighley TC copy award
      ii Bradford MDC sealed original award
      iii Bingley UDC certified copy award and plan (1855,
          buildings, 3 ch=1"
      iv PRO (MAF 1 570) award

326 HAISTHORPE (ER-H)   1723 : 1723
          By agreement. Open fields, meadow, pasture : 267 acres
          estimated
          Commissioners Thomas Coulton, William Hudson, John
          Gotherlesse
          Surveyor Richard Lazenby
      i   HUL DDWB/10/15,16 agreement and sealed original award
      ii HUL DDWB/10/17 copy award

HALDENBY (WR-H) see Adlingfleet

HALIFAX (WR-WY) see Highroad Well

327 HALLAM (UPPER & NETHER), FULWOOD, MOORWOOD, STANNINGTON,
     STORRS, DUNGWORTH (SHEFFIELD AND BRADFIELD) (WR-SY)
                                                      1791 : 1805
          Open fields or mesne inclosures, common or waste : 7231
          acres awarded
          Commissioners Arthur Elliot (died), Joseph Outram,
          Benjamin Chambers, William Rodgers
      i   WRRD B24 p1 enrolled award and 2 plans (1805, surveyors
          William and F. Fairbank and Joseph Thackray; (1) Hallam,
          Fulwood, buildings, whole townships shown, open field
          features, 12 ch=1"; (2) Stannington, Storrs and
          Dungworth, buildings, whole townships shown, 8 ch=1")
      ii Sheffield CL sealed original award and plans
      iii Bradfield parish council award

328 HALTON (WR-NY)   1811 : 1813
          By agreement. Grass Gill and Halton Green Towenfield
          Commissioners William Preston, John Tennant
      i   NRA Raistrick MSS agreement, award and plan (not dated,
          unsigned, 2 ch=1")

329 HALTON EAST (WR-NY)   1767 : 1768
        Stinted pasture called Halton Green : 271 acres awarded
        Commissioners Thomas Midgeley, Richard Clapham, Henry
        Waddington
    i   WRRD B6 p160 enrolled award
    ii NYCRO PR/SKP (HT) 12/1 award and plan

330 HALTON (Leeds) (WR-WY)   1777 : 1783
        Common or waste called Halton Moor : 101 acres awarded
        Commissioners Mordecai Cutts, Richard Warner (did not
        sign), William Leake
    i   WRRD B15 p251 enrolled award
    ii Leeds RO DB sealed original award and related papers

    HALTON (Leeds) (WR-WY) see Temple Newsam

331 HALTON WEST (WR-NY)   1781 : c1792
        No award known. Decisions of commissioners enrolled.
        Moors, other lands and grounds : 2078 acres estimated
        Commissioners John Yorke, Matthew Wilson, Henry
        Waddington
    i   WRRD B12 p326 & B14 p325; B15 pp390,393; B18 p119
        enrolled decisions of commissioners etc.

332 HAMBLETON (WR-NY)   1796 : 1798
        Open fields, other commonable lands and waste : 993
        acres awarded
        Commissioners Thomas Mould, Richard Clark, William
        Whitelock
    i   WRRD B20 p140 enrolled award
    ii Hambleton parish council award and plan (1797, surveyor
        William Shipton)

    HAMPSTHWAITE (WR-NY) see Knaresborough, Forest of

333 HANDSWORTH (Sheffield) (WR-SY)   1802 : 1805
        Commons and waste : 470 acres estimated
        Commissioners Joseph Outram, William Rodgers
    i   CP Wakefield B p3 enrolled award and A69 plan (1805,
        surveyors William and Josiah Fairbank, whole parish,
        buildings, open field features, 12 ch=1")
    ii Sheffield CL ACM 569 sealed original award and 12 plans
        (whole parish, 6 ch=1")
    iii SYCRO 317/X typescript copy of award

334 HANLITH (WR-NY)   1813 : 1817
        By agreement. Two pastures, Hanlith Cow Close and
        Hanlith Moor
        Commissioner Thomas Buttle
    i   WRRD HA p524 memorial of award only, gives some details

    HARDCASTLE (WR-NY) see Bewerley

335 HARDEN (WR-WY) 1847 : 1855
        Harden Moor : 848 acres awarded
        Commissioner Richard Francis Hayward
- i   CP Wakefield A20 sealed original award and A20 two plans (1847, 1848, surveyors Messrs Haywood, (1) Harden Moor, buildings, 3 ch=1"; (2) Harden hamlet, whole hamlet shown, buildings, 6 ch=1")
- ii Bingley UDC sealed original award and plans (surveyor(s dept) and copy award and plans (clerk(s dept)
- iii YAS MD290/7 draft award and plans
- iv Messrs Weatherhead and Butcher, Bingley, award
- v   PRO (MAF 1 389) award

HAREHILLS (WR-WY) see Potternewton

HAREWOOD (WR-WY) see Dunkeswick; East Keswick

HARLINGTON (WR-SY) see Barnburgh

HARLTHORPE (ER-H) see Bubwith

336 HARPHAM (ER-H) 1773 : 1776
        Open fields, meadow, pasture
        Commissioners John Outram, Peter Nevill
- i   ERRD AT/296/31 enrolled award
- ii HCRO PE/61/14 copy award

HARROGATE (WR-WY) see Knaresborough, Forest of

337 HARTHILL WITH WOODALL (WR-SY) 1760 : 1761
        Common or waste called Woodall Moor or Common : 300 acres estimated
        Commissioners William Simpson, William Marsden, Francis Ashbey (died), Thomas Smith
- i   WRRD B4 p21 enrolled award
- ii Rotherham CL award
- iii YAS DD5/3/612 copy award

338 HARTLINGTON (WR-NY) 1857 : 1864
        Hartlington Moor : 600 acres awarded
        Commissioner William Thornton
- i   CP Wakefield A35 sealed original award and plan (1860, unsigned, buildings, 3 ch=1")
- ii NYCRO PR/BNS 16/1/1 award and plan
- iii PRO (MAF 1 730) award

HARTOFT (NR-NY) see Aislaby

339 HARTSHEAD (WR-WY)   1839 : 1842
        Commons or waste : 123 acres awarded
        Commissioner Henry Holt
    i   WRRD B37 p301 enrolled award and 2 plans Vol 2/19 (not
        dated, unsigned, (1) old inclosures, buildings, 6 ch=1";
        (2) Hartshead Common, buildings, 2 ch=1")
    ii WYAS D31/43 award and 2 plans
    iii NRA report Kirklees records 2 copies of award
    iv YAS MD 225 award and plans

340 HARTWITH CUM WINSLEY (WR-NY)   1852 : 1858
        Hartwith High Pasture : 358 acres awarded
        Commissioner Ralph Lodge
    i   CP Wakefield sealed original award A25a and plan (1854
        surveyor W. Thornton, buildings, 3 ch=1")
    ii NYCRO PC/HRW 10 copy award and plan
    iii PRO (MAF 1 554) award

341 HARWOOD DALE (NY-NY)   1858 : 1861
        Moors : 3360 acres awarded
        Commissioner Crayston Webster
    i   NYCRO QDD(I) no.21 enrolled award and plan (Ordnance
        Survey)
    ii NYCRO ZF 9/19 copy award
    iii PRO (MAF 1 284) award

342 HATFIELD, THORNE, FISHLAKE, STAINFORTH AND SYKEHOUSE (WR-SY)
                                                         1811 : 1825
        Open commons, common pastures, moors, broad lands and
        other commonable lands and waste in the parish of
        Hatfield, Thorne and Fishlake; and open fields, meadows,
        ings and pasture in Hatfield, Stainforth, Thorne,
        Fishlake and Sykehouse townships. Also lands in the
        manors of Nunappleton in Fishlake, Dunscroft, Westhall
        in Hatfield and Stocksholdand Westhall in Stainforth :
        2328 acres estimated
        Commissioners Nicholas Brown, William Dawson (died),
        John Bower, William Pilkington
    i   Doncaster RO PR.Tho sealed original award in volume
    ii Hatfield parish council award
    iii Doncaster RO 2 plans (copies) (1811, surveyor J.
        Haywood, whole townships shown, buildings, 12 ch=1")
    iv SYCRO 41/2 microfilm copy of award and copies of plan
    v   Doncaster RO PR.Fish award and plan

343 HAUXWELL, EAST (NR-NY)   1807 : 1808
        Moor or common : 691 acres awarded
        Commissioner Alexander Calvert
    i   NRRD DK no.2 p3 enrolled award and plan (1807, unsigned,
        buildings, scale not stated)

344 HAWES (NR-NY) 1840 : 1859
    Two awards. Common : 787 acres awarded
    Commissioner Richard Garth, Edward Broderick
  i NYCRO QDD(D) Bk S pp157,176 enrolled awards and plans
     (1847, Richard Garth jun. and unsigned, 3 & 6 ch=1")

345 HAWSKER-CUM-STAINSACRE (NR-NY) 1796 : 1797
    By agreement. Pastures
    Commissioners not named, perhaps none
  i NRRD FX no.430 p409 enrolled award
  ii NYCRO ZW sealed original award and 2 plans (1797,
     unsigned, buildings, scale not stated)

346 HAWKSWICK (WR-NY) 1816 : 1824
    Four stinted pastures and leys, open field lands and
    uninclosed grounds : 1880 acres estimated
    Commissioner Thomas Buttle
  i WRRD B47 sealed original award and plans in volume (not
     dated, unsigned, 5 plans on 2 sheets (1) The Moor; (2)
     Clowder; (3) Knotts; (4) The Wood; (5) The Mean Fields;
     buildings, all 6 ch=1". Also insets of Ain Holm and
     Water Lands)
  ii NYCRO PR/ARN 9/2 & 3 sealed original award and plans

347 HAXBY (NR-NY) 1769 : 1771
    Common, arable, moor : 1640 acres estimated
    Commissioners John Graves, John Lund, John Outram
  i NRRD AX no.37 p100 enrolled award
  ii NYCRO ZEY 12 copy award

348 HAYTON (ER-H) 1808 : 1811
    Stinted pastures, waste : 163 acres awarded
    Commissioners William Byass, William Wildon
  i ERRD CQ/143/5 enrolled agreement and CQ/147/6 enrolled
     award
  ii York City RO Acc.124 sealed original award (part only)

    HAYTON (ER-H) see Bielby

    HAYWOOD (WR-SY) see Burghwallis

349 HAZLEWOOD AND SCARCROFT (WR-NY) 1813 : 1815
    By agreement. Common and waste called Scarcroft Moor
    Commissioner William Dawson
  i   WRRD B32 p1 enrolled award
  ii WRRD Map Vol 3/2 sealed original award and plan (1815,
      surveyor John Humphries, buildings, 5 ch=1")
  iii Leeds RO agreement, sealed original award and plan

350 HEADLINGLEY CUM BURLEY (Leeds) (WR-WY) 1829 : 1834
   Common and waste : 88 acres awarded
   Commissioners Jonathan Taylor (died), George Hayward
 i   CP Wakefield A25 sealed original award and plans (1831,
     unsigned, (1) whole township, buildings, 6 ch=1"; (2)
     some small allotments within the township of Bramley,
     Leeds, buildings, 6 ch=1")
 ii Leeds RO original award and plan; also copy award and
     plan
 iv Leeds Civic Hall extract award and plan

351 HEATON (Bradford) (WR-WY) 1780 : 1781
   Commons, moors and waste : 575 acres estimated
   Commissioners Thomas Chippendale, Miles Dawson
 i   WRRD Roll 5 sealed original award
 ii Leeds RO (Bradford diocesan archives) sealed original
     award and plan (not dated, not signed, 4 ch=1")
 iii Bradford RO sealed original award and plan
 iv YAS MS 1348 copy award and plan

352 HEBDEN (WR-NY) 1848 : 1857
   Hebden Moor : 2667 acres awarded
   Commissioner Ralph Lodge
 i   CP Wakefield A12 sealed original award and plan (in 2
     parts, undated, unsigned, buildings, 3 ch=1")
 ii PRO (MAF 1 78) award

   HECK (WR-NY) see Pollington

353 HELLIFIELD (WR-NY) 1846 : 1849
   Hellifield Moor : 254 acres awarded
   Commissioner William Rawsthorne
 i   CP Wakefield A28 sealed original award and plan (not
     dated, surveyor Jno Greenwood, 3 ch=1")
 ii NYCRO PR/PRL 14/1 sealed original award and plan
 iii Leeds RO copy award
 iv PRO (MAF 1 673) award

   HELMSLEY (NR-NY) see Kirkdale; Upper Helmsley

353A HELPERBY (NR-NY) 1772
   By agreement. Common : 394 acres awarded
   Commissioners Miles Dawson, Timothy Mortimer
 i   York Minster Library T2/5/2 agreement, award and plan (4
     ch=1") and related papers

354 HELPERBY (NR-NY) 1809 : 1813
   Open fields, ings and waste : 1284 acres awarded
   Commissioner William Dawson
 i   NRRD DO no.26 p132 enrolled award and plan (1813,
     surveyor John Humphries, buildings, 8 ch=1")

   HELPERTHORPE (ER-NY) see Weaverthorpe

355 HEMINGBROUGH (ER-NY)　　　　　　　　　　　　　　　1836 : 1844
         Open fields, meadow, pasture : 540 acres awarded
         Commissioners William Harper, Joseph Whitle
         Surveyors Joseph Whitle, Samuel Appleby Dawson
    i   ERRD FG/289/3 enrolled award
    ii   HCRO QDB 8 p57 enrolled award
    iii Borthwick Institute York PR HEM/49 award

356 HEMSWORTH (WR-WY)　　　　　　　　　　　　　　　　1803 : 1808
         Open fields, commons and waste : 800 acres estimated
         Commissioner William Whitelock
    i   CP Wakefield A p66 enrolled award
    ii   Wakefield Town Hall sealed original award in volume,
         with plan separate (not dated, perhaps later copy, by
         Gee, Halifax, whole township shown, buildings, open
         field names, 8 ch=1")

357 HENSALL (WR-NY)　　　　　　　　　　　　　　　　　1818 : 1821
         Open fields, ings, meadows, stinted pasture, commons and
         waste : 1012 acres awarded
         Commissioner William Pilkington
    i   WRRD B38 p1 enrolled award and plan Vol 2/17 (1821,
         unsigned, whole township shown, buildings, open field
         names, 6 ch=1")
    ii   HCRO DDCL/243 19 cent copy award and plan in volume
    iii NYCRO ZDS V 4/11 copy award

    HEPWORTH (WR-WY) see Wooldale

    HESLERTON (ER-NY) see East and West Heslerton

358 HESLINGTON (ER-NY)　　　　　　　　　　　　　　　　1761 : 1762
         Common or waste : 786 acres awarded
         Commissioners William Smith, Nathan Hoyle, John
         Dickinson
    i   ERRD AC/139/5 enrolled award

359 HESLINGTON (ER-NY)　　　　　　　　　　　　　　　　1836 : 1857
         Common arable, meadow and pasture lands : 714 acres
         awarded
         Commissioners Francis Carr, Robert William Fenwick Mills
         Umpire Christopher Paver
    i   HCRO QDB 9 p69 enrolled award
    ii   HCRO DDGD Box 1 draft award of 1857
    iii York City RO Acc.80 sealed original award and plan (6
         ch=1")
    iv   Borthwick Institute York PR HES/18 award and plan

    HESLINGTON (ER-NY) see Dunnington

360 HESSAY (WR-NY)　　　　　　　　　　　　　　　　　　1828 : 1831
         Open fields, meadows, pastures, commons and waste : 600
         acres estimated
         Commissioner John Singleton
    i   Councillor Hildreth, Hessay, had award in 1962
    ii   York City RO Vol H enrolled award

361　HESSLE, ANLABY and TRANBY (ER-H)　　　　　　　　　　1792 : 1796
　　　　　　Open fields, meadows, pastures, commons and waste : 3550
　　　　　　acres awarded
　　　　　　Commissioners Peter Nevill, William Hall, John Wood
　　　　　　Surveyors Edward Johnson, Thomas Barrow, Robert Atkinson
　　　i　　ERRD BT/93/16 enrolled award
　　　ii　　Hull CL, copy award with index, two copies of plan
　　　iii　HCRO DDBD/28/1 plan (1794, buildings, 16 ch=1")
　　　iv　　HCRO DDX/202/44 copy plan 30 ch=1"
　　　v　　HUL DX/37/35 copy plan
　　　vi　　Hull City RO original plan
　　　　　　Related documents in HCRO DDHB/1/15-38; Leeds,
　　　　　　Brotherton Library, MS 311

362　HETTON (WR-NY)　　　　　　　　　　　　　　　　　　1771 : 1771
　　　　　　Two pastures : 1060 acres awarded
　　　　　　Commissioners Henry Waddington, George Jackson, Thomas
　　　　　　Hawkshead
　　　i　　WRRD B8 p256 enrolled award
　　　ii　　NYCRO PC/RYL4 sealed original award and plan
　　　iii　Leeds RO sealed original awards 1771 and 1784

363　HETTON (WR-NY)　　　　　　　　　　　　　　　　　　1783 : 1784
　　　　　　By agreement. Open fields
　　　i　　Leeds RO agreement and award

364　HEWORTH (NR-NY)　　　　　　　　　　　　　　　　　　1817 : 1822
　　　　　　Amending act 1818. Moor and green : 242 acres awarded
　　　　　　Commissioners Thomas Gee, James Bulmer
　　　i　　NRRD ES no.1 p1 enrolled award and plan (1822, Daniel
　　　　　　Tuke, buildings, 6 ch=1")
　　　ii　　York City RO TC DP/1/5 sealed original award and plan

365　HEXTHORPE WITH BALBY AND LONG SANDALL (Doncaster) (WR-SY)
　　　　　　1784 : 1785
　　　　　　Open fields, open meadows, commons and waste : 1464
　　　　　　acres awarded
　　　　　　Commissioners Isaac Milbourn, Thomas Fletcher, Miles
　　　　　　Dawson
　　　i　　WRRD B15 p256 enrolled award
　　　ii　　Doncaster RO Enc.3 award and 2 plans

　　　HIGH BRADLEY (WR-NY) see Bradley

366　HIGH AND LOW BISHOPSIDE (WR-NY)　　　　　　　　　1858 : 1865
　　　　　　Moor : 4152 acres awarded
　　　　　　Commissioner George Henry Strafford
　　　i　　NYCRO PC/BPS sealed original award in volume with plan
　　　　　　(not dated, unsigned, buildings, 3 ch=1")
　　　ii　　Borthwick Institute York CC AB./11/71 copy plan
　　　iii　PRO (MAF 1 40 and 1095) award

　　　HIGH CATTON (ER-H) see Catton

　　　HIGH ELLERS (WR-SY) see Cantley

367 HIGH ROAD WELL (Halifax) (WR-WY) 1895 : 1896
    Moor (now known as West View Park)
    Commissioner Benjamin Whitewood Jackson
  i   CP Wakefield A84a sealed original award and plan
       (Ordnance Survey)
  ii   TC Halifax award and plan
  iii PRO (MAF 1 948) award

368 HILLAM (WR-NY) 1797 : 1811
    Amending act 1808 : open fields, commons and waste : 687
    acres awarded
    Commissioners Richard Clark (refused), William Dawson,
    Timothy Bainbridge, Richard Clark jun
  i   WRRD B28 p271 enrolled award and plan Vol 2/14 (not
       dated, surveyor William Shipton, whole township shown,
       buildings, open field names, 6 ch=1")
  0,00 Sealed original awards were to be kept in the town chest
       of Hillam, and by the steward of the manor court of
       Hillam under the act. Neither traced

369 HINDERWELL (NR-NY) 1845 : 1853
    Town fields : 894 acres awarded
    Commissioner Christopher Lonsdale Bradley
  i   NYCRO QDD(I) no.19 original award and plan (1853,
       surveyor C.L. Bradley, 3 ch=1")
  ii   NYCRO DC/WHR original award and plan
  iii PRO (MAF 1 504) award
  iv   NYCRO ZNG draft award

HINDERWELL (NR-NY) see Mulgrave

370 HIRST COURTNEY (WR-NY) 1799 : 1801
    Open fields, ings, marsh and commonable lands and waste
    : 196 acres awarded
    Commissioner William Shipton
  i   WRRD B20 p364 enrolled award and plan Vol 2/15 (1800,
       surveyor William Shipton, whole township shown,
       buildings, open field names, 6 ch=1")
  ii   Chapel Haddlesey church award and plan
  0   Original award to be kept by the Lord of the Manor under
       the act (in addition to that in the church). Not traced

HIVE (ER-H) see Blacktoft

HOLGATE (WR-NY) see Acomb

371 HOLLYM AND WITHERNSEA (ER-H)   1793 : 1797
        Open fields, meadows, pastures, carrs : Hollym 1470
        acres awarded, Withernsea 463 acres awarded
        Commissioners Robert Dunn (died), Peter Nevill, Robert
        Taylor (died), James Dunn, Robert Taylor jun
        Surveyor Thomas Barrow
    i   ERRD BT/364/50 enrolled award
    ii HCRO DX/359 sealed original award and plan (1794,
        buildings, 8 ch=1")
    iii HCRO DDCC/142/18 draft award
    iv HCRO DDCK/35/1 (h) plan
    v   HUL DSJ/89 plan

    HOLME (WR-WY) see Wooldale

372 HOLME ON THE WOLDS (ER-H)   1795 : 1798
        Open fields, pastures, commons : 1461 acres awarded
        Commissioners William Dawson, Joseph Dickinson, John
        Hall
        Surveyor Samuel Dickinson
    i   ERRD BT/432/56 enrolled award and plan A14
    ii ERRD sealed original award and plan (1796, buildings, 8
        ch=1") and DDX/131/7 copies

373 HOLME UPON SPALDING MOOR (ER-H)   1773 : 1777
        Open field, carrs, ings, meadow, waste : 7847 acres
        awarded
        Commissioners James Stovin, John Lund, John Raines,
        Peter Nevill
        Surveyors Joseph Butler, Joseph Dickinson
    i   ERRD AX/357/10 enrolled award and copy plan (1774,
        buildings, 16 ch=1")
    ii HCRO DDMW/5/1 copy award and plan

374 HOLMPTON (ER-H)   1800 : 1807
        Open fields, waste : 882 acres awarded
        Commissioners John Wood, Robert Stickney
        Surveyor Robert Stickney
    i   ERRD CI/202/15 enrolled award
    ii HCRO DDX/218/1 sealed original award and plan (1800,
        buildings, 8 ch=1")
    iii HCRO PR Acc.1433 award and plan
    iv HCRO DDCK/35/1(i) plan
    v   HUL DSJ/77 plan

375 HOLWICK (NR-Durham)   1811 : 1826
        Award under Romaldkirk act, see below. Moor : 6800
        acres awarded
    i   Durham CRO D/HH/2/14/111 award

376   HONLEY (WR-WY)   1782 : 1788
          Commons and waste : 1400 acres estimated
          Commissioners John Sharpe, Nathan Jowett, Benjamin
          Patchett
      i   WRRD B17 p1 enrolled award
      ii Kirklees RO sealed original award and plan; also copy
          award made 1867 and copy plan (1788, surveyor William
          Crossley, whole township shown, buildings, 14 ch=1")
      iv Dartmouth Estate Office, Slaithwaite, copy award and
          plan
      v   Tolson Memorial Museum, Huddersfield, plan
      0   Original award and plan may be at Midland Bank,
          Holmfirth; not traced

377   HOOK (WR-H)   1768 : 1775
          Open fields, marshes, waste, commons, carrs, pasture and
          moor : 1000 acres estimated
          Commissioners John Cleaver, Joseph Pursglove, John Lund
      i   WRRD B10 p285 enrolled award
      ii HCRO DDCL/3436 original award
      iii Goole RDC award and plan
      iv HCRO DDMT/553 and 4, award and copies
      v   YAS MS 564 copy award
      vi York Minster Library BB33 extract of award

378   HORBURY (WR-WY)   1809 : 1815
          Open fields, cow pastures and waste : 360 acres
          estimated
          Commissioner Thomas Gee
      i   Wakefield Town Hall sealed original award and 2 plans in
          volume (not dated, unsigned; (1) Land lying near the
          river, no title, pre-enclosure plan with enclosures
          superimposed, open field features, 3 ch=1"; (2) Land
          lying near the river, no title, pre-enclosure plan with
          enclosures superimposed, buildings, scale not stated)
      ii YAS MS 584 signed draft award and plan
      iii YAS MD 225 plan

379   HORNSEA (ER-H)   1801 : 1809
          Open fields, meadows, pastures, common, waste : 2500
          acres estimated
          Commissioner John Moiser, Joseph Dickinson, John Lee,
          Peter Jackson
          Surveyors Samuel Dickinson, Robert Atkinson
          Arbitrators William Withers, Robert Osborne
      i   ERRD C1/345/7 enrolled award and C6 plan (1809,
          buildings, 8ch=1")
      ii HCRO DDCK/35/1(j) plan and (IA) copy plan
      iii Hull CL plan
          Related documents Hull CL, minutes etc.

380 HORTON IN RIBBLESDALE (WR-NY)   1789 : 1791
         By agreement. Inclosed and stinted pastures called
         Selside, Shaw Park and Lamb Pasture
         Commissioners Thomas Ingilby, Bryan Waller, John Preston
    i   YAS DD 104 sealed original award and plan (not dated,
         unsigned, buildings, 4 and a half ch=1")

381 HORTON IN RIBBLESDALE (WR-NY)   1814 : 1821
         Commons and waste : 3299 acres awarded
         Commissioner Alexander Calvert
    i   WRRD B46 sealed original award and 2 plans bound in
         volume (not dated, surveyor Samuel Swire jun; (1)
         Mooton, Jellet Brea and Horton Wood; (2) Horton High
         Moor and Pennygent, both 12 ch=1")

382 HORTON IN RIBBLESDALE (WR-NY)   1846 : 1847
         Horton Moor : acreage not stated
         Commissioner Richard Clapham
    i   CP Wakefield A13 sealed original award and plan (not
         dated, surveyor John Greenwood, 3 ch=1")
    ii   NCRO ZTW MS copy award
    iii PRO (MAF 1 94) award

383 HOTHAM (ER-H)   1768 : 1771
         Open fields, meadows, pasture : 2700 acres estimated
         Commissioners John Dickinson, John Outram, Robert Bewlay
         jun
         Surveyor Peter Nevill
    i   ERRD AN/83/7 enrolled award

     HOUGHTON (WR-WY) see Glass Houghton

384 HOVINGHAM (NR-NY)   1754 : 1756
         By agreement. Common fields and moor
         Commissioners Robert Bewlay, John Cleaver, George Hebden
    i   NRRD O no.28 p148 enrolled award

385 HOWDEN, EASTRINGTON AND BLACKTOFT (ER-H)   1767 : 1777
         Common or waste ground called Bishopsoil : 3952 acres
         awarded
         Allotments made to 18 surrounding townships
         Commissioners John Cleaver, John Outram, Peter Nevill,
         John Lund, Cornelius Stovin, Edward Cleaver
    i   ERRD AX/184/5 enrolled award and modern copy of plan
         (buildings, 8 and a half ch=1")
    ii   Durham DCM sealed original award
    iii HCRO IA plan
         York Univ. Library Act (vol 7/13) has MS notes on
         implementation of act

386 HOWDEN, EASTRINGTON, NORTH AND SOUTH CAVE (ER-H)
                                        1777 : 1781
          Common pasture called Wallingfen : 5000 acres estimated
          Commissioners William Hill, George Holgate, James
          Keighley, John Danser, Thomas Mould
          Surveyors Joseph Jewitt, Joseph Dickinson
     i   ERRD BE/3/2 enrolled award and A4 copy plan (1778, 8
          ch=1")
     ii   HCRO DDTR/397 original award
     iii HCRO DDTR/793 plan
     iv   HUL CV/169/1 award and copy plan
     v   York Minster Library BB 33 extract of award
          Related documents HUL DDBA/10

387 HOWDEN (ER-H)   ? : 1854
          Open fields
          Commissioner George Alderson
     i   HCRO DDTR/217, DDTR/797 draft awards and plan

388 HOYLAND NETHER (WR-SY)   1794 : 1799
          Open fields, commons and waste
          Commissioners Richard Clark, William Fairbank
     i   WRRD B20 p66 enrolled award
     ii   Sheffield CL Fairbank collection, draft plan (not dated,
          whole township, buildings, scale not stated); also
          drafts and surveys
     iii Sheffield CL NBC 59 award

     HOYLAND SWAINE (WR-SY) see Silkstone

     HUBY (near Harewood) (WR-WY) see Dunkeswick

389 HUBY (Near York) (NR-NY)   1836 : 1841
          Open and common fields, commons and waste : 517 acres
          awarded
          Commissioners James Bulmer, Thomas Scott
     i   NYCRO QDD(D) Bk R no.23 p67 and GZ no.86 p101 enrolled
          awards and 2 plans
     ii   NYCRO PC/HUB 1 & 2 original awards and 2 plans (1841,
          surveyor Francis Carr, buildings, 4 ch=1", 2 ch=1")

390 HUDDERSFIELD (WR-WY)   1786 : 1789
          Commons and waste : 323 acres awarded
          Commissioners John Sharp, William Whitelock
     i   WRRD B17 p130 enrolled award
     ii   Kirklees RO sealed original awards (two)
     iii Huddersfield TC copy award (the copy map belonging to
          this award was taken to York for a law suit and never
          returned. Not traced)
     iv   YAS DD II copy award

     HUDDERSFIELD (WR-WY) see Dalton; Golcar

391 HUDSWELL AND HIPSWELL (NR-NY)   1807 : 1812
        Commons, waste and uninclosed land : 1632 acres awarded
        Commissioners John Tuke, Alexander Calvert
   i   NRRD DO no.10 p39 enrolled award and plan (not dated,
        surveyors Daniel Tuke and Thomas Bradley, buildings, 8
        ch=1")
   ii   NYCRO PC/HUD original award and plan; also copy
        award

392 HUDSWELL (NR-NY)   1755 : 1755
        By agreement. Pasture : 88 and a half acres estimated
   i   NRRD W no.110 p205 enrolled award

393 HUGGATE (ER-H)   1767 : 1773
        Open fields, pastures : 2620 acres estimated
        Commissioners John Outram, John Lund, Isaac Milbourn
   i   ERRD AQ/256/24 enrolled award
   ii   Borthwick Institute York PR HUG/55 extracts of award
HULL (ER-H) see Myton

394 HUNDERTHWAITE (NR-Durham)   1856 : 1858
        Moor : 4020 acres awarded
   i   NRRD no.20 original award and plan
   ii   Durham CRO D/HH/2/14/63 award

395 HUNMANBY (ER-H)   1738,1739
        Act of 1738 confirms agreement. Moor : acreage not
        stated.
        Further act of 1739 enclosed part of moor for warren

396 HUNMANBY AND FORDON (ER-H)   1800 : 1809
        Open fields, meadows, pastures, commons, waste :
        Hunmanby 5005 acres awarded, Fordon 1411 acres awarded
        Commissioners Peter Nevill, Peter Jackson, William
        Shipton, John Hall, John Tuke
        Surveyors Joseph Dickinson, Samuel Dickinson
   i   ERRD CQ/8/1 enrolled award
   ii   HCRO PC/3/1 sealed original award and 2 plans (1801, (1)
        Hunmanby, 12 ch=1"; (2) Fordon, 8 ch=1")
   iii HCRO DDHU/9/80 bound copy award
   iv   HCRO DDX/154/9-10 two copies award

397 HUNSHELF (WR-SY)   1810 : 1813
        Open moors, commons and waste : 700 acres awarded
        Commissioner Thomas Gee
   i   WRRD B29 p230 enrolled award
   ii   Wharncliffe Estates, Wortley, award and plan
   iii Stocksbridge UDC copy award and plan

398 HUNTINGTON (NR-NY)   1764 : 1765
        By agreement. Moor, 4 open fields : 465 acres estimated
        Commissioner Robert Bewlay sen, Robert Bewlay jun
   i   NRRD AH no.22 p97 enrolled award
   ii   Borthwick Institute York PR HUN/10/48-49 awards

399 HUNTON AND PATRICK BROMPTON (NR-NY)   1807 : 1811
         Pasture, common field, waste, moor, common : 730 acres
         estimated
         Commissioner Jonathan Teal
     i   NRRD DA no.83 p219 enrolled award and plan (1811,
         unsigned, buildings, 6 ch=1")
     ii NYCRO ZAW 238 original map

400 HUSTHWAITE (NR-NY)   1840 : 1845

         By agreement. Common and waste
         Commissioner Thomas Scott
     i   NYCRO ZBQ original award and plan (1842, Henry Scott,
         buildings, 2 ch=1")
     ii NYCRO ZBQ copy award

     HUT GREEN (WR-NY) see Eggborough

401 HUTTON BUSCEL (NR-NY)   1699 : 1700
         By agreement.
         Commissioners Richard Osbaldeston, John Beilby, James
         Hebdin, William Rogers
     i   NYCRO ZDS V 2/2/2 sealed original award

402 HUTTON BUSCEL (NR-NY)   1750 : 1751
         Act confirms agreement. Common pasture
         Commissioners Robert Knowsley, George Hebden
     i   NYCRO Z16/2,3 copy award

     HUTTON BUSCEL (NR-NY) see West Ayton

403 HUTTON CONYERS, RAINTON WITH NEWBY, AND MELMERBY (NR-NY)
                                                             1810 : 1815
         Moor and warren, 4 arable fields : 1610 acres awarded
         Commissioners John Humphries, John Bower, William Dawson
     i   NRRD DO no.50 p177 enrolled award and 3 maps (not dated,
         surveyor John Humphries, buildings, 6 or 8 ch=1")
     ii NYCRO PC/RIC sealed original award
     iii PRO (Chancery Lane) CRES 6/145 plan of allotted lands in
         Dishforth 1815

404 HUTTON CRANSWICK (ER-H)   1769 : 1771
         Open fields, meadows, commons, pastures : 4000 acres
         awarded
         Commissioner John Outram, John Raines, George Jackson
     i   ERRD AK/333/24 enrolled award and (IA) copy plan (1770,
         surveyor Peter Nevill, buildings, 8 ch=1")

405 HUTTON-LE-HOLE (NR-NY)   1761 : 1761
         By agreement. Open fields
         Commissioners William Horsley, William Mason, Thomas
         Hutchinson, Robert Benton, Thomas Watson, James Shepherd
     0   Award not known to exist

406　HUTTONS AMBO (HIGH HUTTON & LOW HUTTON) (NR-NY) 1805 : ?
　　　　Act confirms award
　　　　Commissioners Edward Elstob, Thomas Goulton, Robert
　　　　Stamper, James Ebden, Robert Ward, William List
　　0　Act only known

407 IDLE (Bradford) (WR-WY) 1809 : 1814
　　　Commons or waste : 175 acres awarded
　　　Commissioners Jonathan Teal (died), Jonathan Taylor, Henry Teal
　i　WRRD B29 p345 & B31 p1 enrolled award and 4 plans Vol 2/20 (1813, surveyor Jonathan Taylor; (1) Part of Idle Moor, Tithe Laith Green, Thorp Green and Simpson Green, buildings, 4 ch=1"; (2) Idle Moor, buildings, 3 ch=1"; (3) Thackley Common, buildings, 3 ch=1"; (4) Commons called Wrose Brown and Gawcliffe Cragg, buildings, 3 ch=1")
　ii　Bradford TC copy award and plan
　iii　Weatherhead and Butcher, Bingley, award
　iii　Leeds RO copy award and plan (1878, whole manor, 6 ch=1")
　iv　Leeds RO sealed original award; also copy
　v　Bradford RO copy award and copy plan made 1878

408 ILKLEY (WR-WY) 1855 : 1858
　　　Cow Pasture : 73 acres awarded
　　　Commissioner Joseph Smith jun
　i　CP Wakefield A47 sealed original award and plan (not dated, not signed, buildings, 3 ch=1" with insets on a larger scale)

　ii　PRO (MAF 1 1889) award

409 INGBIRCHWORTH (WR-SY) 1800 : 1813
　　　Commons, moors and waste : 580 acres awarded
　　　Commissioners William Fairbank (died), William Fairbank jun
　i　WRRD B30 p218 enrolled award
　ii　Gunthwaite and Ingbirchworth parish council award
　iii　Sheffield CL draft plan (not dated, surveyor William Fairbank (died), William Fairbank jun. whole township shown, buildings, 6 ch=1")

　　　IRTON (NR-NY) see Seamer

410 KEARBY WITH NETHERBY (WR-NY)   1800 : 1804
          Open fields, stinted pastures, common pastures, commons
          and waste : 459 acres awarded
          Commissioner William Dawson
     i   WRRD B21 p368 enrolled award and plan Vol 2/24 (1804,
          surveyor Jonathan Taylor, whole township shown,
          buildings, open field names, 6 ch=1")
     ii   Kirkby Overblow parish church award and plan

411 KEIGHLEY, THWAITES AND NEWSHOLME (WR-WY)   1780 : 1782
          Open fields, arable lands, meadows, commons and waste :
          5080 acres estimated
          Commissioners William Hobson, Nathan Jowett, John Sharpe
     i   WRRD B15 p7 enrolled award and plan Vol 2/22 (not dated,
          surveyor Benjamin Chambers, buildings, open field names,
          16 ch=1")
     ii   Keighley TC award and plan

     KEIGHLEY (WR-WY) see Hainworth

     KELBROOK (WR-Lancs) see Barnoldswick

412 KELFIELD (ER-NY)   1744 : 1746
          Agreement 1744 confirmed by act 1746. Common fields,
          commons, waste : 661 acres estimated
          Commissioner and surveyor Robert Keighley
     i   HUL DDFA/7/4 copy agreement

413 KELFIELD (ER-NY)   1806 : 1812
          Open meadows, commons, waste : 282 acres awarded
          Commissioners William Dawson, Richard Clark jun
          Umpire William Shipton
     i   ERRD CQ/189/9 enrolled award
     ii   York Minster Library sealed original award and plan (not
          dated, buildings, 6 ch=1")
     iii HCRO IA plan (not dated, buildings, 12 ch=1")
     iv   HCRO DDCL/248 copy award

     KELLINGLEY (WR-NY) see Beal

414 KELLINGTON (WR-NY)   1791 : 1793
          Commissioners John Beighton, Richard Clark, William
          Whitelock
     i   WRRD B18 p330 enrolled award and plan Vol 2/ 23 (1793,
          surveyor Jonathan Teal, whole townships, buildings, open
          field names, 6ch=1")

     KELLINGTON (WR-NY) see Beal

415 KETTLEWELL CUM CONISTON (WR-NY)   1801 : 1803
         Commons or moors, stinted pastures, open fields, waste :
         8690 acres awarded
         Commissioner Alexander Calvert
    i   WRRD Roll 7 sealed original award and 2 plans annexed
         (1802, surveyor Alexander Calvert; (1) Kettlewell; (2)
         Coniston, open field features in both maps, 8 ch=1")
    ii   NRA Raistrick MSS draft award
    0   Two sealed original awards to be kept in Kettlewell
         church and Conistone chapel under the act. Not found

     KEX MOOR (WR-NY) see Kirkby Malzeard

416 KEYINGHAM (ER-H)   1802 : 1805
         Open fields, meadow, pasture : 1418 acres awarded
         Commissioners Thomas Wilson, John Hall, Robert Stickney
         Surveyor Thomas Barrow
    i   ERRD CI/89/5 enrolled award and E6 plan (1805, 8 ch=1")
    ii   HCRO DDCC/142/19 copy award
    iii HCRO PC/18/16 award and plan
    iv   HCRO DDCK/35/1 (k) plan
         Related documents Hull CL, act and commissioners
         minutes; also HCRO DDIV/8/1-20 papers

417 KILBURN (HIGH AND LOW) (NR-NY)   1813 : 1829
         Common or moor and waste and stinted pasture called the
         Thickett : 1800 acres awarded
         Commissioners William Lockwood, John Bower
    i   NRRD ES no.51 p147 enrolled award and plan (not dated,
         unsigned, buildings, 8ich=1")
    ii   NRRD no.20 original award

418 KILDALE (NR-NY)   1775 : 1755
         Following agreement. Commons and waste : 2944 acres
         estimated. Act only (2 different dates in secondary sources)
         Commissioners not named

419 KILDWICK (WR-WY)   1848 : 1850
         Kildwick West Common, East Common and Parkinson Hill :
         82 acres awarded
         Commissioner Ralph Lodge
    i   CP Wakefield A43 sealed original award and plan (1850,
         buildings, 3 ch=1")
    ii   Kildwick parish church sealed original award and plan
    iii PRO (MAF 1 664) award

420 KILHAM ON THE WOLDS (ER-H)   1771 : 1773
         Open fields : 7017 acres awarded
         Commissioners William Hill, Samuel Milbourn , John
         Raines
         Surveyors Miles Dawson, Peter Nevill
     i   ERRD AQ/351/29 enrolled award
     ii HCRO DDX/154/6 copy award
     iii HUL DDDU/11/12 bound copy award and DDDU/11/277 plan
         (1772, buildings, 6 ch=1") and DDDU/11/13 copy plan
         (fragile)
         Related documents HCRO DDX/40/190 prposal for enclosure
         c1774

     KILDWICK (WR-WY) see Skipton; Steeton; Sutton

     KILLINGHALL (WR-NY) see Knaresborough, Forest of

421 KILNSEA (ER-H)   1836 : 1843
         Open fields, meadow, pasture : 542 acres awarded
         Commissioner and surveyor Richard Fowler
     i   HCRO/PC 15/21 sealed original award and plan (1840,
         buildings, 8 ch=1")
     ii HCRO QDB 8 p40 enrolled award
     iii HCRO DDCK/32/20-22 award and copy plan
     iv Hull CL copy award
     v   HUL DDCV/92/1 plan
         Related documents HCRO DDX/92/4 and DX/127 plan of
         Kilnsea and Spurn prior to enclosure showing strips 1818

422 KILNWICK (ER-H)   1785 : 1788
         Open arable fields, ings, pasture, comon : 1465 acres
         awarded
         Commissioners William Wilkinson (resigned), Edward
         Cleaver, Joseph Dickinson, Isaac Leatham
         Surveyor Joseph Dickinson
     i   ERRD BG/202/16 enrolled award

     KILNWICK (ER-H) see Wilfholme

423 KIMBERWORTH (Rotherham) (WR-SY)   1796 : 1800
         Common fields, undivided inclosures, commons and waste :
         424 acres awarded
         Commissioners Arthur Elliot, Joseph Outram
     i   WRRD B20 p226 enrolled award and plan Vol 2/26 (1800,
         surveyor William Fairbank jun, buildings, open field
         names, 8 ch=1")
     ii Rotherham CL sealed original award and plan

     KIMBERWORTH (Rotherham) (WR-SY) see Wentworth

     KINGTHORPE (NR-NY) see Thornton Dale

424 KIPPAX (WR-WY) 1791 : 1793
      Seven common town fields, a common stined pasture, a common or waste : 695 acres awarded
      Commissioners John Sharp, Richard Clark, William Whitelock
- i   WRRD B18 p286 enrolled award
- ii Leeds RO sealed original award and plan (1792, surveyor William Dawson, whole township shown, buildings, 6 ch=1"). Also modern copy award and plans
- iii Leeds RO copy award and plan

425 KIRBY GRINDALYTHE AND MOWTHORPE (ER-NY) 1755 : 1755
      Agreement in deed of 1755. Open field, meadow, pasture : 2243 acres estimated
      Commissioners and surveyors Robert Bewlay, Samuel Milbourn
- i   HUL DDSY/38/51 deed
- ii Borthwick Institute York PR/KG/2 19th cent. copy plan (1755, buildings, 9 ch=1")
- iii HCRO DPX/60 photograph of plan copy

KIRK BRAMWITH (WR-SY) see Moss

426 KIRKBURN (ER-H) 1836 : 1851
      Common meadow and pasture lands : 34 acres awarded
      Commissioners Edward Page, Richard Foster
      Umpire Isaac Staveley
- i   HCRO QDB 9 p54 enrolled award
- ii HCRO IA award and plan (1851, buildings, part of Kirkburn, 3 ch=1")
- iii HCRO DX/77 award

      Related documents HCRO DX/63-79 papers relating to enclosure

KIRKBURN see Southburn

427 KIRKBURTON (WR-WY) 1813 : 1816
      Commons, moors and waste : 206 acres awarded
      Commissioners Jonathan Teal (died), Henry Teal
- i   WRRD B32 p245 enrolled award and plans Vol 2/28 (4 plans, 1816, surveyor Henry Teal; (1) Kirkburton, whole township, shows buildings, 6 ch=1"; (2) Harry Hower and Burton Royd, buildings, 3 ch=1"; (3) Grice Common and Thorncliffe Green, buildings, 3 ch=1"; (4) Dean, Green Common and Hartley Bank, buildings, 3 ch=1")
- ii Kirklees RO sealed original award and plans in volume; also photocopy award

KIRKBURTON (WR-WY) see Whitley

KIRBY HILL (NR-NY) see Langthorpe

428   KIRKBY MALHAM (WR-NY)   ? : 1832
            By agreement. Two stinted pastures called Kirkby
            Grainsand and Kirkby Cow Close
            Commissioner William Pilkington
      i   WRRD LI p456, 461 memorial of agreement only
      ii   NRA Raistrick MSS copy award and plan (9 ch=1")

429   KIRKBY MALZEARD, LAVERTON, GALPHAY, MICKLEY AND KEX MOOR
            (WR-NY)   1787 : 1789
            Moors, commons or wastes called Kirkby High and Low
            Moors, Laverton Moor, Galphay Moor, Mickley High and Low
            Moors : 3637 acres awarded
            Commissioners Richard Beckwith, John Bradford, Francis
            Sands
      i   YAS MS 884 18 cent. copy award
      ii   Leeds RO copy award
      iii   Kirkby Malzeard parish council copy award
      0   Original probably lost in fire at Kirkby Malzeard church
            1908

430   KIRKBYMOORSIDE, FADMOOR AND GILLAMOOR (NR-NY)   1788 : 1793
            Three common arable fields in Kirkbymoorside, commons
            and waste in all 3 places : 2125 acres awarded
            Commissioners Richard Clarke, Peter Merry
            Umpire Joseph Dickinson
      i   NRRD CR ONT 13/9 typed copy award
      ii   Messrs Pearson and Mackirdy of Helmsley original award
            and plan
      iii   NRRD no.8 original award and plan
      iv   NYCRO ZEW sealed original and 6 plans; (i) West Field
            and Lund Common part of Low Commons, decorated
            cartouche, 3 ch=1"; (2,3,4) other parts of Low Commons,
            scale not dated; (5) part of High Commons, 8 ch=1"; (6)
            land to be exchanged

431   KIRKBY OVERBLOW (WR-NY)   1798 : 1799
            Common and waste and commonable lands : 71 acres awarded
            Commissioner Jonathan Teal
      i   WRRD Map Vol 2/27 sealed original award and plan (1799,
            surveyor Jonathan Teal, buildings, 5ch=1")
      ii   Kirkby Overblow parish church award and plan

432   KIRKBY RAVENSWORTH (NR-NY)   1777 : 1778
            Moors : 1527 acres awarded
      i   NRRD BL no.13 p65 enrolled award
      ii   NYCRO PR/KRR original award and plan

433   KIRKDALE AND HELMSLEY (NR-NY)   1806 : 1816
            Amending act of 1814. Open fields and commons : 877
            acres awarded
            Commissioners Edward Cleaver, John Tuke
      i   NRRD no.1 orignal award and plan (buildings, 8 ch=1")
      ii   NYCRO ZEW original award and plan

KIRK ELLA (ER-H) see North Ferriby

434 KIRK HAMMERTON (WR-NY)   1765 : 1768
        Four open fields, common stinted pasture called Low Moor
        Commissioners Joseph Butler, Robert Bewlay sen. Robert
        Bewlay jun (last two refused)
    i   WRRD B7 p1 enrolled award
    ii NYCRO PR/HMK/16/2 sealed original award and plan (1767,
        unsigned, buildings, open field names, scale not stated)

435 KIRK HAMMERTON (WR-NY)   1857 : 1861
        Moor : 35 acres awarded
        Commissioner George Alderson
    i   CP Wakefield A56 sealed original award and plan (1857/8,
        buildings, 3 ch=1")
    ii NYCRO PR/HMK 16/2 sealed original award and plan
    iii PRO (MAF 1 819) award

436 KIRKHEATON (HUDDERSFIELD) (WR-WY)   1799 : 1804
        Act of 1799 confirms agreement. Amending act passed
        1804. Commons, moors and waste, open fields : 400 acres
        estimated
        Commissioners John Sunderland, Joshua Ingham, John
        Sutcliffe
        Related papers and act, Huddersfield public library

     KIRKLEATHAM (NR-Cleveland) see Coatham

437 KIRK SANDALL (WR-SY)   1806 : 1808
        Open fields, common or waste : 445 acres awarded
        Commissioners William Dawson, Richard Tilburn
    i   WRRD B27 p4 enrolled award and 2 plans Vol 2/21 (1807,
        surveyor Joseph Haywood; (1) Kirk Sandall, whole
        township shown, buildings, 6 ch=1"; (2) Lands set out
        for the tithes of Streetthorpe, 3 ch=1")
    ii Doncaster RO Enc.18 photocopy award and plan
    0   Sealed original award to be kept in church under the
        act. Not found

     KIRK SANDALL (WR-SY) see Barnby Dun

438 KIRK SMEATON (WR-WY)   1808 : 1811
        Open fields, pastures, commons, waste and commonable
        lands : 1011 acres awarded
        Commissioners William Whitelock (died), William Shipton
    i   WRRD B28 p358 enrolled award
    ii Kirk Smeaton parish council sealed original award and
        plan (1810, surveyor William Shipton, whole township
        shown, buildings, open field features, 6 ch=1")
    iii Sheffield CL Baxter Collection 61610-61611 and NBC 74
        copies of award
    iv PRO DL/45/8/11 enrolled extract of award

439 KNAPTON (WR-NY) 1788 : 1791
    Five common fields and common : 241 acres awarded
    Commissioner Miles Dawson
- i   York City RO Vol G enrolled award
- 0   Sealed original award to be deposited with the owner of the manor of Knapton under the act. Not found

440 KNARESBOROUGH, FOREST OF (WR-NY) 1770 : 1778
    Amending acts 1774, 1789 and 1795. Those parts of the Forest in the 11 constableries of Killinghall, Bilton and Harrogate, Beckwithshaw with Rossett Green or Panall, Clifton, Timble, Thruscross, Menwith with Darley, Felliscliff, Birstwith, Hampsthwaite and Clint : 20,000 acres estimated
    Commissioners William Hill, Joseph Butler (died), William Chippendale (died), John Flintoff (died), Thomas Furness (died), John Bainbridge, Richard Richardson
- i   WRRD Roll 8 enrolled award (marked B16) and 2 plans Vol 4/17, 4/18 (not dated, not signed, both very large; (1) all open commonable grounds and waste within the 11 constableries, showing boundaries, 12 ch=1"; (2) the whole of all the 11 constableries, buildings, decorated cartouche showing Knaresborough Castle, 12 ch=1")
- ii   D of L sealed original award and plans
- iii   Part of the plan (Harrogate, Bilton, parts of Pannal and Killinghall) was printed in 1892. Copies of this printed map in Harrogate CL and Leeds RO

441 KNAYTON (NR-NY) 1799 : 1802
    Commons and waste : 195 acres awarded
    Commissioner Arthur Mowbray
    Surveyor John Bell
- i   NRRD 24 original award and plan (buildings, 3 ch=1")

442 KNEDLINGTON (ER-H) 1836 : 1839
    Open fields : 250 acres awarded
    Commissioner and surveyor Henry Hutchcroft
- i   HCRO QDB 7 p159 enrolled award and plan (1839, buildings, scale not stated)

443 KNOTTINGLEY (WR-WY) 1793 : 1795
    Commons and waste and ings or meadow : 257 acres awarded
    Commissioners Isaac Leatham, William Shipton
- i   WRRD B19 p136 enrolled award and plan Vol 2/25 (1793, surveyor Richard Clark jun. shows Knottingley South Moor, Little Marsh and Ings, buildings, 4 ch=1")
- 0   Sealed original award to be kept in Knottingley chapel under the act. Not found

444 LANGBAR AND NESFIELD (WR-NY)   1881 : 1883
         Moor : 668 acres estimated
         Commissioner Joseph Smith
     i   CP Wakefield A82 award and plan (Ordnance Survey)
     ii PRO (MAF 1 587) award

445 LANGCLIFFE (WR-NY)   1789 : 1793
         Six stinted pastures : 1400 acres estimated
         Commissioners Henry Waddington, Thomas Ingleby, William
         Clapham
     i   WRRD Map Vol 3/1 sealed original award and plan (1789,
         unsigned, buildings, 8 ch=1")
     ii NYCRO PC/LAC sealed original with plan

446 LANGSETT (WR-SY)   1811 : 1814/20
         Amending act 1820 and new award 1820. Commons, waste
         and moors or heaths : 3041 acres awarded
         Commissioner Thomas Gee (for both awards)
     i   CP Wakefield C p86 (1814 enrolled award) and E p57 (1820
         enrolled award) and plans A80a and A63 (1) 1814,
         surveyorsW. & J. Fairbank, buildings, 3 furlongs=1"; (2)
         1820, surveyor E. Taylor, buildings, 15 ch=1")
     ii WYAS D 28/6-7 two awards and 2 plans
     iii Sheffield CL draft plan
     iv Leeds RO copy award and plan
     v   PRO DL/45/9/6 enrolled extract of award

447 LANGTHORPE AND KIRBY HILL (NR-NY)   1806 : 1812
         Kirby Hill common and wastes, 3 open fields in
         Langthorpe and common and wastes : 504 acres awarded
         Commissioner William Dawson
     i   NYCRO QDD(D) Bk O p1 enrolled award and plan (surveyor
         John Humphries, buildings, 6 ch=1")
     ii NYCRO PC/LAP sealed original award

448 LANGTOFT (ER-H)   1801 : 1805
         Open fields, common fields, common pasture : 3434 acres
         awarded
         Commissioners William Dawson, John Hall
         Surveyors Benjamin Outram, Samuel Dickinson
     i   ERRD CI/14/2 enrolled award and plan (not dated,
         buildings, 8 ch=1")
     ii HCRO DDX/154/24 copy award
         Related documents HCRO DDIN/40/191-8; also HUL DDSY/98/1

449 LASTINGHAM (NR-NY)   1787 : 1788
         Common fields : 238 acres awarded
         Commissioners Edward Watterson, Timothy Parke
     i   NRRD no.31 sealed original award and plan (1787, town
         fields and old enclosures, scale not stated)

450 LAUGHTON EN LE MORTHEN, SLADE HOOTON (WR-SY) 1769 : 1771
    Open fields, arable lands, waste and common : 1160 acres awarded
    Commissioners Edward Oates, George Ingman, Henson Kirkby
  i   WRRD B9 p1 enrolled award
  ii NRA Report Lumley MSS copy award
  iii Original award and plan from parish church with Laughton church school in 1983
  iv Rotherham CL photocopy of plan
  v   Sheffield CL LD 1096 copy award and plan; also photocopy plan (1769, 8 ch=1")

LAVERTON (WR-NY) see Kirkby Malzeard

451 LAYTON, EAST (NR-NY) 1801 : 1802
    Common and waste : 178 acres awarded
    Commissioner Alexander Calvert
  i   NRRD CP no.102, p176 enrolled award

452 LEAKE (NR-NY) 1845 & 1864 : 1869
    Ings : 143 acres awarded
    Commissioner Francis Carr
  i   NYCRO ZES 94 award and plan (3 ch=1")
  ii NYCRO QDD(I) 25 original award and plan
  iii PRO (MAF 1 1037) award

453 LEATHLEY (WR-NY) 1740 : 1753
    Agreements of 1740 and 1748 confirmed by act 1753
    Common and waste : no acreage stated
  i   YAS DD 161 pre-enclosure award and plan

454 LEAVENING (ER-NY) 1804 : 1804
    Open and stinted pasture, common and waste : 236 acres awarded
    Commissioner William Whitelock
    Surveyor John Dalton
  i   ERRD CA/403/48 enrolled award and C8 plan (1804, buildings, 6 ch=1")
  ii NYCRO PC/LUN original award and plan

LEEDS (WR-WY) see Bramley; Halton; Headingley; Wortley

LEES (WR-WY) see Hainworth

455 LELLEY (ER-H) 1769 : 1770
    Open fields, meadow, pasture : 700 acres awarded
    Commissioners Joseph Butler, John Raines, James Strutt, Edward Johnson, Charles Tate
    Surveyors Edward Johnson, Charles Tate
  i   ERRD AK/213/19 enrolled award
  ii HCRO DDCK/32/8-9 award
  iii HCRO DDCC/142/13,32 draft award and bound copy
  iv HCRO DDX/92/1 copy plan made 1843 (buildings, 6 ch=1")

LENNERTON (WR-WY) see Sherburn in Elmet

456   LEPTON (WR-WY)   1779 : 1780
          Open commons and waste : 300 acres awarded
          Commissioners John Kent, John Birks, Joseph Jagger
      i   WRRD B12 p262 enrolled award and copy plan
      ii   Kirklees RO sealed original award and plan (1780,
           surveyor William Shipton, whole township shown,
           buildings, 7 ch=1")
      0   Sealed original award to be kept by the Lord of the
           manor under the act. Not found

457   LEVEN (ER-H)   1791 : 1796
          Arable, meadow, pasture : 1250 acres awarded
          Commissioners John Wood sen (died), William Mosey
          (died), Wiliam Hall (died), John Wood jun, John Hall,
          Joseph Dickinson
          Surveyors Robert Atkinson, John Wood jun
      i   ERRD BT/182/24 enrolled award
      ii   HCRO PE/128/45 award
      iii HCRO DDCC/142/17 award
      iv   HUL DSJ/63 copy award
      v   HCRO IA plan (1792, buildings, 8 ch=1")

458   LEVISHAM (NR-NY)   1770 : 1770
          By agreement. Common fields : 525 acres awarded
          Commissioners Robert Lyth, John Foord, Thomas Dodsworth,
          Robert King
      i   NRRD BA no.35 p181 enrolled award

459   LEYBURN (NR-NY)   1783 : 1783
          Leyburn moor : 950 acres awarded
          Commissioner Ingram Gill
          Surveyor John Rodham
      i   NYCRO CR ONT 13(4) typed transcript award
      ii   NYCRO PC/LEY original award and plan (buildings, scale
           not stated)

460   LINDLEY (WR-WY)   1798 : 1798
          By agreement. Open fields : 220 acres awarded
          Commissioners John Sharp, William Newton, William
          Whitelock
      i   WRRD B24 p339 enrolled award
      ii   Huddersfield TC sealed original award
      iii Tolson Memorial Museum Huddersfield, plan

461   LINDLEY (WR-WY)   1812 : 1817
          Commons, moors, warren and waste : 220 acres awarded
          Commissioners Jonathan Teal (did not sign), Elihu
          Dickinson, Nicholas Brown
      i   CP Wakefield C p214 enrolled award and plan A50 (1818,
           surveyor G. Charlesworth, buildings, 6 ch=1"). Also
           plan of road diversion, C p217
      ii   Kirklees RO sealed original award and plan; also extract
           of award in volume

      LINDLEY (WR-WY) see Old Lindley

462 LINTON (Collingham) (WR-NY) 1861 : 1864
       Linton Common
       Commissioner Richard Gouthwaite
- i   CP Wakefield A59 sealed original award and plan (1862, 2 ch=1"); copy plan Z3(L)
- ii Collingham with Linton parish council award and plan
- iii PRO (MAF 1 969) award

463 LINTON (Craven) (WR-NY) 1790 : 1793
       Open fields, a stinted pasture called Linton Pasture : 431 acres awarded
       Commissioners Miles Dawson (refused), William Dawson
- i   WRRD B18 p254 enrolled award and map Vol 2/30 (not dated, unsigned, Linton Pasture and other open ground, buildings, scale not stat1ed)
- ii NRA Raistrick MSS original award and plan

464 LISSETT (ER-H) 1771 : 1772
       Open fields, meadow, pastures, carrs : 1000 acres estimated
       Commissioners Thomas Simpson, Michael Ake, Thomas Milner
       Surveyor Robert Atkinson
- i   ERRD AN/391/27 enrolled award

LITTLE COWDEN (ER-H) see Great Cowden

LITTLE DRIFFIELD (ER-H) see Driffield

LITTLE FENTON (WR-NY) see Sherburn in Elmet

465 LITTLE NEWSHAM AND BARNINGHAM (NR-Durham) 1777 : 1781
       Common, waste and stinted pasture : 1809 acres awarded
- i   NRRD BR no.35 p114 enrolled award
- ii NYCRO ZMD 13 original award
- iii NYCRO ZDL a2 plan (12 ch=1")

466 LITTLE OUSEBURN (WR-NY) 1801 : 1806
       Open fields, ings, carr lands, stinted pastures, commonable lands and wastes : 562 acres awarded
       Commissioner William Dawson
- i   WRRD Roll 10 sealed original award and plan (not dated, surveyor Richard Birks, whole township shown, buildings, 6 ch=1")

467 LITTLE SMEATON AND STUBBS WALDEN (WR-NY) 1786 : 1788
       Open fields, stinted pasture, ings or meadow, commons and waste (3 open fields in each township) : 1158 acres awarded
       Commissioners Richard Clark, Miles Dawson, John Lund jun
- i   WRRD B15 p326 enrolled award
- ii NYCRO PC/SMT sealed original award and plan (1787, surveyor William Shipton, whole townships shown, buildings, 6 ch=1")
- 0   Another sealed original award to be kept in manor court records under the act. Not found

468 LITTLETHORPE (WR-NY)   1741 : 1742
         By agreement. Moor or stinted pastures called
         Littlethorpe Moor
         Commissioners William Wrather, John Harrison, William
         Wood
    i   YAS MD 284/7 sealed original award and plan (1742,
         surveyor M. Beckwith, buildings, 4 ch=1") ; also copy
         award made 1819
    ii   Leeds RO three copies award

     LITTLETHORPE (WR-NY) see Ripon

469 LITTLE WEIGHTON (ER-H)   1801 : 1804
         Open fields, sheep walks, commons, waste : 1677 acres
         awarded
         Commissioners Peter Nevill, Joseph Dickinson, John Hall,
         William Whitelock
         Surveyor Samuel Dickinson
    i   ERRD CA/283/39 enrolled award and E3 plan (1801,
         buildings, 8 ch=1")
    ii   HCRO PE/62/36 sealed original award and plan
    iii HCRO DX/4 copy plan
    iv   Hull CL copy award and plan
         Related documents HUL DDDU/10/7

470 LITTON (WR-NY)   1768 : 1769
         Several stinted pastures : 3000 acres estimated
         Commissioners Henry Waddington, John Foster, Richard
         Clapham
    i   WRRD B7 p34 enrolled award
    ii   Leeds RO sealed original award

471 LOCKINGTON AND AIKE (ER-H)   1770 : 1772
         Open fields, meadows, pastures, commons, carrs : 2629
         acres awarded
         Commissioners Peter Nevill, William Hall, Robert
         Sherwood
         Surveyor Joseph Dickinson
    i   ERRD AQ/176/18 enrolled award and E7 plan (1771, scale
         not stated)
    ii   HCRO DDX/191/1 two copies of plan
    iii HUL DDHO/16/52 copy plan; related account DDHO/42/162

472 LOCKTON (NR-NY)   1784 : 1785
         Common arable fields, common pastures and waste : 1142
         acres awarded
         Commissioners John Foord, Robert King
    i   NYCRO ZPC 1/2 sealed original award and plan (buildings,
         17 ch=1")
    ii   NYCRO PC/LOC sealed original award and plan
    iii NYCRO CR ONT 13/14 and ZPC 1/3 typed transcript and
         photocopy plan

473 LOCKTON AND SALTERGATE (NR-NY)　　　　　　　　　　1866 : 1872
　　　　　Lockton Low Moor and Saltergate Moor : 2894 acres
　　　　　awarded
　　　　　Commissioners not named
　　i　　NYCRO PR/LOC 9/1 certified copy award and plan (in 3
　　　　　parts, 4 ch=1")
　　ii　　NYCRO ZPC 1/5 certified copy
　　iii　　PRO (MAF 1 129,922) award
　　iv　　PRO DL/45/10/6 enrolled award and extract

LOCKWOOD (WR-WY) see North Crosland

LODGE (WR-NY) see Stonebeck Up

474 LOFTHOUSE AND CARLTON (WR-NY)　　　　　　　　　　1837 : 1844
　　　　　Open fields, commons and waste : 373 acres awarded
　　　　　Commissioner Christopher Paver
　　i　　WRRD B45 p247 enrolled award and 2 plans Vol 3/4 (1842,
　　　　　surveyor, Richard Gouthwaite; (1) Lofthouse in 4 parts,
　　　　　Aaron Green, Langley, Lee Moor Park, buildings, 2ch=1";
　　　　　(2) Carlton, whole hamlet shown, buildings, open field
　　　　　features, 5 ch=about 1 and a half ")
　　ii　　CP Wakefield A7 sealed original award and plans annexed
　　iii　　Leeds RO award and plans
　　iv　　Messrs Farrer & Co, Oulton, copy award and plan

LOFTHOUSE (WR-WY) see Rothwell

475 LONDESBOROUGH (ER-H)　　　　　　　　　　　　　　　1816 : 1821
　　　　　Commons, wastes, moors, pastures, fields, mesne
　　　　　inclosures : 1401 acres awarded
　　　　　Commissioner and surveyor John Bower
　　i　　ERRD sealed original award and C3 plan (not dated,
　　　　　buildings, 8 ch=1")
　　ii　　HCRO typescript copy award

476 LONG MARSTON (WR-NY)　　　　　　　　　　　　　　　1766 : 1767
　　　　　Five open fields, common and waste : 1741 acres awarded
　　　　　Commissioners John Dawson, Robert Bewlay, Ambrose Gray
　　i　　York City RO Vol F enrolled award

477 LONG PRESTON (NR-NY)　　　　　　　　　　　　　　　1773 : 1775
　　　　　By agreement. Land called the Flat : 94 acres estimated
　　　　　Commissioners Richard Clapham, John Preston, William
　　　　　Preston
　　i　　NYCRO ZXF sealed original award

478 LONG PRESTON (WR-NY) 1799 : 1815
   Open fields, stinted pastures and ings : 784 acres awarded
   Commissioners Thomas Ingilby (died), John Preston (died), Thomas Buttle, Robert Waddington
   i   WRRD Map Vol 3/2 sealed original award and 2 plans (not dated, surveyor Thomas Ingilby ; (1) Stinted pastures of Rag Birk, Cracoe Mire, Langbar, Ridding Banks, 6 ch=1"; (2) Ings 4 and a half ch=1")
   ii Leeds RO award

479 LONG RISTON AND ARNOLD (ER-H) 1771 : 1778
   Open fields, grounds, commons, carrs, ings : 1600 acres estimated
   Commissioners John Outram, Robert Foster, Henry Raines
   Surveyor Joseph Dickinson
   i   ERRD BB/73/13 enrolled award
   ii HUL DSJ/62 copy award

LONG SANDALL (WR-SY) see Hexthorpe

480 LONGWOOD AND DEANHEAD (WR-WY) 1813 : 1825
   Commons, moors and waste : 1500 acres estimated
   Commissioners Jonathan Teal (died), William Roberts (died), Thomas Dinsley, Nicholas Brown
   i   CP Wakefield E p309 enrolled award
   ii   Kirklees RO sealed original award and 2 plans (1818, surveyor Henry Teal, buildings, various scales)
   iii Kirklees RO copy award
   iv   YAS DD II copy award

481 LOTHERTON CUM ABERFORD AND STURTON GRANGE (WR-WY) 1818 : 1821
   By agreement. Three town fields
   Commissioner John Humphries
   i   WRRD HL p31 enrolled award
   ii Leeds RO draft plan

LOW BISHOPSIDE (WR-NY) see High and Low Bishopside

482 LOWER DUNSFORTH (WR-NY) 1807 : 1809
   Open fields, meadows, pastures, commons and waste : 630 acres estimated
   Commissioners John Tuke, William Dawson
   i   WRRD B27 p174 enrolled award and plan Vol 2/29 (1809, surveyors William Shipton and Daniel Tuke, whole township shown, buildings, open field names, 6 ch=1")
   ii   Aldborough parish church award and plan
   iii Borthwick Institute York CC/D/C/11/2 award

LOW MOOR (WR-WY) see Wibsey Slack

LOW BRADLEY (WR-NY) see Bradley

LOW CATTON (ER-H) see Catton

LOXLEY (WR-SY) see Wadsley

LUMBY (WR-NY) see South Milford

483 LUND (ER-H)   1794 : 1796
     Open fields, pastures, commons, waste : 2263 acres awarded
     Commissioners Robert Dunn (died), Joseph Dickinson, William Dawson, John Hall
     Surveyors Robert Stickney, Samuel Dickinson
  i   ERRD BT/244/31 enrolled award and plan (1795, 12 ch=1"); (IA) tracing of plan
  ii Hull CL award and copy plan
  iii HCRO DDX/202/49 plan

LUND (WR-NY) see Brayton; Cliffe

LUTTONS (ER-NY) see East and West Lutton

LYTHE (NR-NY) see Mulgrave

484 MALHAM (WR-NY)   1847 : 1849
         Malham Moors : acreage not stated
         Commissioner Ralph Lodge
     i   CP Wakefield A19 sealed original award and plans (not
         dated, surveyor John Greenwood, in 3 parts (1) West
         Malham Moors; (2 and 3) East Malham Moors, 3 ch=1")
     ii NYCRO PR/KMA/16/1 sealed original award
     iii PRO (MAF 1 225) award

485 MALTBY (WR-SY)   1837 : 1841
         Open fields : 125 acres awarded
         Commissioner Robert Smith
     i   CP Wakefield E p411 enrolled award
     ii Maltby church award and plan
     iii Lumley MSS typed copy award

     MALTON (NR-NY) see Old Malton

486 MANFIELD (NR-NY)   1815 : 1817
         By agreement. Waste ground called Manfield Green : 18
         acres
         Commissioner Thomas Bradley
     i   NRRD EE no.53 p89 enrolled award and plan (buildings, 2
         ch=1")
     ii Durham CRO D/HH 2/14/63

487 MAPPLETON (ER-H)   1846 : 1849
         Agreement 1846, order 1847. Open fields : 1070 acres
         awarded
         Commissioner John George Weddall
         Surveyor Gregory Page
     i   HCRO IA award and plan (1849, buildings, 4 ch=1")
     ii HCRO DX/17 copy award; DX/16 agreement
     iii PRO (MAF 1 436) award

488 MARFLEET (ER-H)   1763 : 1764
         Common fields, pastures, meadows, common grounds : 987
         acres awarded
         Commissioners John Dickinson, Joseph Thompson, John
         Outram
     i   ERRD AF/122/8 enrolled award
     ii HCRO DDCC/142/10 bound copy award
     iii HCRO PE/28/50 copy award; also typescript copy
     iv Hull City RO sealed original award

489 MARKET WEIGHTON AND SHIPTON (ER-H)   1773 : 1776
        Open fields, commons, waste : 6172 acres awarded
        Commissioners Samuel Brailsford, Samuel Milbourn,
        William Hall
   i   ERRD AX/2/2 enrolled award and printed copy plan
   ii   HCRO IA copy award and copy plan made 1970 (1776,
        buildings, scale not stated)
   iii HCRO DDBD/45/6 printed copy award
   iv   HUL DDLA/15/4 printed copy award
   vi   Borthwick Institute, York PR M/W/28 printed copy award
   vii York Minster Library copy award in volume
        Related documents Borthwick Institute York PR M/W/38
        survey and plan of old enclosures of Shipton; HCRO
        DDPY/14/2 plan of old enclosures

490 MARKINGTON (WR-NY)   1792 : 1792
        By deed poll. Four common fields and ings
        Commissioners Richard Clark, William Barker
   i   NYCRO DC/RIC sealed original award and plan (1792,
        surveyor Alexander Calvert, buildings, open field names,
        3 ch=1")
   ii   NYCRO DC/RIC later copy award

491 MARRICK (NR-NY)   1812 : 1841
        Marrick Moor, common and waste : 4091 acres awarded
        Commissioner*
        Surveyor Thomas Bradley
   i   NRRD GW no.103 p161 enrolled award
   ii   Marrick parish council sealed original award
        Related papers NYCRO ZQA

492 MARRICK (NR-NY)   1856 : 1861
        Lea Pasture : 19 acres
        Commissioner and surveyor William Lay
   i   NYCRO QDD(I) no.28 and plan (2 ch=1")
   ii   PRO (MAF 1 902) award

493 MARSKE (near Redcar) (NR-NY)   1755 : 1756
        Some open field : 1371 acres awarded
   i   NRRD AB no.1 p1 enrolled award
   ii   NYCRO ZNK original award; also copy

494 MARSKE (near Richmond) (NR-NY)   1809 : 1842
        Moors and common : 1285 acres awarded
        Commissioner and surveyor John Humphries
   i   NYCRO QDD(D) Bk S no.30 p135
   ii   NYCRO QDD(I) no.27 original award
   iii NYCRO ZAZ plan made 1810 by T. Bradley

495 MARTON AND SEWERBY (ER-H)   1802 : 1811
        Open fields, common pastures, waste : 1624 acres awarded
        Commissioners Joseph Dickinson, John Hall, Isaac Leatham
        Surveyor Samuel Dickinson
    i   ERRD CQ/113/4 enrolled award and B4 plan (1811,
        buildings, 8 ch=1")
    ii HCRO DDX/154/12 copy award
    iii HUL DDLG/30/346 sealed original award and plan
    iv Bridlington Public Library copy award and plan
        Related documents HCRO DDLG/30/897 pre-enclosure plan
        1802

496 MARTON CUM GRAFTON (WR-NY)   1798 : 1799
        Open fields in Marton : 439 acres awarded
        Commissioners Isaac Leatham, John Tuke
    i   WRRD B20 p53 enrolled award and plan Vol 2/12 (1799,
        surveyor John Tuke, open fields showing uninclosed
        furlongs, grass balks and enclosure allotments
        overmarked, 3 ch=1")
    ii NYCRO PR/MAG 12/1 sealed original award

    MARTON (NR-NY) see Sinnington

    MARTON (WR-NY) see Grafton

497 MASBROUGH (WR-SY)   1765 : 1766
        Common fields, meadows, ancient undivided enclosures,
        commons and wastes : 103 acres awarded
        Commissioners Edward Oates, Leonard Webster, James
        Wright, William Marsden (refused)
    i   WRRD B5 p1 enrolled award
    ii Rotherham CL sealed original award and plan (1763,
        surveyor W. Fairbank)

498 MASHAM (NR-NY)   1793 : 1797
        Moors and commons : 4657 acres awarded
        Commissioners Richard Clark , John Mowbray, John
        Bradford
    i   NRRD no.3 and no.35, sealed original award with 2 plans
        (two scale not stated, one 8 ch=1"), 2 draft plans, 2
        deeds of exchange

499 MELBOURNE AND STORTHWAITE (ER-H)   1777 : 1782
        Open fields, commons, waste, carrs, ings or meadow :
        2478 acres awarded
        Commissioners John Outram, John Raines, Miles Dawson,
        Peter Nevill
        Surveyor William Dawson
    i   ERRD BB/311/40 enrolled award and plan (1777, buildings,
        8 ch=1")
    ii ERRD sealed original

    MELMERBY (NR-NY) see Hutton Conyers

500 MELSONBY (NR-NY) 1815 : 1820
Commons and waste : 600 acres awarded
Commissioners Humphries, Leafe and Calvert (sic)
i NRRD EI no.23 p91 enrolled award and plan (buildings, 6 ch=1")
ii NYCRO sealed original award and plan

501 MELTHAM (WR-WY) 1817 : 1832
Amending act 1830. Commons, moors and waste : 3545 acres awarded
Commissioners William Rayner (bankrupt and in prison), Joseph Taylor, John Buckley (died), Frederick Robert Jones
i WRRD B45 p1 enrolled award and plan Vol 3/8 (not dated, surveyors James Bulmer, John Johnson (resigned), William Porter, Joseph Hall, whole township shown, buildings, 6 ch=1", very large plan)
ii Kirklees RO sealed original award and plan in volume: also award
iii YAS photocopy of 1877 copy of map

502 MELTON (ER-H) 1771 : 1773
Fields, lands and waste : 864 acres awarded
Commissioners John Lund, John Outram, Robert Dunn
Surveyor Charles Tate
i ERRD AQ/249/22 enrolled award and modern copy of plan (buildings, scale not stated)
ii Hull CL copy award and plan (8 ch=1")
iii Durham HCR sealed original award and plan

MELTONBY (ER-H) see Yapham

503 MENSTON (WR-WY) 1821 : 1825
By agreement. Menston common and some small pieces of waste
Commissioner Jonathan Taylor
i CP Wakefield C 346/1-2 sealed original award and plan (1822, surveyor Jonathan Taylor, buildings, 6 ch=1")

MENWITH WITH DARLEY (WR-NY) see Knaresborough, Forest of

504 METHLEY (WR-WY) 1786 : 1789
Commons, common fields, wastes and commonable lands : 800 acres awarded
Commissioner Miles Dawson, George Travis, Richard Clark
i WRRD B17 p237 enrolled award and plan Vol 3/5 (1787, surveyor William Whitelock, whole township shown, buildings, scale not stated)
ii Leeds RO sealed original award and 2 plans
iii WYAS Z35 copy award
iv WYAS Z98 two photocopies of plans from original at Leeds (1786,1787, surveyor William Whitelock, one unsigned, buildings, whole township shown, similar but not identical plans, 5 ch=1" and 6 ch=half an inch)

MEXBOROUGH (WR-SY) see Dolcliffe

505 MICKLETON (NR-Durham)   1802 : 1810
         Not open field. 4356 acres awarded
      i   Durham CRO D/HH 2/14/114 award

     MICKLEY (NR-NY) see Mulgrave

     MICKLEY (WR-NY) see Kirkby Malzeard

     MIDDLESMOOR (WR-NY) see Stonebeck Up

     MIDDLETHORPE (WR-York) see Dringhouses

     MIDDLETON (NR-NY) see Aislaby

506 MIDDLETON ON THE WOLDS (ER-H)   1803 : 1805
         Supplementary award 1816. Open fields, waste : 3463
         acres awarded
         Commissioners William Dawson, John Lee, Joseph Dickinson
         (supplementary award added John Bower in place of
         William Dawson who died)
      i   ERRD CI/47/3 enrolled award and plan (not dated,
          buildings, 8 ch=1"); enrolled supplementary award
          CQ/451/38 and plan
      ii HCRO DDX/131/8 copy both plans; also DDX/239

507 MIDHOPE, UPPER (WR-SY)   1818 :
         Award never completed. Commons and waste : 3600 acres
         estimated
         Commissioner William Pilkington
      i   Bradfield parish council uncompleted MS award

508 MILLINGTON (ER-H)   1768 : 1770
         Open fields, common pastures, commons, waste : 2300
         acres estimated
         Commissioners Robert Bewlay jun, John Outram, Edward
         Cleaver
         Surveyor Miles Dawson
      i   ERRD AK/297/22 enrolled award
      ii   HCRO IA typescript copy award and copy plan (undated,
           buildings, scale not stated)
      iii HUL DDCV/113/1 sealed original award

509 MINSKIP (WR-NY)   1835 : 1839
         By agreement. Open fields, uninclosed grounds, common
         or stinted pasture and waste
         Commissioner John Howgate
      i   WRRD B45 p134 enrolled award and plan Vol 3/9 (1839,
          surveyor John Howgate, whole township shown, buildings,
          open field names, 6 ch=1")
      ii Aldborough parish church award

510 MIRFIELD (WR-WY)   1796 : 1806
       Commons, 3 common fields and other commonable lands :
       560 acres estimated
       Commissioners John Sykes, John Sharp (died), Charles
       Brooke
   i   WRRD B22 p293 enrolled award
   ii NRA Report Kirklees records 2 copies of award and 2
       plans (1798, surveyor Elias Stott, buildings, open field
       names, 3 ch=1")
   iii Messrs Goodall & Son solicitors, Mirfield, typewritten
       copy of award and copy plan

     MITTON (WR-Lancs) see Grindleton

511 MOLESCROFT (ER-H)   1801 : 1803
       Supplementary award 1812. Open fields, common or carr :
       685 acres awarded, and 75 in supplementary award
       Commissioners Richard Clark, John Hall, Joseph Dickinson
       Surveyors Samuel Dickinson, John Dalton
   i   ERRD CA/208/30 enrolled award and F4 plan; supplementary
       award CQ/109/3
   ii HUL DDCV/209/11-12 sealed original award with
       supplementary award and plan (not dated, buildings, 8
       ch=1")
   iii HUL DDSY/47/63 copy award and DDSY/98/1 related paper

512 MONK BRETTON (WR-SY)   1777 : 1778
       Common fields, mesne inclosures, commons or waste : 419
       acres awarded
       Commissioners John Outram Thomas Tofield, William Hill
   i   WRRD B12 p1 enrolled award
   ii Sheffield CL NBC 60 award

513 MONK FRYSTON (WR-NY)   1792 : 1794
       Open fields, meadows, ings, commons and waste : 558
       acres awarded
       Commissioners Richard Clark, Miles Dawson (refused),
       Isaac Leatham, William Dawson
   i   WRRD B19 p245 enrolled award and plan with 2 copies
       Z55(L) (1798, unsigned, buildings, whole township shown,
       scale not stated)
   0,00 Sealed original awards to be kept in parish church and
       with manorial records under the act. Neither found

514 MOOR MONKTON (WR-NY)   1786 : 1787?

       Three open fields, meadow, pasture, Moor Monkton Common
       : 1080 acres estimated
       Commissioners John Graves, Richard Clark
   i   Moor Monkton parish church award and plan (dated 1787)
   ii Borthwick Institute York M/M/14 copy award

515 MOORSHOLM (NR-Cleveland) 1858 : 1864
        Low Moor and High Moor : 605 acres awarded
        Commissioner James Fair
   i   NYCRO No.29 original award and plan
   ii   Cleveland County Archives PR/MO original award and plan
   iii NYCRO ZPY (L) 123 copy award
   iv   PRO (MAF 1 975 and 505) award

   MOORWOOD (WR-SY) see Hallam

516 MORLEY (WR-WY) 1816 : 1833
        Commons and waste : 119 acres awarded
        Commissioner Nicholas Brown
   i   WRRD B41 sealed original award and 2 plans bound in
        volume (1818,1821, surveyor G. Charlesworth, buildings,
        3 ch=1")
   ii   Morley Public Library sealed original award and 2 plans

517 MORTHEN (WR-SY) 1766 : 1766
        By agreement. Two common fields
        Commissioners George Townsend, Joseph Purslove, John Hay
   i   WRRD B5 p98 enrolled award
   ii   Notts CRO DD 48/20 sealed original award, and DD 48/21-2
        copy and draft award
        Related papers Sheffield CL Fairbank Collection

   MORTON (WR-WY) see Riddlesden

518 MOSS AND KIRK BRAMWITH (WR-SY) 1780 : 1783
        Commons and waste, and in Kirk Bramwith open fields,
        meadows and pastures : 1060 acres awarded
        Commissioners John Lund jun. George Kelk (died), Thomas
        Fletcher, William Kelk
   i   WRRD B15 p134 enrolled award
   ii   Doncaster RO P16 award and plans
   iii SYCRO 281/P microfilm of award and plan

   MOWTHORPE (ER-NY) see Kirby Grindalythe

519 MUKER (NR-NY) ? : 1817
        By agreement
        Surveyors A. Clarkson and J. Swailes
   i   Original award in private possession

520 MUKER (NR-NY) 1828 : 1832
        By agreement. Stinted pasture : 899 acres awarded
        Commissioners Richard Garth, Anthony Clarkson
   i   NYCRO Acc 866 sealed original award and plan (1829,
        4ch=1")
   ii   NYCRO plan (1836, 8ch=1")

521 MULGRAVE IN LYTHE AND HINDERWELL (NR-NY)　　　　1776 : 1782
    Moors, common and waste in Lythe; arable and meadow in
    Lythe, Burnby and Mickley : 4586 acres awarded
    Commissioners not named
    Surveyors Richard Richardson, Joseph Foord
  i   NRRD BR no.26 p32 enrolled award
  ii   NYCRO ZPA original award and plan (buildings, 8 ch=1")
  iii NYCRO ZW copy award

522 MYTON (Hull) (ER-H)　　　　1771 : 1773
    Pasture called Myton Carr : 188 acres awarded
    Commissioners John Outram, Peter Nevill
    Surveyor Charles Tate
  i   ERRD AT/45/5 enrolled award
  ii   HCRO DDTH/15 copy award and plan (copy of 1844, 4 ch=1")
  iii Hull CL copy award and plan
  iv   Hull City RO copy award and plan
  v   HUL DSJ/61 copy award
  vi   Leeds Brotherton Library MS 311/5 19 cent. copy award
       and plan

523 NABURN (ER-NY) 1766 : 1768
    Common fields, meadows, moor, common : 706 acres awarded
    Commissioners Edward Cleaver, John Cleaver, John Lund, John Graves
  i   ERRD AH/378/16 enrolled award
  ii   HUL DDPA/7/291 sealed original award
  iii HUL DDBH/12/17 sealed original award

524 NAFFERTON AND WANSFORD (ER-H) 1769 : 1772
    Open fields, common pastures, open lands : 4200 acres estimated
    Commissioners John Outram, Robert Bewlay jun (refused), John Raines, Peter Nevill
    Surveyors Peter Nevill, Isaac Milbourn
  i   ERRD AQ/97/13 enrolled award
  ii   HCRO DDX/154/10 copy award

NESFIELD (WR-NY) see Langbar

NETHERBY (WR-NY) see Kearby

NETHER POPPLETON (WR-NY) see Poppleton

525 NETHERTHONG (WR-WY) 1826 : 1829
    Commons and waste, Netherthong Common : 280 acres estimated
    Commissioner George Crowther
  i   WRRD B38 p251 enrolled award and plan Vol 3/13 (1829, surveyor Thomas Dinsley, buildings, 4 ch=1")
  ii   Kirklees RO sealed original award; also copy award and copy plan plan

NEWALL (WR-WY) see Otley

NEWBALD (ER-H) see North Newbald

526 NEWBIGGIN, BISHOPDALE AND BURTON (NR-NY)   1811 : 1816
        Pasture, common : 2957 acres awarded
        Commissioners John Humphries, William Morton
    i   NRRD DZ no.9 p57 enrolled award and 3 plans (not dated,
        surveyor not named, 6 ch=1")

NEWBY (NR-NY) see Hutton Conyers ; Scalby

NEWBY (WR-NY) see Clapham

NEWHOLM (NR-NY) see Dunsforth

NEWLAND (ER-H) see Eastrington

527 NEWSHAM (Bempton) (ER-H)   1836 : 1843
        Open fields : 218 acres awarded
        Commissioner Leonard Brooks Earnshaw
        Surveyor Henry Scott
    i   ERRD FG/430/15 enrolled award
    ii HCRO QDB 8 p31 enrolled award
    iii HCRO DDX/154/24 award
    iv NYCRO ZDV plan (1841, 4 ch=1")

NEWSHOLME (WR-WY) see Keighley

NEWTON (ER-H) see Out Newton; Wold Newton

528 NEWTON (Kirkdale) (NR-NY)   1784 : 1787

        By agreement. Stinted pasture
        Commissioner Edward Cleaver
        Surveyor Ralph Burton
    i   NYCRO PR/KRD sealed original award and plan (4ch=1")
    ii NRRD BU no.65 p150 enrolled award

NEWTON (NR-NY) see Pickering

529 NEWTON-LE-WILLOWS AND THORNTON STEWARD (NR-NY)   1800 : 1803
        Normans' Moor : 716 acres awarded
        Commissioner and surveyor Alexander Calvert
    i   NRRD no.5 sealed original award and plan (buildings, 8
        ch=1")

530 NEWTON-ON-OUSE (NR-NY)   1758 : ?
        Act 1758, award not found : not executed?

531 NEWTON ON RAWCLIFFE (NR-NY)   1774 : 1775
        By agreement. Three open fields : 300 acres awarded
        Commissioner Robert Lyth, William Willmott, John Kendall
        Surveyors Thomas Dodsworth, Robert King
    i   NRRD BB no.61 p194 enrolled agreement
    ii NRRD BH no.2 p60 enrolled award

NEWTON UPON DERWENT (ER-H) see Catton

532 NORMANBY (Ormesby) (NR-Cleveland) 1809 : 1811
        Moor : 87 acres
        Commissioner John Humphries
    i   NRRD DO no.4 p27 plan in volume

533 NORMANTON AND WOODHOUSE (WR-WY) 1804 : 1810
        Open fields, commons and waste : 630 acres awarded
        Commissioners William Whitelock (died), Thomas Gee
    i   WRRD B28 p200 enrolled award
    ii Wakefield Town Hall award and plan (not dated, surveyor
        Thomas Gee, buildings, whole township shown, scale not
        stated)
    iii YAS MD 225 plans

534 NORTHALLERTON (NR-NY) 1637
        Warrant from the bishop of Durham allowing his
        Northallerton tenants to enclose all their arable,
        meadow and pasture
    i   Durham DCM 221344 f3

535 NORTH ANSTON AND TODWICK (WR-SY) 1767 : 1768
        Four open fields, commons, moor or waste : 785 acres
        awarded
        Commissioners Edward Oates, William Hill, John Kay,
        Jonathan Bromehead, George Jackson
    i   WRRD B7 p117 enrolled award
    ii Rotherham CL sealed award
    iii Sheffield CL MD 5720 copy award

536 NORTH CAVE (ER-H) 1764 : 1765
        Open fields, meadow, pastures : 1400 acres estimated
        Commissioners Joseph Thompson, John Lund, John Outram
        Surveyors Charles Tate, Isaac Milbourn
    i   ERRD AF/265/12 enrolled award
    ii HCRO DDBD/52/5 copy part award

     NORTH CAVE (ER-H) see Howden

537 NORTH CLIFFE (ER-H) 1799 : 1801
        By agreement. Common and commonable grounds : 522 acres
        awarded
        Commissioner and surveyor Richard Clark
    i   HUL DDLA/42/3 award and plan (not dated, 7 ch=1")
    ii ERRD copy plan made 1932

538   NORTH CROSLAND (lost, in South Crosland or Lockwood) (WR-WY)
                                                            1799 : 1803
            Commons, moors and waste : 824 acres awarded
            Commissioners William Newton, Jonathan Teal
      i   WRRD B21 p271 enrolled award and plan Vol 3/10 (1802,
            surveyor Jonathan Teal, buildings, 6 ch=1")
      ii   Kirklees RO copy award
      iii   Kirklees RO,   19 cent copy award and plan; also later
            copy plan
      iv   Leeds RO DB/M638 award and plan
      0   Sealed original award to be kept in parish church of
            Almondbury under the act. Not found

539   NORTH DALTON (ER-H)   1778 : 1779
            Open fields, stinted pastures, waste : 4330 acres
            awarded
            Commissioners William Hall, Miles Dawson, Robert Dunn
            Surveyor William Hildyard
      i   ERRD BB/184/22 enrolled award
      ii   HCRO DDX/96/1 sealed original award and plan (1779,
            buildings, 8ch=1")
            Related documents HUL DDCV/118/1-10

540   NORTH DEIGHTON (WR-NY)   1783 : 1785
            Four open fields, meadow : 511 acres awarded
            Commissioners George Hayes, John Graves, John Lund jun
      i   WRRD Map Vol 3/12 sealed original award and plan (not
            dated, surveyor William Dawson, buildings, open field
            names, 6 ch=1")
      ii   NRA Report Ingilby Records, sealed original award and
            plan

541   NORTH DUFFIELD (ER-NY)   1809 : 1814
            Open fields, ings, carrs, commons, waste : 1080 acres
            awarded
            Commissioners John Tuke, Richard Clark
            Surveyor William Shipton
      i   HCRO QDB 7 p64 enrolled award
      ii   HCRO DDTR/350 copy award

542   NORTH FERRIBY, SWANLAND, KIRK ELLA, WEST ELLA AND WILLERBY
            (ER-H)   1824 : 1837
            Opewn fields, balks, medows, pastures : 3645 acres
            awarded
            Commissioners John Hall, Leonard Brooks Earnshaw,
            Cornelius Collett, William Stickney
            Surveyors Robert Iveson, James Bulmer, William Rawson
      i   ERRD FG/87/2 enrolled award and A1 plan (not dated,
            buildings, 6 ch=1")
      ii   Hull CL, copy award with index and copy plan
      iii   HCRO IA copy plan
      iv   Leeds Brotherton Library MS 311/1 copy award
            Related documents HCRO DX/128 and DDX/25/5, and Hull CL,
            3 copies pre-enclosure plan of Swanland and Ferriby,
            1824. HCRO HD/34 plan 1829 showing old and new roads

543 NORTH FRODINGHAM (ER-H)   1801 : 1808
        Open fields, meadows, pasture, carrs, common waste :
        2384 acres awarded
        Commissioners John Moiser (refused), Robert Spofforth,
        Joseph Dickinson, Peter Jackson
        Surveyors Robert Atkinson, Francis Haigh
   i   ERRD CI/276/20 enrolled award and plan (1808, buildings,
        8 ch=1")
   ii HCRO PE/118/57 sealed original award
        Related documents HUL DDCV/120/8-10 Commissioners'
        minute book

544 NORTH GRIMSTON (ER-NY)   1792 : 1794
        Certain open fields : 691 acres awarded
        Commissioners Samuel Milbourn, William Dawson, Isaac
        Milbourn
   i   ERRD BG/403/61 enrolled award
        Related document NYCRO ZDS late 18 cent survey

545 NORTH NEWBALD AND SOUTH NEWBALD (ER-H)   1771 : 1783
        Open fields, wolds, commons, waste : 5497 acres awarded
        Commissioners John Outram (died), John Wood, Miles
        Dawson,Edward Watterson
        Surveyors Joseph Dickinson, William Dawson
   i   ERRD BG/4/3 enrolled award and copy plan made 1930
        (1778, buildings, 8 ch=1")
   ii HCRO IA copy plan
   iii York Minster Library X2 sealed original award and plan
   iv Hull CL copy award

546 NORTHOWRAM (WR-WY)   1778 : 1780
        Commons, moors and waste : 600 acres estimated
        Commissioners John Sharpe, Joseph Jagger, Benjamin
        Patchett
   i   WRRD B14 p121 enrolled award and 5 plans Vol 3/11 (not
        signed (1) Northowram Green etc. (2) Green Lane etc. (3)
        Hainworth Moor etc. (4) Priestly Hill etc. (5) Pepper
        Hill etc, buildings, 4 ch=1"; volume also contains
        survey 1779)
   ii Queensbury and Shelf UDC award and plans

    NORTON (Near Doncaster (WR-SY) see Campsall

547 NORTON-LE-CLAY (NR-NY)   1791 : 1792
        Open fields and common pastures : 770 acres awarded
        Commissioners Edward Watterson, Richard Clark
   i   NRRD CA no.40 p110 enrolled award and plan (buildings, 6
        ch=1")
   ii NRRD no.2 original award and plan

    NORWOOD (WR-NY) see Clifton

548 NUNBURNHOLME (ER-H)　　　　　　　　　　　　　　　　1754 : 1755
    　　　By agreement of 1754; act 1755, award 1755
    　　　Commissioners John Dealtry, Ralph Featherstone, John
    　　　Dickinson, John Conyers
    　i　ERRD Y/28/12 copy award
    　ii　HCRO DDX/131/9 copy award and 2 reconstructions of plan
    　　　(20 cent?)

549 NUN MONKTON (WR-NY)　　　　　　　　　　　　　　　　1767 : 1776
    　　　Open fields, ings, meadow or pasture : 1100 acres
    　　　estimated
    　　　Commissioners John Outram, William George Nicholson,
    　　　Robert Bewlay
    　i　WRRD B10 p312 enrolled award

    NUNNINGTON (NR-NY) see Stonegrave

550 OAKWORTH (WR-WY) 1849 : 1855
      Oakworth Common : 975 acres awarded
      Commissioner Joseph Smith
- i CP Wakefield A34 sealed original award and plans (1854, surveyor Joseph Smith, buildings, various scales)
- ii TC Keighley award and plan
- iii PRO (MAF 1 699) award
- iv Bradford RO copy award and copy plan

OCTON (ER-H) see Thwing

551 OLD LINDLEY (WR-WY) 1807 : 1810
      Two open fields, commons, moors and waste : 242 acres awarded
      Commissioner James Garside
- i WRRD B27 p273 enrolled award
- ii Tolson Museum, Huddersfield, enclosure plan (not dated, surveyor J. Garside)

552 OLD MALTON (NR-NY) 1794 : 1805
      Open fields, common waste and ings : 1516 acres awarded
      Commissioners Isaac Milbourn, Peter Merry, William Dawson
      Surveyor Ralph Burton
- i NYCRO I original award and plan (buildings, 8 ch=1")
- ii NRRD DA no.3 p3 enrolled award
- iii NYCRO DC/MLU copy award

553 ORGREAVE (WR-SY) 1808 : 1810
      By agreement. Commons and waste
      Commissioner William Rodgers
- i WRRD B27 p319 enrolled award
- ii Sheffield CL NBC 75 sealed original award and plan (1809, survey made by Mr Fairbank, plan by William Bingley, buildings, 4 ch=1")
- ii Sheffield CL MS copy award and plan

554 OSBALDWICK AND GATE HELMSLEY (NR-NY) 1769 : 1772
      3 parcels of ground called Osbaldwick High Moor, Osbaldwick Carr and Gate Helmsley stinted pasture : 232 acres awarded
- i NYCRO ZEY 15 p9 copy award
- ii NYCRO ZOW original award and plan (4 ch=1")

555 OSGODBY (near Selby) (ER-NY) 1811 : 1819
      Open fields, ings, commons, waste : 475 acres awarded
      Commissioner John Tuke
      Surveyor Daniel Tuke
- i ERRD DA/207/50 enrolled award and plan (not dated, buildings, 6 ch=1")

556 OSMOTHERLEY (NR-NY)   1755 : 1755
        Act confirms agreement. Moor or common : 1030 acres
        awarded
        Commissioners not named
    i   NRRD W no.107 p175 enrolled award
    ii Durham HCR M76 enrolled award
    iii Durham DCM 184973 p574 enrolled award; also 54322
        related papers

557 OSSETT (WR-WY)   1807 : 1813
        Open fields, common or waste : 580 acres estimated
        Commissioners William Whitelock (died), Thomas Gee
    i   Wakefield Town Hall award and 3 plans
    ii YAS MD 225 copy award made 1814 and 3 plans (not dated,
        surveyor Thomas Gee, (1) Ossett, 6ch=1"l (2) Town of
        Ossett, 3 ch=1"; (3) Thornes, Sowood Green and Ossett, 3
        ch=1", all show buildings. Also plan of Ossett Common,
        Green, and Storrs Hill, made at time of enclosure,
        showing buildings, 3 ch=1")

    OSWALDKIRK (NR-NY) see Ampleforth

558 OTLEY AND NEWALL WITH CLIFTON (WR-NY)   1778 : 1783
        Commons called Otley Chevin and Newall Carr and waste :
        1236 acres awarded
        Commissioners Robert Bewlay, Thomas Midgeley, John
        Bainbridge
    i   Otley UDC copy award
    ii Copy award and 2 plans, in private possession, Otley
    iii Church Commissioners, copy award
    iv Borthwick Institute York CC/A6/11/17 and CC/A6/11/63
        plans
    v   YAS award and MS 209 copy plan

559 OTTRINGHAM (ER-H)   1758 : 1760
        By agreement. Open fields, pasture : 2900 acres awarded
        Commissioners John Cleaver, John Dickinson, Richard
        North
        Surveyors John Lund, Thomas Lazenby
    i   ERRD AC/45/2 enrolled award and agreement AC/1/1
    ii HCRO DDCK 32/4 award
    iii Ottringham church award : plan not found 1985

560 OUGHTERSHAW (WR-NY)   1845 : 1849
        Stinted pastures called Cow Close and Moss or West
        Pasture : 2850 acres awarded
        Commissioner Richard Garth jun
    i   CP Wakefield A24 sealed original award and plan (1848,
        surveyor Richard Garth jun, buildings, 4 ch=1")
    ii PRO (MAF 1 271) award

    OULTON (WR-WY) see Rothwell

561 OUSEFLEET (WR-H) 1828 : 1832
Open fields, ings, meadows, stinted pastures, commons, moors and waste : 1119 acres awarded
Commissioners William Pilkington, John Ireland
- i   WRRD B38 p369 enrolled award and 2 plans Vol 3/15 (not dated, surveyor William Pilkington, whole township on 2 sheets, buildings, open field names, 9 ch=1")
- ii HCRO DDCL/242 draft award
- iii Sealed original award to be kept in Whitgift parish church under the act. Not found

562 OUT NEWTON (ER-H) 1756 : 1757
By agreement. Open fields : 601 acres awarded
Commissioners Joseph Thompson, Robert Bell, Richard North
Surveyors Peter Nevill, Charles Tate
- i   ERRD Y/117/25 enrolled agreement, Y/99/24 enrolled award
- ii HCRO DDCK/32/3 copy award
- iii HCRO IA copy plan (1756, buildings, 10 ch=1")
- iv HCRO DDCC(2)G(5) plan

563 OVENDEN (WR-WY) 1814 : 1817
Commons, moors and waste : 1200 acres awarded
Commissioners Thomas Gee, John Watkinson
- i   WRRD B31 p156 enrolled award
- ii Halifax TC award
- iii YAS MD 225 draft award, commissioners' minute book
- iv Calderdale RO copy award

564 OWSTON (WR-SY) 1760 : 1761
Commons and waste : 375 acres awarded
Commissioners Richard Frank, Anthony Eyre, Edward Forster
- i   WRRD B4 p1 enrolled award
- ii Doncaster RO PR.Ow sealed original award
- iii Doncaster RO DD.DC sealed original award

565 OWTHORNE (ER-H) 1806 : 1815
Open arable fields, meadow, pasture : 586 acres awarded
Commissioners John Hall, Thomas Wilson
Surveyor Robert Stickney
- i   ERRD CQ/401/23 enrolled award and plan
- ii HCRO PE/59/19 sealed original award and plan (1812, buildings, 4 ch=1")
- iii HCRO DDCC/142/21 draft award
- iv HUL DX/38/1 plan
Related documents HCRO DDIV/13/1-16

566 OXENHOPE (WR-WY) 1771 - 1777
Oxenhope moor : 2500 acres awarded
Commissioners Francis Fourness (withdrew), John Clapham, Robert Lang, John Smith
- i   WRRD B11 p199 enrolled award and 3 plans Vol 3/14 (1774, (1) Great Moor (2) Black Moor (3) The Marsh, buildings on all plans, scale not stated
- ii TC Keighley award and plans

567 OXSPRING (WR-SY)   1818 : 1831
        Commons and waste : 250 acres estimated
        Commissioner William Pilkington
    i   Oxspring parish council award and plan, deposited with
        the Midland Bank, Penistone
    ii SYCRO 114/P sealed original award and plan (1831,
        surveyor William Bingley, whole township shown,
        buildings, 6 ch=1")

PANNAL (WR-NY) see Knaresborough, Forest of

PATRICK BROMPTON (NR-NY) see Hunton

568   PATRINGTON (ER-H)   1766 : 1768
        Open fields : 2093 acres awarded
        Commissioners John Dealtry, John Raines, Edward Holgate
        Surveyor Peter Nevill
- i   ERRD AK/98/8 enrolled award and plan (1769, buildings, 10 ch=1")
- ii ERRD sealed original award
- iii HCRO DCK/35/1 (c) copy plan
- iv HUL DDKG/188 copy plan
- v   HUL DX/26/4 tracing plan

569   PAULL (ER-H)   1811 : 1822
        Open fields, meadow, pasture : 402 acres awarded
        Commissioners John Lee, John Hall, John Singleton
- i   ERRD DQ/3/1 enrolled award and plan
- ii HCRO DDIV/40/3 sealed original award and plan (not dated, buildings, 8 ch=1")
- iii HCRO DDCC/142/10 copy award
- iv HCRO PE/39/22 enrolled award
- v   HCRO DDX/92/5 copy plan
- vi HUL DX/26/5 tracing plan

570   PENISTONE (WR-SY)   1819 : 1826
        Open fields, mesne inclosures, commons, moors and waste : 420 acres estimated
        Commissioners John Housman (died), Richard Birks, Michael Ellison
- i   WRRD B38 p141 enrolled award and plan Vol 3/17 (not dated, unsigned, some buildings, open field features, scale not stated)
- ii Sheffield CL NBC 61 award and plan

571   PICKERING AND NEWTON (NR-NY)   1785 : 1789
        Further award 1790. Common and waste : 10,130 acres awarded
        Commissioners Timothy Parke, Robert King, Samuel Milbourn, William Hall, John Bainbridge
        Surveyors Robert King, Richard Simpson
- i   NRRD no.9 sealed original award
- ii NYCRO PR/PI 11/1, 11/12 sealed original awards and 2 plans , differing scales
- iii NYCRO QDD 1 and 2 no.49 copies of awards
- iv PRO DL/45/8/9 enrolled award and DL/41/71 related papers

572   POCKLINGTON (ER-H)   1757 : 1759
        Open fields, meadow, common : 1896 acres awarded
        Commissioners Samuel Milbourn, John Dickinson, John Dealtry
- i   ERRD Y/230/39 enrolled award
- ii HCRO DDBD/56/1(a) bound copy award
- iii York City RO M20 p1

573 POLLINGTON, BALNE, WHITLEY, WHITLEY THORPE, GREAT AND LITTLE
          HECK (WR-H)   1772 : 1775
          Open fields, common meadow, pasture, commons and waste :
          2670 acres awarded
          Commissioners William Hill, Henson Kirkby, Richard
          Richardson
     i   WRRD B10 p229 enrolled award
     ii   Doncaster archives award
     iii Doncaster RO P50 award
     iv   HCRO DDCL/250 18 cent copy award in volume

574 PONTEFRACT (WR-WY)   1780
          Act: no award? Open area of the park, allottments of 325
          acres for the use of the inhabitants of Pontefract and
          Tanshelf : 900 acres estimated
     i   PRO DL/31/33 plan (surveyor J Crowder) ; DL/41/68
          enclosure papers

575 PONTEFRACT, CARLETON, TANSHELF, EAST AND WEST HARDWICK,
          FERRYBRIDGE AND KNOTTINGLEY (WR-WY)   1797 : 1800
          Open fields and other lands and compensation for tithes :
          180 acres awarded
          Commissioners Richard Clark, Jonathan Teal
     i   WRRD B21 p7 enrolled award and 4 plans Vol 1/24 and Vol
          2/11 (1800, surveyor William Shipton, (1) Pontefract,
          whole township shown, buildings, scale not stated; (2)
          Tanshelf and Carleton, whole townships shown, buildings,
          scale not stated; (3) East Hardwick and Spittle Hardwick,
          whole townships shown, buildings, scale not stated; (4)
          Ferrybridge, whole township shown, buildings, open field
          names and features 6 ch=1")
     ii   Pontefract TC copy award
     iii WRRD Map Vol 2/25 plan of Knottingley (1800, open field
          features and names, scale not stated)
     iv   J.F. Goodchild copies of plans

576 POOL (WR-WY)   1774
          By agreement. Common
     i   YAS DD 161 plan (1774, surveyor J. Teal, 4 ch=1")
     ii   Leeds RO agreement, award and plan
     iii Pool parish council copy plan

577 POPPLETON, NETHER POPPLETON AND SCAGGLETHORPE (WR-NY)
                                                           1769 : 1775
          Five open fields, meadow, ings, pastures and waste : 2288
          acres awarded
          Commissioners John Dawson (died), Robert Bewlay jun
          (refused), Ambrose Gray, Miles Dawson
     i   York City RO Vols F & G enrolled award
     ii   Borthwick Institute York PR POP/1 sealed original award
     0   Sealed original award to be kept by Lord of the Manor
          under the act. Not found

     POTTER BROMPTON (ER-NY) see BINNINGTON

578 POTTERNEWTON AND GIPTON (WR-WY) 1803 : 1806
　　　　　Common or waste : 149 acres awarded
　　　　　Commissioner William Whitelock
　　i　　WRRD B25 p1 enrolled award and plan Vol 2/13 (1806,
　　　　　surveyor Jonathan Taylor, Potternewton and Harehills
　　　　　commons, buildings, 6 ch=1")
　　ii　　Leeds Civic Hall copy award and plan
　　iii　Leeds RO copy award and plan
　　iv　　PRO (Chancery Lane) MPC 280 plan of Potternewton
　　　　　allotments 1810
　　v　　PRO DL/45/8/2 enrolled extract of award and DL/41/70
　　　　　papers
　　0　　Sealed original award to be kept in Leeds parish
　　　　　church under the act. Not found

579 PRESTON (ER-H) 1773 : 1777
　　　　　Open fields, meadows, pastures : 4374 acres awarded
　　　　　Commissioners John Raines, John Outram, Robert Dunn
　　　　　Surveyors Charles Tate, Peter Nevill
　　i　　ERRD AX/92/4 enrolled award
　　ii　　HCRO IA award and copy plan (1774, buildings, 8 ch=1")
　　iii　HCRO DDCC/142/22 bound copy award
　　iv　　HCRO DDCK/32/14 award and DDCK/35/16 (f) and 25/2
　　　　　tracings of plan
　　v　　HCRO DDIV/41/3 copy award
　　vi　　HCRO PE 123/83 bound copy award
　　vii　HUL DDKG/190 photograph of plan

580 PUDSEY (WR-WY) 1811 : 1820
　　　　　Commons and waste : 360 acres awarded
　　　　　Commissioners Jonathan Teal (died), Henry Teal
　　i　　WRRD B35 p264 enrolled award and 4 plans Vol 3/16 (1820,
　　　　　surveyor Henry Teal (1) Upper Moor, Green Side,
　　　　　Bankhouse and Stocks Greens; (2) Crimbles and Waver
　　　　　Greens; (3) Rickardshaw; (4) Little Moor, all have
　　　　　buildings, 2 or 4 ch=1")
　　ii　　TC Pudsey award and 5 plans

　　PUDSEY (WR-WY) see Calverley

581 PURSTON JAGLIN (WR-WY) 1809 : 1811
　　　　　Open fields, commons and wastes : 123 acres awarded
　　　　　Commissioner Thomas Gee
　　i　　WRRD B49 enrolled award and plan bound in volume (1810,
　　　　　surveyor Thomas Gee, whole township shown, buildings,
　　　　　open field names, 6 ch=1")
　　ii　　Wakefield Town Hall award and plan (20 cent copy, not
　　　　　dated, not signed, buildings, whole township shown, 6
　　　　　ch=1")
　　iii　PRO DL/45/8/6 enrolled extract of award

　　QUICK (Lancs-Greater Manchester) see Denshaw

RAINTON (NR-NY) see Hutton Conyers

582 RASKELF (NR-NY) 1834 : 1838
    Common and waste : 873 acres awarded
    Commissioners Thomas Scott, Charles Greaves
  i NRRD GN no.2 p2 enrolled award

583 RAWCLIFFE (WR-H) 1836 : 1854
    Open fields : 345 acres awarded
    Commissioners Robert Smith, William Perrott Ingram (both refused), Makin Durham
  i CP Wakefield A p156 enrolled award and plan A46 (not dated, unsigned, buildings, open field names, 6 ch=1" and inset, scale not stated)
  ii HCRO DDCL/247 sealed original award and plan in volume
  iii HCRO DDCL/243 copy award in volume; copy plan DDCL/3410 and related papers DDCL/254-64
    Related papers Leeds RO Thorpe Arch estate

RAWCLIFFE (WR-H) see Snaith

584 RAWMARSH (WR-WY) 1774 : 1781
    Common fields, common ings, mesne inclosures, commons or waste : 1323 acres awarded
    Commissioners Christopher Alderson, William Fillingham, Henson Kirkby (died), John Parker
  i WRRD B14 p241 enrolled award and plan Vol 3/18 (1780, unsigned, whole parish shown, buildings, open field features, scale not stateld)
  ii Rotherham CL sealed original award and plan
  iii Sheffield CL printed copy award and plan

REDMIRE (NR-NY) see Wensley

585 REEDNESS AND SWINEFLEET (WR-H) 1759 : 1760
    Act confirms agreement. Commons or waste called Reedness and Swinefleet Pastures : 1200 acres estimated
    Commissioners William Simpson, Edward Forster, Marmaduke Lawson
  i WRRD B3 p83 enrolled award

586 REEDNESS AND SWINEFLEET (WR-H) 1793 : 1801
    Open lands called the Moors : 2000 acres estimated
    Commissioners Thomas Mould, John Wood
  i WRRD B20 p335 enrolled award
  ii YAS MS 560 early 19 cent copy award, also copy award made 1857
  0 Award said to be in Swinefleet parish church. Not found

587 REIGHTON (ER-NY)   1811 : 1820
        Lands : 1593 acres awarded
        Commissioner John Tuke
    i   ERRD H sealed original award and plan (not dated,
        buildings, 8 ch=1")
    ii HCRO DDX/154/12 (vi) copy award
    iii HCRO IA copy plan
    iv HUL DDCV/130/1 sealed original award and plan

588 RICCALL (ER-NY)   1845 : 1883
        Amending award 1907. Open field, common, dam
        Commissioners and surveyors Edmund Smith (died), Spencer
        Gore
    i   HCRO sealed original award and plan (1884, buildings, 3
        ch=1")
    ii HCRO QDB 9 p157 enrolled award
    iii HUL DDFA plan
    iv PRO (MAF 1 514) award

589 RICHMOND (NR-NY)   1802 : 1810
        Four open fields, stinted pasture, moor : 1726 acres
        awarded
        Commissioners William Dawson, John Rodham
    i   NYCRO DC/RMB original award, also bound copy
    ii PRO (Chancery Land) KB Plea Roll no.858 enrolled award

590 RIDDLESDEN AND EAST AND WEST MORTON (WR-WY)   1788 : 1790
        Common or waste called Morton Moor or Rumbles Moor :
        2254 acres awarded
        Commissioners Miles Dawson, Nathan Jowett (did not
        sign), John Sharp
    i   WRRD Map Vol 3/7 sealed original award and plan (1788,
        unsigned, buildings, 8 ch=1")
    ii WRRD B18 p29 enrolled award
    iii Keighley TC copy award
    iv Messrs Weatherhead & Butcher, solicitors, Bingley, copy
        award
    v   Leeds RO xerox copy award

591 RIGTON (WR-WY)   1775 : 1778
        Two commons, meadows, closes of arable, a coney warren :
        2056 acres awarded
        Commissioners Richard Richardson, Benjamin Chambers,
        Ambrose Gray
    i   WRRD Roll 12 sealed original award
    ii Leeds RO Harewood archives, sealed original award and
        pre-enclosure plan (1776, surveyor Benjamin Chambers,
        buildings, open field features 5 ch=1")
    iii Kirkby Overblow parish church award

592 RILLINGTON (ER-NY)   1657
         Open lands
         Commissioners Thomas Langdale, Francis Danby, John
         Burgess, James Mawe, Robert Denison
     i   Leeds RO Thorp Arch estate records 2/15 award and
         boundary description 1677

593 RILLINGTON (ER-NY)   1778 : 1780
         By agreement. Open fields, ings, pasture : 795 acres
         estimated
         Commissioners Samuel Milbourn, Robert Dunn, William
         Wilmott
         Surveyor Isaac Milbourn
     i   ERRD BB/226/26 enrolled agreement and BB/231/27 enrolled
         award

594 RIMSWELL (ER-H)   1818 : 1822
         Carr or low ground : 68 acres awarded
         Commissioner William Stickney
         Surveyor Thomas Thornton
     i   ERRD EU/355/370 enrolled award
     ii HCRO DDCK/32/19 award and plan (unsigned, drawn on
         award, scale not stated)
     iii HCRO DDPK/29/2 bound copy

595 RIPLEY (WR-NY)   1778
         Act to confirm agreement. Open and enclosed lands and
         common : Scarah Moor

596 RIPLINGHAM (ER-H)   1801 : 1803
         Open fields, sheep walks, commons, waste : 1413 acres
         awarded
         Commissioners Peter Nevill, John Hall, William Whitelock
         Surveyor Samuel Dickinson
     i   ERRD CA/180/28 enrolled award and plan (1802, buildings,
         8ch=1")
     ii HCRO PE 62/35 sealed original award and plan
     iii HCRO DDHB/35/67 copy award and plan DDHB/35/64
     iv Hull CL award and plan
         Related documents HUL DDDU/10/7,70,86

597 RIPON, LITTLETHORPE AND BONDGATE (WR-NY)
                                                           1744 : 1747
         Common right called average in the open fields : 1197
         acres awarded
         Commissioners Sir Miles Staplyton, Sir John Ingleby, Sir
         Reginald Graham, Andrew Wilkinson, William Danby, John
         Milbank, Gabatis Norton, Fletcher Norton, John Hutton,
         Gregory Rhodes, John Moyer, William Crompton
     i   WRRD Roll 3 enrolled award
     ii TC Ripon sealed original award and plan (1744, surveyor
         M. Beckwith, plan of common field lands, buildings drawn
         pictorially, including Minster, open field features, 4
         and a half ch=1")
     iii Leeds RO photocopy of map

598 RIPON, BISHOPTON, SHAROW, LITTLETHORPE (WR-NY)   1826 : 1858
   Commons and waste, Bishopton High and Low Ellers, Sharow
   Oxclose and Littlethorpe Oxclose, also to exonerate
   lands enclosed 1747 from average rents : 358 acres
   awarded
   Commissioners John Humphries (died), Robert Telford
   i   WRRD B52 p154 enrolled award
   ii   WRRD Map Vol 4/24 sealed original award
   iii NYCRO DC/RIC sealed original award and 10 plans in
        volume (not dated, surveyor Robert Telford, buildings
        including part of city, open field features, various
        scales)

   RIPON (WR-NY) see Skelton

599 RISHWORTH (WR-WY)   1819 : 1820
   By agreement. Mosleden Pasture
   Commissioner William Pilkington
   i   WRRD B33 p364 enrolled award
   ii   Notts CRO Savile of Rufford, enclosure papers
   0   Original awards to be given to 6 separate persons under
        the act: 5 untraced 1962 (one probably (ii) above)

600 ROECLIFFE (WR-NY)   1836 : 1841
   Open fields : 599 acres awarded
   Commissioner James Potter
   i   WRRD B37 p248 enrolled award and plan Vol 3/19 (not
        dated, signed by commissioner, whole township shown,
        buildings, open field names and features, 8 ch=1")
   ii   CP Wakefield A79 sealed original award and plan (dated
        1841)
   iii NYCRO PR/ROC 2/2
   iv   Leeds RO photocopy of plan

601 ROLSTON (ER-H)   1836 : 1860
   Open fields, meadow, pasture : 673 acres awarded
   Commissioner and surveyor Robert Wise
   i   HCRO IA award and plan (1859, buildings, 6 ch=1")
   ii   HCRO QDB 9 p109 enrolled award
   iii HCRO DX/20 copy award
   iv   HUL DDCV/136/1 award

   ROMALDKIRK (NR-NY) see Cotherstone; Hunderthwaite

602 ROOS (ER-H)   1783 : 1786
   Open fields, meadow, pasture : 1593 acres awarded
   Commissioners Robert Dunn, Edward Lorrimar, Peter Nevill
   Surveyor William Hildyard
   i   ERRD BG/103/9 enrolled award
   ii   HCRO PE/44/32 sealed original award and plan (1794,
        buildings, scale not stateld)
   iii HCRO DDCK/35/1(g) copy plan; DDCK/32/15 copy schedule
        Related documents, HUL DDSY(3)/3/10

   ROSSETT GREEN (WR-NY) see Knaresborough, Forest of

603 ROSSINGTON (WR-SY)   1810
        Act confirms agreement. No award. Acreage not stated

ROSSINGTON (WR-SY) see Doncaster

604 ROTHERHAM (WR-SY)   1761 : 1764
        Common fields, moors and common : 1034 acres awarded
        Commissioners George Walker, William Marsden, Thomas
        Smith, Joseph Pursglove, Henson Kirkby
- i   WRRD B4 p75 enrolled award
- ii Rotherham CL sealed original award, also copy award and tracing and photocopy of plan

ROTHERHAM (WR-SY) see Brinsworth; Dalton; Kimberworth

605 ROTHWELL, LOFTHOUSE, CARLTON, OULTON AND WOODLESFORD (WR-WY)
                                                                         1785 : 1793
        Act amended 1796. Uninclosed ground called Rothwell
        Haigh : 542 acres awarded
        Commissioners John Sharp, Richard Clark
- i   WRRD B18 p173 enrolled award
- ii Rothwell UDC sealed original award and plan (1783, surveyor Charles H. Turner), buildings, open field features, 273'=1")
- iii Messrs John Farrar & Co Oulton, copy award and plan

606 ROTHWELL, ROYDS GREEN, OULTON AND WOODLESFORD (WR-WY)
                                                      1809 : 1818
        Open fields, commons and waste : 397 acres awarded
        Commissioners Jonathan Teal, Richard Clark
- i   CP Wakefield C p303 enrolled award and A37 eight plans (not dated, surveyor Henry Teal; (1) Patrick Green; (2) Church Field; (3) Ashwell and Quarry Fields; (4) Holmesley Fields; (5) Orgrove and North Fields; (6) Stone Bridge Green and Rothwell Marsh; (7) Oulton and Oulton Green; (8) Royds Green and Farlightnings
- ii Rothwell UDC sealed original award and plan
- iii Messrs John Farrer & Co Oulton, copy award and copies of plan
- iv PRO DL/45/9/5 enrolled extract of award

ROYDS GREEN (WR-WY) see Rothwell

607 ROYSTON (WR-SY)   1772 : 1773
        Two open commons or moors called West Moor and Low
        Common : 169 acres awarded
        Commissioners William Hill, Matthew Ash, John Kay
- i   WRRD B10 p23 enrolled award and B11 p197 correction
- ii D of L Lib.2 p59 enrolled award
- iii Sheffield CL NBC 77 copy award

608 RUDSTON (ER-H)   1774 : 1777
       Open arable fields : 4000 acres estimated
       Commissioners John Outram, William Hall, Robert Dunn
       Surveyors Peter Nevill, Joseph Dickinson
     i   ERRD BB/18/7 enrolled award
     ii   HCRO DDX/154/7,20 two copies award
     iii HCRO PE 84/24 copy award

609 RUFFORTH (WR-NY)   1794 : 1806
       Open fields, ings, common and waste : 858 acres awarded
       Commissioner William Dawson
     i   York City RO TC DP/1/6 sealed original award and plan
          annexed (1795, surveyor not named, buildings, 6 ch=1")
     ii   Rufforth parish church award

610 RUSTON PARVA (ER-H)   1801 : 1805
       Common fields, pastures : 908 acres awarded
       Commissioners John Hall, Joseph Dickinson
       Surveyor Samuel Dickinson
     i   ERRD CI/2/1 enrolled award and plan (1801, buildings, 8
          ch=1")
     ii   HCRO DDX/154/15 copy award
     iii HCRO DX/5 plan

611 RYHILL AND CAMERTON (ER-H)   1805 : 1810
       Open fields, meadows, pasture : 1385 acres awarded
       Commissioners John Hall, John Lee, Joseph Dickinson
       Surveyors Robert Stickney, Thomas Barrow
     i   ERRD CQ/68/2 enrolled award and plan (not dated,
          buildings, 9 and a half ch=1")
     ii   HCRO PE 73/32 sealed original award and plan
     iii HCRO DDCC/142/2 bound copy award
     iv   HUL DDKG/192 photograph of plan showing strips
          Related documents HCRO DDIV/42/1

612 RYLSTONE (WR-NY)   1771 : 1772
       Four stinted pastures : 769 acres awarded
       Commissioners Henry Waddington, John Squire, George
       Jackson
     i   WRRD B9 p136 enrolled award
     ii   Messrs Weatherhead & Butcher, solicitors, Bingley, TS
          copies of award. Original award destroyed by fire
          (information from W.E. Tate)

613   SADDLEWORTH (WR-Greater Manchester)   1830 : 1834
            Commons, moors and waste : 7220 acres awarded
            Commissioners Ralph Fletcher (died), Joseph Shaw
      i   WRRD Map Vol 4/4 sealed original award and plan (not
            dated, surveyor Joel Hawkyard (died), Joseph
            Hesslegrave, buildings, 8 ch=1")
      ii   CP Wakefield F p209 enrolled award and plan A42
      iii   Saddleworth UDC copy award made 1840, copy map
      iv   Saddleworth Museum printed copy of award 1840 and 2
            copies of plan
      v   Saddleworth CL, copy award

      ST JOHN'S (WR-SY) see Dinnington

      SALTERFORTH (WR-Lancs) see Barnoldswick

      SALTERGATE (NR-NY) see Lockton

614   SANCTON (ER-H)   1769 : 1771
            Arable fields, meadows, pastures, common, waste : 1615
            acres awarded
            Commissioners Robert Bewlay jun (refused), John Outram,
            Peter Nevill, John Raines
            Surveyor David Tate
      i   ERRD AN/2/2 enrolled award and copy plan
      ii   HUL DDLA/42/1 sealed original award and plan (1770,
            buildings, 4 ch=1")
            Related document HCRO DDX/299

615 SANDAL MAGNA, WALTON AND CRIGGLESTONE (WR-WY)   1799 : 1806
        Open fields, undivided inclosures, commons, waste and
        commonable places : 638 acres awarded
        Commissioners Isaac Leatham, William Whitelock, Richard
        Clark (refused), Arthur Elliot (died), Thomas Gee
    i   WRRD B22 p199 enrolled award and Z8 copy plan
    ii YAS Map 67-70, later copy of plan (1800, surveyor Thomas
        Gee, whole township of Crigglestone shown, buildings,
        scale not stated)
    iii WYAS D20/395 award and plans

    SANDAL MAGNA (WR-WY) see Wakefield

    SAND BRAMWITH (WR-SY) see South Bramwith

    SANDHOLME (ER-H) see Eastrington

616 SAND HUTTON (near Stamford Bridge) (NR-NY)   1806 : 1808
        Common : 779 acres awarded
        Commissioners Richard Clark, John Flintoff
    i   NRRD DO no.13 p72 enrolled award and plan (buildings, 12
        ch=1")
    ii NYCRO ZQD original award and plan

617 SANDHUTTON (near Thirsk) (NR-NY)   1793 : 1799
        Common : 212 acres awarded
        Commissioner Richard Clark
    i   NRRD no.28 sealed original award

618 SANDHUTTON (near Thirsk) (NR-NY)   1836 : 1841
        Eight open and common arable fields : 82 acres
    i   NYCRO QDD(D) Bk S no.36 p119 enrolled award and plan (2
        ch=1")
    ii NRRD GW no.63,p104 enrolled award
    iii NRRD QDD(I) 34 original award and plan

    SAWDON (NR-NY) see Brompton

619 SAWLEY AND WINKSLEY (WR-NY)   1797 : 1799
        Commons, moors and waste : 1395 acres awarded
        Commissioners William Downing, Jonathan Teal, Francis
        Sands
    i   Leeds RO sealed original award and plans (1799, surveyor
        Thomas Robinson; (1) Sawley, buildings, 9 ch=1"; (2)
        Winksley, 6ch=1")
    ii Sawley parish council award and plan
    iii WYAS Z extract from plan

620 SAXTON WITH SCARTHINGWELL (WR-NY)   1847 : 1849
        Open fields, meadow and pasture : 306 acres awarded
        Commissioner Christopher Paver
    i   CP Wakefield F p344 enrolled award and plan A33 (1849,
        whole township shown, buildings, 6 ch=1")
    ii Leeds RO sealed original award and plan
    iii Leeds RO copy award and plan made 1895

621 SCAGGLETHORPE (ER-NY)   1725 : 1726
        By agreement. Fields, common meadows, lands : 956 acres
        estimated
        Commissioners William Lister, Francis Wright, William
        Cossins, Timothy Wastling (died), John Carr
    i   HCRO DDX/15/1 typescript copy award

    SCAGGLETHORPE (WR-NY) see Poppleton

622 SCALBY AND THROXENBY OR NEWBY (NR-NY)   1771 : 1777
        Open fields, commons and wastes : 4000 acres estimated
        Commissioners Edward Cleaver, John Butler, William
        Willmott, John Foord, Edward Hebb
        Surveyor John Foord
    i   NRRD BQ no.1 p1
    ii PRO DL/41/68 enclosure papers
    iii Scarborough RDC original award and plan, and typescript
        copy
    iv NYCRO I/SCA copy plan (12ch=1")
    v   Scalby parish records copy award

    SCALBY (NR-NY) see Ebberston

623 SCALING AND ROXBY (NR-NY)   1804 : 1813
        Commons and wastes : 1200 acres awarded
        Commissioners Dymoke Wells, Thomas Scott
    i   NYCRO ZPA copy award

624 SCAMMONDEN (WR-WY)   1814 : 1816
        Commons, moors and waste called Scammonden Moor : 260
        acres awarded
        Commissioner Thomas Gee
    i   WRRD B32 p110 enrolled award and plan Vol 3/30 (1815,
        surveyor W. Pilkington, whole manor or graveship shown,
        buildings, 6 ch=1")
    ii YAS MD 225 copy award, plan, draft award and minute book
    0   Sealed original award to be kept in Huddersfield parish
        church under the act. Not found

SCARCROFT (WR-WY) see Hazlewood

SCARTHINGWELL (WR-NY) see Saxton

SCHOLES (WR-WY) see Cleckheaton

SCHOLES (WR-WY) see Wooldale

625 SCOSTHROP (WR-NY) 1796 : 1799
    By agreement. Common fields and stinted pastures
    Commissioner William Dawson
- i WRRD Map Vol 3/26 sealed original award and plan (1798, surveyor Jonathan Teal, 10 ch=1")

626 SCOTTON (NR-NY) 1808 : 1812
    By agreement. Common or waste : 241 acres awarded
    Commissioner and surveyor John Humphries
- i NRRD no.32 sealed agreement
- ii NRRD DT no.56 p91 enrolled agreement
- iii NRRD no.32 sealed original award and plan (buildings, 12 ch=1")

SCOTTON (WR-NY) see Scriven

627 SCRAYINGHAM (ER-NY) 1825 : 1830
    Open pasture, unclosed lands : 284 acres awarded
    Commissioner William Ware
    Surveyor James Bulmer
- i ERRD DQ/223/9 enrolled award and plan
- ii Borthwick Institute York PR SCR/1 sealed original award and plan (not dated, buildings, 6 ch=1")

628 SCRIVEN WITH TENTERGATE, SCOTTON AND FARNHAM (WR-NY)
1828 : 1830
    Three moors or commons called Scriven Moor, Scotton Moor and SCotton Low Moor, open fields in Scotton : 545 acres awarded
    Commissioner William Pilkington
- i WRRD B39 p1 enrolled award and plan Vol 4/2 (1830, surveyor John Howgate, all township shown, including part of Knaresborough, buildings, open field names in Scotton, 10 ch=1")
- ii Messrs Powell, Eddison, Freeman & Wilks, solicitors, Knaresborough, award
- iii PRO DL/45/9/9 enrolled extract of award
- iv YAS DD 56/C2 plan

629 SEAMER AND IRTON (NR-NY) 1809 : 1810
    Open pasture and commons, moor and ings : 779 acres awarded
    Commissioner John Dalton
- i NRRD DA no.77 p208

SEAMER (NR-NY) see Ebberston

630 SEATON ROSS (ER-H)   1811 : 1814
        Open stinted pasture, common : 766 acres awarded
        Commissioner John Hall
        Surveyor John Foster
    i   ERRD CQ/358/20 enrolled award and plan F3 (1814,
        buildings, 8 ch=1")
    ii Borthwick Institute York PR S/R/10 award and plan

631 SELBY (WR-NY)   1797 : 1808
        Commons and waste grounds : 597 acres awarded
        Commissioner Richard Clark
    i   WRRD B27 p50 enrolled award and plan Vol 3/25 (not
        dated, surveyor Benjamin Mitchell, whole parish shown,
        buildings, 8 ch=1")
    ii Selby UDC award and plan
    0   Sealed original awards to be kept in parish church, and
        in manor court, under act. One of these may be (ii)
        above; the other not found

632 SETTLE (WR-NY)   1758 : 1759
        By agreement. Two stinted common pastures called Settle
        Banks High Scarr, and Scaleber : 1468 acres awarded
        Commissioners Richard Clapham, Stephen Knowles, William
        Bradley, Henry Waddington, Thomas Carr
    i   WRRD Map Vol 3/27 signed award, no plan
    ii Leeds RO plan of Scaleber

633 SETTLE (WR-NY)   1803 : 1806
        By agreement. Highhill and Halstead pastures : 264
        acres awarded
        Commissioners Thomas Buttle, Richard Holmes
    i   NYCRO ZXF sealed original award

634 SETTRINGTON (ER-NY)   1797 : 1799
        Open fields, common pasture, common, waste : 1944 acres
        awarded
        Commissioners John Hall, Isaac Leatham
        Surveyors Robert Stickney, Samuel Dickinson
    i   ERRD CA/102/9 enrolled award
    ii HUL DDKG/229 rough tracing of plan of 1799

     SEWERBY (ER-H) see Marton

635 SHADWELL (WR-WY)   1803 : 1807
        Commons or waste and other commonable lands : 625 acres
        awarded
        Commissioner William Dawson
    i   WRRD B25 p191 enrolled award and plan Vol 3/20 (1807,
        surveyor Samuel Gawthorpe, whole township shown,
        buildings, open field features, 6 ch=1")
    ii Leeds Civic Hall sealed original award and plan. Also
        copy award
    iii Leeds RO photocopy plan

     SHAROW (WR-NY) see Ripon

SHEFFIELD (WR-SY) see Attercliffe; Brightside; Ecclesall; Hallam; Handsworth

636 SHELLEY (WR-WY) 1803 : 1807
   Uninclosed woodland called Hartley Bank, commons, moors and waste : 288 acres awarded
   Commissioner Timothy Bainbridge
   i WRRD B26 p59 enrolled award and plan Vol 3/21 (1807, surveyor Samuel Gawthorpe, whole township shown, buildings, 6 ch=1")
   ii Kirklees RO   sealed original award and plan. Also modern copy award

637 SHEPLEY (WR-WY) 1827 : 1830
   Commons, Shepley Common : 220 acres awarded
   Commissioner William Fairbank
   i WRRD B39 p70 enrolled award and plan Vol 4/3 (1829, surveyor Frederick Robert Jones, whole township shown, buildings, 6 ch=1")
   ii Kirklees RO sealed original award and plan in volume. Also 1910 copy award

638 SHERBURN (ER-NY) 1755 : 1756
   By agreement. Large open fields, meadow, common : 375 acres estimated
   Commissioners George Hebden, Samuel Milbourn, John Foord
   i ERRD Y/331/41 enrolled award
   ii HCRO DDCS/38/6 copy award

639 SHERBURN IN ELMET, LENNERTON, BARKSTON ASH, CHURCH FENTON, LITTLE FENTON AND BIGGIN (WR-NY) 1770 : 1775
   Common fields, common meadow, pasture : 4413 acres awarded
   Commissioners John Cleaver, William Hill, William George Nicholson, John Outram, John Graves
   i   WRRD B11 p4 enrolled award and plan Z/6(L)
   ii Sherburn parish council sealed original award and plan (1770, surveyors Joseph Butler, Miles Dawson, whole townships shown, buildings, 1 mile =10"
   iii PRO DL/41/72 enclosure papers, Barkston Ash
   iv Leeds RO copy plan

640 SHERIFF HUTTON AND WEST LILLING (NR-NY) 1769 : 1776
   Open fields, common pastures, ings, balks, commons and waste, moor and West Lilling Green : 1908 acres awarded
   Commissioners John Cleaver, John Lund, John Outram
   i NRRD BH no.1 p1 enrolled award

SHERWOOD (WR-NY) see Eggborough

641 SHIPLEY (WR-WY) 1815 : 1825
       Commons or waste called High Bank and Low Moor, and other waste : 277 acres awarded
       Commissioner John Bower
  i   WRRD B38 p82 enrolled award
  ii Shipley UDC sealed original award and 2 plans in volume (based on 1806 survey by Joseph Heaton, plans by William Pilkington; (1) Allotments on common, High Moor and Low Moor, scale not stated; (2) enlarged part of Low Moor allotments, buildings, scale not stated)

642 SHIPTON (NR-NY) 1758 : 1759
       Moor or common
       Commissioners Robert Bewlay sen, Robert Bewlay jun, Samuel Milbourn
  i   NRRD AL no.26 p53 enrolled award

643 SHIPTON AND NEWTON-ON-OUSE (NR-NY) 1812 : 1815
       Open fields, commonable land and waste : 989 acres awarded
       Commissioners William Dawson, John Tuke
       Surveyor William Bingley
  i   NYCRO QDD(I) no.31 sealed original award and 2 plans (one with buildings, 6 ch=1")

SHIPTON THORPE (ER-H) see Market Weighton

644 SICKLINGHALL WITH WOODHALL (WR-NY) 1789 : 1799
       Common and waste : 176 acres awarded
       Commissioner William Dawson
  i   WRRD B21 p1 enrolled award
  ii Kirkby Overblow parish church award

645 SIGGLESTHORNE (ER-H) 1772 : 1781
       Open fields, lands : 934 acres awarded
       Commissioners Peter Nevill, Christopher Keld, John Outram, Anthony Bower
       Surveyors Joseph Dickinson
  i   ERRD BB/264/32 enrolled award
       Related papers PRO (Chancery Lane) MPE 528 survey, plan, valuation and extract of award

646 SILKSTONE, HOYLAND SWAINE AND CAWTHORNE (WR-SY) 1802 : 1809
       Open fields and mesne inclosures, commons and waste
       Commissioner Jonathan Teal
  i   CP Wakefield B p241 and C p1 enrolled award and plans A62 (3 plans, not dated, surveyor Richard Birks; (1) Silkstone; (2) Hoyland Swaine (3) Cawthorne, surveyor J. Haywood, buildings, scale not stated
  ii SYCRO 359/P sealed original award and 3 plans
  iii Penistone UDC modern copy of part of award and of plan

SILKSTONE (WR-SY) see Thurgoland

SILPHO (NR-NY) see Hackness

SILSDEN (WR-WY) see Skipton

647 SILTON, NETHER (NR-NY) 1794 : 1796
    By agreement. Moor : 526 acres awarded
    Commissioners John Rodham and others
    Surveyor John Rodham
  i   NYCRO ZW Hickes family original agreement
  ii   NRRD CP no.33 p40 enrolled award and plan (5 ch=1")

648 SINNINGTON WITH MARTON AND GREAT AND LITTLE EDSTONE (NR-NY)
                                                                     1786 : 1788
    Common pastures, commons and wastes: 1086 acres awarded
    Commissioners John Kendall, Edward Watterson, Peter
    Merry, umpire Peter Johnson
  i   NRRD CA no.20 p56 enrolled award
  ii   NYCRO ZPC 1/7 copy award
  iii Messrs Pearson & Mackirdy, Helmsley, original award and plan
  iv   YAS MS 667 award

SKECKLING (ER-H) see Burstwick

649 SKEFFLING (ER-H) 1764 : 1765
    Open and common fields : 1191 acres awarded
    Commissioners John Dickinson, John Outram, Edward Holgate
    Surveyors Thomas Lazenby, Charles Tate
  i   ERRD ALH/126/4 enrolled award and copy plan (buildings, scale not stated9
  ii   HCRO DDCC/142/2,12 2 copies award
  iii Hull CL copy award and plan
  iv   HCRO IA copy plan; DDCK/35/1(b); DDCV/148/1 copies of plan

650 SKELDING AND GRANTLEY (WR-NY) 1813 : 1844
    Two moors, Skelding Moor and Grantley Moor : 728 acres awarded
    Commissioner John Humphries
  i   WRRD B34 p358 enrolled award and 2 plans 4/1 (1820, unsigned, buildings, 5ch=1")
  ii   NYCRO PC/RIC sealed original award with plan and minutes

651 SKELLOW (WR-SY) 1801 : 1806
    Open fields, ings, common and waste : 888 acres awarded
    Commissioners Isaac Leatham, William Whitelock, Samuel Turner
  i   WRRD B22 p321 enrolled award and plan Vol 3/24 (1801, surveyor Joseph Colbeck, whole manor shown, buildings, open field names, scale not stated, decorated cartouche
  ii   Adwick le Street UDC award and plan
  iii Thorp Arch estate office copy award
  iv   Doncaster RO DD.DC.E1/2/2, three copies of award

652 SKELMANTHORPE (WR-WY)   1800 : 1802
         Common, moor and waste : 191 acres awarded
         Commissioner Jonathan Teal
     i   WRRD B21 p158 enrolled award
     ii   Kirklees RO copy award and plan (surveyor Thomas
          Gee, whole township shown, 3 ch=1")
     iii Leeds RO photocopy plan
     0   Sealed original award to be kept in town chest under
          act. Not found 1962

653 SKELTON (ER-H)   1809 : 1815
         Open fields, meadows, pastures, waste : 330 acres
         awarded
         Commissioner Joseph Dickinson
     i   HCRO QDB 7 p100 enrolled award and IA plan (not dated,
          buildings, 8 ch=1")
     ii   HCRO DDTR/795 tracing of plan

654 SKELTON (near Middlesborough) (NR-Cleveland)   1813 : 1844
         Moors : 6000 acres awarded
         Commissioner and surveyor John Humphries
     i   NYCRO Box S p1 award and 4 plans
     ii   NRRD enrolled award

655 SKELTON (near Ripon) (WR-NY)   1794 : 1798
         Open fields, ings, moors, commons and waste : 276 acres
         awarded
         Commissioner John Bradford
     i   WRRD B19 p314 enrolled award
     0,00 Sealed original awards to be kept by the Canon Fee Court
          of Ripon, and in Skelton chapel chest: neither found

656 SKELTON (near York) (NR-NY)   1806 : 1807
         Open fields, commons and waste : 784 acres awarded
         Commissioner William Dawson
     i   NRRD DA no.31 p93 enrolled award and no.15 plan (6
          ch=1")

657 SKIDBY (ER-H)   1793 : 1795
         Open fields, meadow, pasture and waste : 833 acres
         awarded
         Commissioners Jonathan Teal, Robert Dunn, Peter Nevill
         Surveyor John Wood
     i   ERRD BT/2/3 enrolled award and IA plan (1793, 8 ch=1");
          also copy award and plan
     ii   HCRO PC 4/1 award and plan
     iii Hull CL copy award and plan
          Related documents Hull CL, copy of Teal's survey

     SKIDBY (ER-H) see Woodmansey

658 SKIPSEA (ER-H)   1764 : 1765
        Open fields, meadow, pasture : 1765 acres awarded
        Commissioners John Dickinson, John Outram, John Raines
        Surveyors John Lund, Peter Nevill
    i   ERRD AF/180/9 enrolled award and plan IA (1764,
         buildings, no scale
    ii   HCRO DDCC/142/2,12,23 two copies and draft
    iii HCRO DDX/154/1 copy award

    SKIPTON BROUGH (ER-H) see Dringhoe

659 SKIPTON, KILDWICK,STIRTON WITH THORLBY,SILSDEN (WR-NY)1773 : 1774
              An open meadow field, commons, common pasture,
        waste including Rumblesmoor : 2479 acres awarded
        Commissioners John Heelis, Thomas Watkinson, Richard
        Clapham
    i   WRRD B10 p132 enrolled award and 4 plans Roll 9 (not
         dated, unsigned; (1) Skipton Ings, 10 poles=1"; (2)
         Rumbles Moor, 20 poles=1"; (3 & 4) Parts of Silsden
         Moor, 20 poles=1")
    ii   NYCRO PR/SKP copy plan
    iii Leeds RO copy award
    0   Sealed original award to be kept by the earl of Thanet
         and his heirs. Not found

660 SKIPTON-ON-SWALE (NR-NY)   : 1765
        By undated agreement. Stinted pasture 220 acres awarded
        Commissioners William Reynard, John Allanson, Marmaduke
        Hodgson, Thomas Coopland
    i   NRRD AO no.87 p237 enrolled award
    ii   NYCRO ZTF 2/1 plan (4 ch=1")

661 SKIPWITH (ER-H)   1901 : 1904
        Open field, common : 318 acres estimated
        Commissioner and surveyor John Farrer
    i   HCRO IA award and plan (not dated, buildings, 5 ch=1")
    ii   HCRO DDX/165/1 plan (1904)
    iii HUL DDFA plan
    iv   Borthwick Institute York SKIP 62,63 plan and 1905
         amendment to award
         Related documents HCRO DDX/165

    SKIRETHORNE (WR-NY) see Threshfield

662 SKIRPENBECK (ER-H)   1758 :
        No award. Six large open fields and pastures : 1980
        acres estimated
    i   HCRO DDDA/4/34 act and DDDA/4/39 1761 plan

    SLADE HOOTON (WR-SY) see Laughton en le Morthen

663 SLINGSBY (NR-NY)   1754 : 1755
        By agreement. Acreage not stated
        Commissioners Samuel Milbourn, William Richardson, John
        Conyers
    i   NRRD O no.15 p88 enrolled award

664   SNAITH, COWICK AND RAWCLIFFE (WR-H)   1752 : 1754
        Act confirms agreement dated 1751   :1160 acres estimated
        Commissioners Thomas Yarburgh, William Simpson, William
        Sotheron, Richard Worsop, Edward Forster
    i   CP Wakefield A61 18 cent. copy award
    ii   HCRO DDCL/243,251,252 award and two copies; DDCL/3393-4
          three plans (1754, surveyor Sam. Brailsford; (1)
          Commons, buildings represented pictorially, open field
          features, 12 ch=1"; (2) Langham and Hales, scale not
          stated; (3) plan separate, not dated, surveyor John
          Read, buildings, some represented pictorially, open
          field names and features, 20 ch=1")
    iii   Thorp Arch estate office copy award
    iv   Doncaster RO P50/9/A1 award

665   SNAITH AND COWICK (WR-H)   1773 : 1781
        Open fields and meadow : 1160 acres estimated
        Commissioners Thomas Tofield (died), John Outram (died),
        Isaac Milborn, Benjamin Outram, Edward Watterson
    i   WRRD B14 p199 enrolled award and plan 1/23 (not dated,
          surveyor Isaac Milbourn, open field names, 7 ch=1")
    ii   HCRO DDCL/3444 (copy) and 3445 (original) award and 3
          plans in volume
    iii   NYCRO 18 cent. plan relating to enclosure
    iv   Doncaster RO P50/9/A4 award

      SNAITH (WR-H) see Carlton

666   SNAINTON AND EBBERSTON (NR-NY)   1768 : 1772
        Open arable fields, open grounds, Low and High Common :
        3933 acres awarded
        Commissioners John Outram, John Cleaver, Robert Bewlay
    i   NRRD BE no.1 p1 enrolled award
(no number 667)

668   SNEATON (NR-NY)   1797 : 1824
        Commons and waste : 1800 acres estimated
        Commissioners Richard Scarth, Peter Merry, Dymoke Wells
    i   PRO (Chancery Lane) C 54 10210 and MPA 50 award and 2
          plans

669   SOUTHBURN (ER-H)   1793 : 1797
        Open fields, meadows, pastures, wastes : 1034 acres
        awarded
        Commissioners Robert Dunn, Joseph Dickinson, William
        Hall, Francis Haigh, John Hall
        Surveyor Robert Atkinson
    i   ERRD BT/277/37 enrolled award
    ii   HCRO IA sealed original award and plan (1793, buildings,
          10 ch=1")
        Related documents HCRO DDBV/43/1 and 2, including open
        field plan

669 SOUTH BRAMWITH OR SAND BRAMWITH (WR-SY)   1842 : 1846
    Open fields, meadow and pasture
    Commissioners William Simpson, James Alexander
  i   CP Wakefield Vol F p323 enrolled award and plan (1845, surveyor James Alexander, buildings, open field names, 6 ch=1")
  ii Lincs AO 2T.G.H 7/3 copy award

670 SOUTH CAVE (ER-H)   1785 : 1787
    Open fields, stinted pastures, wolds, ings, sands, meadows, waste : 2379 acres awarded
    Commissioners John Levitt, John Wood, Peter Nevill
    Surveyor Joseph Dickinson
  i   ERRD BG/139/12 enrolled award and copy plan made 1929 (1785, buildings, 12 ch=1")
  ii   HCRO IA copy plan
  iii Hull CL copy award
  iv   HUL DDBA/4/58 plan
       Related documents HCRO DDBA/4; also HUL DDBA/4/31, DDBA/5/27, DDBD/68/9-10

SOUTH CAVE (ER-H) see Howden

671 SOUTH CLIFFE (ER-H)   1775
  i   HCRO IA plan, 19 cent copy (1780, unsigned, buildings, scale not stated)
  ii HUL DDLO/72/2 award

672 SOUTHCOATES (ER-H)   1756 : 1757
    By agreement 1756 and act 1764. Three large open fields : 323 acres awarded
    Commissioners Joseph Thompson, Robert Bell, Richard North
  i   ERRD AC/358/17 enrolled agreement
  ii   ERRD Y/124/26 enrolled award
  iii HCRO DDCC/142/6 copy award
  iv   HCRO DDHB/8/2 sealed original award
  v   Hull CL copy award and plan (not dated, buildings, 8 ch=1")
  vi   Hull City RO copy award and plna
  vii HUL DSJ/60 copy award

SOUTH CROSLAND (WR-WY) see North Crosland

673 SOUTH DALTON (ER-H) 1822 : 1827
Open fields, common pasture, commons, waste : 1622 acres awarded
Commissioners John Hall, Thomas Musgrave
Surveyor Edward Page
Umpire John Lee
- i ERRD D/107/4 enrolled award and plan
- ii ERRD sealed original award and plan (1822-3, buildings, 5 ch=1")
- iii HCRO DX/23 draft award
- iv HUL DDHO/16/56 copy plan

Related documents HCRO DX/9 commissioners' minutes

674 SOUTH DUFFIELD (ER-NY) 1820 : 1834
Amending act 1821. Open fields, ings, commons, waste : 450 acres awarded
Commissioners William Pilkington, John Bower
Surveyor William Shipton
- i HCRO QDB 7 p129 enrolled award and IA plan (1828, buildings, 8 ch=1")

SOUTH ELMSALL (WR-WY) see South Kirkby

675 SOUTH KIRKBY AND SOUTH ELMSALL (WR-WY) 1807 : 1813
Open fields, common and waste : 795 acres awarded
Commissioners William Whitelock (died), Thomas Gee
- i WRRD B30 p88 enrolled award
- ii South Kirkby parish church award and plans (in 1962 temporarily with the Public Trustee Office, London WC2)
- iii PRO DL/45/9/2 enrolled extract of award 1816

676 SOUTH MILFORD AND LUMBY (WR-NY) 1793 : 1799
Common fields, commons or waste (3 fields in each township) : 1077 acres awarded
Commissioners John Crowder, William Dawson, William Whitelock
- i WRRD B19 p346 enrolled award
- ii Leeds RO tracing of plan
- 0 Sealed original award to be kept in town chest of South Milford under act. Not found 1962

Related papers YAS MS 1069

SOUTH NEWBALD (ER-H) see North Newbald

677 SOWERBY (NR-NY) 1798 : 1803
Open field, stinted pasture, common and waste : 929 acres awarded
Commissioner Edward Cleaver
Surveyor J. Colbeck
- i NRRD CS no.20 p161 enrolled award
- ii NRRD no.10 original award and 2 plans; (1) Sowerby, buildings, 8 ch=1"; (2) South Moor, scale not stated

678 SOWERBY AND SOYLAND (WR-WY) 1843 : 1849
       Commons, waste and moors : 3881 acres awarded
       Commissioner Thomas Bradley
   i   WRRD B53 sealed original award (printed) with plan (not
       dated, surveyor Thomas Bradley, whole townships shown,
       buildings, 6 ch=1", very large
   ii Calderdale RO sealed original award and plan
   iii Leeds RO printed award
   iv YAS MD 225 printed award and plans
   v   NRA Report Rawson Records, copy plan

   SOYLAND (WR-WY) see Sowerby

679 SPEETON (ER-NY) 1793 : 1794
       Open fields, lands, pastures, waste : 1754 acres awarded
       Commissioners Peter Nevill, Joseph Dickinson, John Wood
       Surveyor John Wood
   i   ERRD BG/415/65 enrolled award
   ii HCRO DDX/154/9 copy award
   Related document HCRO IA pre-enclosure plan 1772

   SPITTAL (ER-H) see Fangfoss

680 SPOFFORTH (WR-NY) 1787 : 1792
       Open fields, meadows, pastures, commons and waste : 464
       acres awarded
       Commissioners William Hill, Miles Dawson, James Hebdin
   i   WRRD B18 p83 enrolled award
   0   Sealed original award to be kept in parish church. Not
       found

681 SPROATLEY (ER-H) 1762 : 1763
       Open fields, pastures, meadows : 1235 acres awarded
       Commissioners John Dickinson, Henry Raines, Peter Nevill
   i   ERRD AC/221/10 enrolled award
   ii HCRO DDCC/142/5,7 two copies award
   iii Hull CL copy award and plan
   iv HCRO DDPK/25/1 tracing plan (1763, buildings, 7 ch=1")
   v   HCRO DDCK 35/1(a) copy plan
       Related documents HCRO DDCC (2nd deposit, plan no.12)
       pre-enclosure plan and survey 1762

682 STAINBURN (WR-NY) 1776 : 1777
       Stainburn common : 1048 acres awarded
       Commissioners John Bainbridge, Benjamin Chambers,
       Ambrose Gray
   i   WRRD Map Vol 3/28 sealed original award
   ii YAS DD 61 sealed original award and plan (1777, surveyor
       J. Bainbridge, buildings, 8 ch=1")
   0   Sealed original award to be kept by Lord of the Manor
       under the act. Not found

   STAINFORTH (WR-SY) see Hatfield

683 STAINLAND (WR-WY)   1816 : 1819
        Commons, moors and waste : 400 acres awarded
        Commissioners Thomas Gee, Nicholas Brown
    i   WRRD B33 p267 enrolled award
    ii Halifax TC sealed original award in volume and plan
        (1816, surveyor Thomas Dinsley, whole manor shown, 6
        ch=1")
    iii YAS MD 225 copy award and plan in volume

684 STAINTON AND EDLINGTON (WR-SY)   1810 : 1815
        Common called Cockhill Common and other common or waste
        : 370 acres estimated
        Commissioners Francis Raynes, James Colbeck
    i   CP Wakefield C p165 enrolled award and 2 plans A66 and
        A67 (1815, surveyor Joseph Young; (1) part of Stainton,
        buildings, 6 ch=1"; (2) Cockhill Common, 2 and a half
        ch=1")
    ii Doncaster RO Enc.15 award and plans

685 STAINTON DALE (NR-NY)   ? : 1829
    i   NRRD FS no.306 p345 enrolled memorial of award only

STALLINGBUSK (NR-NY) see Bainbridge
STANLEY (WR-WY) see Wakefield

STANNINGTON (WR-SY) see Hallam

686 STANSFIELD (WR-WY)   1815 : 1818
        Commons, moors and waste : 1962 acres awarded
        Commissioner Thomas Gee
    i   WRRD B34 p53 enrolled award
    ii Calderdale RO sealed original award and 2 plans (1816,
        surveyors William Pilkington, James Scholefield
        (refused), William Bingley, (1) West part of township
        (2) east part : together plans show whole township,
        buildings, 6 ch=1")
    iii Leeds RO copy award

STARBOTTON (WR-NY) see Buckden

687 STAVELEY (WR-NY)   1801 : 1806
        Open fields, stinted pastures, ings, carrs, commons,
        commonable lands and waste : 398 acres awarded
        Commissioner William Dawson
    i   WRRD Roll 13 sealed original award
    ii Farnham vicarage sealed original award and plan (not
        dated, surveyor Jonathan Teal, whole parish shown,
        buildings, open field names, 6 ch=1")
    iii NYCRO I Acc no.7112 plan

688 STAXTON (ER-NY) 1801 : 1803
     Open fields, common pasture, carr, waste : 1500 acres estimated
     Commissioners John Hall, Joseph Dickinson, Isaac Leatham
     Surveyors Thomas Barrow, Ralph Burton
- i   ERRD CA/235/32 enrolled award and F5 plan (1801, 8 ch=1")
- ii HCRO DX/3 copy plan (1801, 16 ch=1")

     Related documents HUL DDDU/10/7 commissioners' papers

689 STEETON WITH EASTBURN (WR-WY) 1787 : ?
     Moors and wastes : 960 acres estimated
     Commissioners Joshua Hirst, John Sharp, J. Asquith
- 0   No award found, perhaps never made

690 STILLINGFLEET (ER-NY) 1753 : 1756
     By agreement. Open fields, meadows, pastures, moors, greens : 800 acres estimated
     Commissioners Samuel Milbourn, William George Nicholson, Robert Bewlay, Marmaduke Lawson
- i   HCRO DX/2 agreement
- ii   ERRD Y/49/15 enrolled award
- iii HUL DDFA/45/1 sealed original award
- iv   Borthwick Institute York PR/STIL/1600 award

691 STILLINGTON (NR-NY) 1766 : 1767
     Common, waste, open fields, medow, grounds and ings : 1361 acres awarded
     Commissioners Robert Bewlay jun, John Dealtry, William George Nicholson
- i   NRRD AH no.38 p167 enrolled award
- ii NYCRO PC/STL award

STIRTON WITH THORLBY (WR-NY) see Skipton

692 STOCKTON-ON-THE-FOREST (NR-NY) 1813 : 1817
     Open common lands and waste : 1200 acres estimated
     Commissioners John Tuke, John Humphries
     Surveyors James Bulmer, Edmund Gray
- i   NRRD no.33 sealed original award and plan (buildings, 5 ch=1")

693 STONEBECK UP (WR-NY) 1804 : 1825
     Moors : 9700 acres estimated
- i   Stonebeck Up parish council award and 4 plans (1805, surveyor Alexander Calvert; (1) Carle Fell, 8 ch=1"1 (2) Riggs or West and Netherdale Head Moors, 12 ch=1"; (3) Part of Riggs or West Moor called Moresdale, 12ch=1"; (4) Middlesmoor Inn Moor 4 ch=1")
- ii   Bradford Corporation draft award
- iii Leeds RO photocopies of plans
- iv   NYCRO PC/SBU sealed original award

694 STONEBECK UP (WR-NY)   1835 : 1835
        By agreement. Two stinted pastures in Lodge in
        Stonebeck Up called the High and Low Pastures
        Commissioner Thomas Bradley
    i   WRRD B39 p3435 enrolled award and plan Vol 3/3 (1835,
        unsigned, some buildings shown, 4 ch=1")

695 STONEBECK UP (WR-NY)   1839 : 1840
        By agreement. Common stinted pastures called Haden Carr
        Pasture and Haden Carr Calf Pasture
        Commissioner Thomas Bradley
    i   WRRD B45 p215 enrolled award and plan Vol 2/18 (1840,
        surveyors T. Bradley & Son, buildings, 3 ch=1")
    ii Bradford Corporation agreement and award

696 STONEGRAVE, WEST NESS AND NUNNINGTON (NR-NY)   1776 : 1781
        Open fields : 647 acres awarded
        Commissioners Edward Cleaver, John Carter, John Graves
    i   NRRD BL nos 40-42, p188

    STORRS (BRADFIELD) (WR-SY) see Hallam

    STORWOOD (ER-H) or STORTHWAITE see Melbourne

697 STRENSALL (NR-NY)   1757 : 1758
        Common ground, 675 acres estimated
        Commissioners John Cleaver, Samuel Milbourn, John Lund
    i   NRRD AB no.38 p158 enrolled award
    ii Borthwick Institute York PR STR/11 and 12 award

    STUBBS WALDEN (WR-NY) see Little Smeaton

    STURTON GRANGE (WR-WY) see Lotherton

698 STUTTON (WR-NY)   1796 : 1798
        By agreement. Open fields, meadows, pastures, ings,
        commons and waste
        Commissioner William Dawson, John Sharpe
    i   WRRD B20 p44 enrolled award and plan Vol 3/2 (not dated,
        unsigned, whole township shown, buildings, scale not
        stated)

    SUFFIELD (NR-NY) see Hackness

699   SUMMERGANGS (ER-H)   1749 : 1749
          By agreement. Open common pasture
          Commissioners Richard North, John Raines, Joseph
          Thompson
      i   ERRD B/250/47 enrolled award
      ii HCRO DDCC/142/3 copy award
      iii HUL DBJ copy award
      iv Hull City RO copy award and plan
      v   Leeds Brotherton Library MS 311, 19 copy of part of
          award

700   SUTTON, CAMPSALL AND BURGHWALLIS (WR-SY)   1854 : 1858
          Commons and commonable lands : 589 acres awarded
          Commissioner William Paver
      i   CP Wakefield A22 sealed original award and plan (not
          dated, surveyor William Paver, whole township shown,
          buildings, pre-enclosure plan with overmarkings, open
          field furlongs and names, 3 ch=1")
      ii Northants RO tracings of 3 plans relating to enclosure
      iii Doncaster RO PR.Nor/1 award
      iv PRO (MAF 1 447) award

701   SUTTON (in Kildwick) (WR-NY)   1815 : 1824
          Moor, common and waste : 1000 acres estimated
          Commissioners William Burton (died), Richard Ayrton
      i   WRRD Roll 14 sealed original award and plan (not dated,
          surveyor Samuel Swire jun, buildings, 6 ch=1")
      ii Skipton RDC sealed original award

702   SUTTON (in Norton) (ER-NY)   1769 : 1772
          Town fields, common fields, pastures, waste : 606 acres
          awarded
          Commissioners William Fordon, John Outram, John Cleaver
      i   ERRD AN/379/25 enrolled award

703   SUTTON-ON-THE-FOREST (NR-NY)   1756 : 1759
          By agreement. Open fields, meadows, Commissioners John
          Conyers, Robert Bewlay, John Cleaver
      i   NRRD AL no.33 p91 enrolled award
      ii NYCRO PR/SUF original award

704   SUTTON UPON DERWENT (ER-H)   1776 : 1777
          Open arable fields, meadows, pastures : 742 acres
          awarded
          Commissioners John Dealtry, Edward Cleaver, Miles Dawson
          Surveyor Miles Dawson
      i   ERRD BB/4/4 enrolled award
      ii HCRO DDX/31/181 sealed original award
      iii Borthwick Institute York PR S/D/40 award

705   SUTTON ON HULL (ER-H)   1763 : 1768
         Open fields, meadow, pasture, ings, common : 4236 acres
           awarded
         Commissioners John Dickinson, William Iveson, John
           Outram, John Lund, Edward Holgate
         Surveyors Robert Bewlay jun (refused), Peter Nevill
    i   ERRD AK/228/20 enrolled award
    ii   HCRO DDCK/32/6 enrolled award
    iii HCRO PE 120/55 sealed original award
       iv   Hull City RO copy award and plan
    v   HUL DSJ/60 copy award
    vi   HUL DDMM(2)/2/1 summary award
    vii HUL DDKG/199 photograph of copy of plan made 1824,
           buildings, scale not stated

SWANLAND (ER-H) see North Ferriby

706   SWILLINGTON (WR-WY)   1795 : 1799
         Open fields, ings, commons and waste : 360 acres awarded
         Commissioner John Sharpe
    i   WRRD B20 p1 enrolled award and plan 3/23 (1799, surveyor
           Jonathan Teal, whole parish shown, buildings, open field
           names, 6 ch=1")
    ii   Leeds RO modern tracing of map misdated 1779
    iii Messrs Farrer & Co Oulton, tracing of plan
    0   Sealed original award to be deposited in parish chest
           under act. Not found

SWINEFLEET (WR-H) see Reedness

SWINTON (WR-WY) see Brampton Bierlow

707   SWINTON (NR-NY)   1774 : 1776
         Open fields, common pstures : 815 acres awarded
         Commissioners John Graves, William Hall, Isaac Leatham
    i   NRRD Vol BE no.14 p168 enrolled award

SYKEHOUSE (WR-SY) see Hatfield

708 TADCASTER (WR-NY)   1791 : 1798
       Common fields, three common ings, a stinted pasture, common and waste : 1721 acres awarded
       Commissioners John Bainbridge, Miles Dawson (refused), Richard Clark, William Dawson
- i   WRRD Roll 15 sealed original award
- ii   NYCRO DC/TD sealed original award
- iii Tadcaster Ark Museum copy award and reconstructed plan

TANSHELF (WR-WY) see Pontefract

TEMPLE HIRST (WR-NY) see West Haddlesey

709 TEMPLE NEWSAM (WR-WY)   1820 : 1834
       Open fields, intermixed enclosures, commons, commonable and waste lands : 525 acres awarded
       Commissioner Nicholas Brown
- i   WRRD B39 p221 enrolled award and 3 plans Vol 4/9 (1821, surveyor Alfred Smith (1) Manor of Temple Newsam including Halton, Colton and Newsam, whole township shown, buildings, open field features, 6 ch=1"; (2) Halton, buildings, open field names, 6 ch=1"); (3) Colton and Newsam, buildings, open field names, 6 ch=1")
- ii   Leeds Civic Hall sealed original award and plans
- iii Messrs John Farrar & Co Oulton, copy award
- iv   Leeds RO copy award, copies of plans with surveyor's papers

TENTERGATE (WR-NY) see Scriven

710 TERRINGTON (NR-NY)   1772 : 1779
       Open fields, commons, pastures, moors : 1804 acres awarded
       Commissioners John Outram, John Graves, Christopher Wilkinson
- i   NRRD BH nos 72-3, p185 enrolled award
- ii   Borthwick Institute York PR TER/49,50 copy award and related papers

THEARNE (ER-H) see Woodmansey

711 THIRSK (NR-NY)   1793 : 1797
       East Moor and West Moor : 743 acres awarded
       Commissioner John Flintoff
- i   NRRD no.23 with 2 plans (scale not stated)

712 THIRSK (NR-NY)   1836 : 1845
       Open and arable fields : 314 acres awarded
       Commissioner and surveyor Henry Scott
- i   NYCRO QDD(D) Book S no.41, p99 enrolled award and plan (1840, 4 ch=1")

705 SUTTON ON HULL (ER-H) 1763 : 1768
      Open fields, meadow, pasture, ings, common : 4236 acres awarded
      Commissioners John Dickinson, William Iveson, John Outram, John Lund, Edward Holgate
      Surveyors Robert Bewlay jun (refused), Peter Nevill
- i   ERRD AK/228/20 enrolled award
- ii   HCRO DDCK/32/6 enrolled award
- iii HCRO PE 120/55 sealed original award
- iv   Hull City RO copy award and plan
- v   HUL DSJ/60 copy award
- vi   HUL DDMM(2)/2/1 summary award
- vii HUL DDKG/199 photograph of copy of plan made 1824, buildings, scale not stated

SWANLAND (ER-H) see North Ferriby

706 SWILLINGTON (WR-WY) 1795 : 1799
      Open fields, ings, commons and waste : 360 acres awarded
      Commissioner John Sharpe
- i   WRRD B20 p1 enrolled award and plan 3/23 (1799, surveyor Jonathan Teal, whole parish shown, buildings, open field names, 6 ch=1")
- ii   Leeds RO modern tracing of map misdated 1779
- iii Messrs Farrer & Co Oulton, tracing of plan
- 0   Sealed original award to be deposited in parish chest under act. Not found

SWINEFLEET (WR-H) see Reedness

SWINTON (WR-WY) see Brampton Bierlow

707 SWINTON (NR-NY) 1774 : 1776
      Open fields, common pstures : 815 acres awarded
      Commissioners John Graves, William Hall, Isaac Leatham
- i   NRRD Vol BE no.14 p168 enrolled award

SYKEHOUSE (WR-SY) see Hatfield

708 TADCASTER (WR-NY)　　　　　　　　　　　　　　　1791 : 1798
　　　　Common fields, three common ings, a stinted pasture,
　　　　common and waste : 1721 acres awarded
　　　　Commissioners John Bainbridge, Miles Dawson (refused),
　　　　Richard Clark, William Dawson
　　i　　WRRD Roll 15 sealed original award
　　ii　 NYCRO DC/TD sealed original award
　　iii　Tadcaster Ark Museum copy award and reconstructed plan

　　TANSHELF (WR-WY) see Pontefract

　　TEMPLE HIRST (WR-NY) see West Haddlesey

709 TEMPLE NEWSAM (WR-WY)　　　　　　　　　　　　　1820 : 1834
　　　　Open fields, intermixed enclosures, commons, commonable
　　　　and waste lands : 525 acres awarded
　　　　Commissioner Nicholas Brown
　　i　　WRRD B39 p221 enrolled award and 3 plans Vol 4/9 (1821,
　　　　surveyor Alfred Smith (1) Manor of Temple Newsam
　　　　including Halton, Colton and Newsam, whole township
　　　　shown, buildings, open field features, 6 ch=1"; (2)
　　　　Halton, buildings, open field names, 6 ch=1"); (3)
　　　　Colton and Newsam, buildings, open field names, 6 ch=1")
　　ii　 Leeds Civic Hall sealed original award and plans
　　iii　Messrs John Farrar & Co Oulton, copy award
　　iv　 Leeds RO copy award, copies of plans with surveyor's
　　　　papers

　　TENTERGATE (WR-NY) see Scriven

710 TERRINGTON (NR-NY)　　　　　　　　　　　　　　　1772 : 1779
　　　　Open fields, commons, pastures, moors : 1804 acres
　　　　awarded
　　　　Commissioners John Outram, John Graves, Christopher
　　　　Wilkinson
　　i　　NRRD BH nos 72-3, p185 enrolled award
　　ii　 Borthwick Institute York PR TER/49,50 copy award and
　　　　related papers

　　THEARNE (ER-H) see Woodmansey

711 THIRSK (NR-NY)　　　　　　　　　　　　　　　　　1793 : 1797
　　　　East Moor and West Moor : 743 acres awarded
　　　　Commissioner John Flintoff
　　i　　NRRD no.23 with 2 plans (scale not stated)

712 THIRSK (NR-NY)　　　　　　　　　　　　　　　　　1836 : 1845
　　　　Open and arable fields : 314 acres awarded
　　　　Commissioner and surveyor Henry Scott
　　i　　NYCRO QDD(D) Book S no.41, p99 enrolled award and plan
　　　　(1840, 4 ch=1")

713 THIXENDALE (ER-NY) 1794 : 1795
   Open fields, stinted common pstures : 2437 acres awarded
   Commissioners Robert Dunn, William Hall (died) John Hall
   Surveyor Robert Stickney
   Umpire Joseph Dickinson
   i   ERRD BG/426/67 enrolled agreement
   ii   HUL DDSY/66/286 enrolled agreement
   iii ERRD BG/433/67 enrolled award
   iv   HUL DDSY/66/287 sealed original award and plan (1793, buildings, 16 ch=1")

714 THOLTHORPE AND FLAWITH (NR-NY) 1800 : 1804
   Open fields, ings, commons and waste : 1265 acres in Tholthorpe and 410 acres in Flawith
   Commissioners John Hall, William Dawson
   Surveyor John Dalton
   i   NRRD CS no.22 p191 enrolled award and plan (8 ch=1")

   THORGANBY (ER-NY) see West Cottingwith

715 THORALBY AND BISHOPDALE (NR-NY) 1809 : 1814
   Stinted pastures : 2412 acres awarded
   Commissioner Alexander Calvert
   i   NRRD DZ no.10 p101 enrolled award and 2 plans (8 ch=1")
   ii   NYCRO ZQF copy award

716 THORALBY (NR-NY) 1861 : 1863
   Pasture : 174 acres awarded
   Commissioner Edward Broderick
   i   NYCRO QDD(I) 40 certified copy award and plan (3 ch=1")
   ii   NYCRO ZBH certified coopy award
   iii PRO (MAF 1 952) award

   THORLBY (WR-NY) see Skipton

717 THORMANBY (NR-NY) 1782 : 1785
   Common : acreage not given
   Commissioners Robert Moore, John Graves, George Plummer
   i   NRRD BU nos 21-2 p34 enrolled award and plan (scale not stated)
   ii   NYCRO ZDS V 1/6 copy award and copy plan
   iii Borthwick Institute York original award and plan

718 THORNBOROUGH (West Tanfield) (NR-NY) 1793 : 1799
   Open fields and moor : 523 acres awarded
   Commissioner John Mowbray
   Surveyor Ralph Burton
   i   NYCRO QDD(I) no.42 original award and 2 plans (1796, 1797, Thornborough, West Tanfield, 6 ch=1" and scale not stated)
   ii   NYCRO PR/TAN 5 copy award

   THORNE (WR-SY) see Hatfield

719 THORNER (WR-WY)   1777 : 1779

         Commons, open fields, undivided inclosures and commonable lands : 870 acres estimated
         Commissioners Miles Dawson, Joseph Pursglove sen (died), Henry Waddington, William Hill

- i   WRRD B12 p135 enrolled award and plan Vol 4/5 (1777, surveyor John Lund jun, whole township shown, buildings, 8 ch=1")
- ii   Leeds RO award and copy plan
- iii   YAS MD 225 award and plan

THORNES (WR-WY) see Wakefield

720 THORNGUMBALD (ER-H)   1757 : 1757

         By agreement. Open fields, pasture : 976 acres estimated
         Commissioners Joseph Thompson, Robert Bell, John Dickinson
         Surveyors Charles Tate, Peter Nevill

- i   ERRD Y/142/27 enrolled award
- ii   HCRO DDIV/44/1 sealed original award
- iii   HCRO DDCC/142/5 copy award
- iv   HCRO DDCK/32/2 copy award

721 THORNHILL (near Dewsbury) (WR-WY)   1815 : 1823

         Commons and waste : 230 acres awarded
         Commissioner Jonathan Taylor

- i   WRRD B36 p205 enrolled award
- 0   Sealed original award to be kept with manor records under the act. Not traced

THORNHILL (WR-WY) see Briestfield

722 THORNTON (Bradford) (WR-WY)   1770 : 1772

         Thornton Common : 1600 acres estimated
         Commissioners Hugh Oldham, Thomas Leach, William Eden (died), Nathan Jowett

- i   WRRD B9 p226 enrolled award
- ii   PRO DL/41/72 enclosure papers
- 0   Sealed original award to be kept at Thornton chapel under the act. Not found

723 THORNTON DALE (NR-NY)   1780 : 1781

         Open fields, commons, carrs and wastes : 1389 acres awarded
         Commissioners William Willmott, Samuel Milbourn, Robert Dunn

- i   NRRD BR p77 enrolled award
- ii   PRO DL/45/7/1 enrolled extract of award

724 THORNTON DALE, FARMANBY, ELLERBURN AND KINGTHORPE (NR-NY)
1796 : 1799   1796 : 1799
Common and waste : 1066 acres awarded
Commissioners William Whitelock, John Hall, Timothy Parke
- i   NRRD CS no.7 p39 enrolled award
- ii NYCRO ZPC 1/10 copy award

725 THORNTON IN CRAVEN (WR-NY)   1819 : 1825
Commons, moors and waste : 950 acres awarded
Commissioner William Pilkington
- i   WRRD B38 p112 enrolled award and plan Vol 4/8 (1825, surveyor Henry Teal, whole township shown, buildings, 12 ch=1")
- ii Lancs RO award and plan
- iii Leeds RO copy award and plan

726 THORNTON IN LONSDALE (WR-NY)   1814 : 1820
Awards for 1819 and 1820, the second for Thornton Fell only. Moor, common and waste : 3948 acres awarded
- i   CP Wakefield E p1 enrolled award and plan A52 (not dated, unsigned, buildings, 10 ch=1")
- ii Lancs RO enclosure papers
- iii NYCRO PC/TNL sealed original awards and plans (1 1817, unsigned, whole township, buildings, 9 ch=1"; 2 Thornton Fell, signed TW and WP, 3 small plans incorporated in award 9 ch=1")

727 THORNTON LE CLAY (NR-NY)   1777 : 1778
Open fields, moor, carrs, ings, green : 872 acres awarded
Commissioners John Flintoff, Christopher Pickering, John Outram
- i   NRRD BL no.17 p117 enrolled award
- ii Borthwick Institute York PR TC/1 award

728 THORNTON RUST (NR-NY)   1848 : 1855
Moor and pastures : 1114 acres awarded
Commissioner Edward Broderick
Surveyor Francis Garth
- i   NYCRO QDD(I) 38,39 sealed original awards (2) and 2 plans (buildings, 3 ch=1")
- ii PRO (MAF 1 423 and 992) award

THORNTON STEWARD (NR-NY) see Newton-le-Willows

729 THORNTON WATLASS (NR-NY)   1753 : 1754
Act confirms agreement. Canswick or Watlass Moor
Commissioners Thomas Raper, John Harrison, John Telford, Thomas Ascough, Edward Norsdale, Edmund Smith
- i   NYCRO ZBW sealed original award
- ii NYCRO QDD (D) M p45

730 THORP ARCH AND WALTON (WR-WY)　　　　　　　　　　1816 : 1829
　　　　　Open fields, ings, stinted pastures, commons and waste :
　　　　　800 acres estimated
　　　　　Commissioners Daniel Tuke, George Addinell
　　i　　York City RO Vol H enrolled award
　　ii　　Thorp Arch estate office copy award
　　iii　Borthwick Institute York PR WAL/18 award

731 THORP AUDLIN (WR-WY)　　　　　　　　　　　　　　　1810 : 1814
　　　　　Open fields, stinted pastures, commons, wastes and
　　　　　commonable lands : 509 acres awarded
　　　　　Commissioner Thomas Gee
　　i　　WRRD B30 p315 enrolled award and plan Vol 4/7 (1814,
　　　　　surveyor William Bingley, whole township shown,
　　　　　buildings, open field names, 6 ch=1")
　　ii　　PRO DL/45/9/1 enrolled extract of award
　　0　　Sealed original award to be in Badsworth parish church
　　　　　under the act. Not found

　　THORPE IN BALNE (WR-SY) see Barnby Dun

732 THORPE IN BURNSALL (WR-NY)　　　　　　　　　　　1789 : 1793
　　　　　Open fields and stinted pastures : 603 acres awarded
　　　　　Commissioners Henry Wadddington, Henry Wrathall, Thomas
　　　　　Ingelby
　　i　　WRRD Map Vol 4/6 sealed original award and plan (1789,
　　　　　surveyor Thomas Ingleby, buildings, open field names, 4
　　　　　and a half ch=1")
　　0　　Sealed original award also to be kept by John Batty, a
　　　　　landholder, under the act. Not found

733 THORPE SALVIN (WR-SY)　　　　　　　　　　　　　　　　　1823
　　i　　SYCRO 150/Z abstract of agreement for private enclosure

　　THORPE WILLOUGHBY (WR-NY) see Brayton

734 THRESHFIELD, SKIRETHORNE AND BURNSALL (WR-NY) 1805 : 1827
　　　　　Common, commonable lands, stinted pasture, an open field
　　　　　: 1670 acres awarded
　　　　　Commissioners Thomas Buttle, John Preston sen (died),
　　　　　John Binns (died), John Preston jun
　　i　　WRRD B40 sealed original award and 5 plans (not dated,
　　　　　surveyor not named, some buildings, 6 or 4 ch=1")
　　ii　　Threshfield parish council modern copy award and 3 plans
　　iii　Broughton Hall, award and 5 plans

THROXENBY (NR-NY) see Scalby

THRUSCROSS (WR-NY) see Knaresborough, Forest of

735 THURGOLAND IN SILKSTONE (WR-SY)   1813 : 1815
        Commons, waste and moors : 400 acres estimated
        Commissioner Thomas Gee
    i   WRRD B32 p17 enrolled award
    ii Thurgoland parish council award and plan
    iii SYCRO 56/P sealed original award and plan (1815,
        surveyor William Bingley, whole township shown,
        buildings, 6 ch=1")

736 THURLSTONE (WR-SY)   1812 : 1816
        Commons, waste and moors : 5001 acres awarded
        Commissioner Thomas Gee
    i   WRRD B31 p49 enrolled award
    ii Penistone UDC award and plan

737 THURNSCOE (WR-SY)   1729 : 1738
        Act confirms agreement. Moor or common called Whinny
        Moor : 500 acres estimated
        Commissioners not named
    i   WRRD B p291

738 THURNSCOE (WR-SY)   1825 : 1833
        By agreement. Commons or waste
        Commissioner William Bingley
    i   WRRD B38 p324 enrolled award
    ii Dearne UDC award

739 THURSTONLAND (WR-WY)   1800 : 1805
        Commons and waste : 500 acres awarded
        Commissioners Richard Clark, replaced by Joseph Outram
    i   WRRD B22 p124 enrolled award
    ii Kirkburton UDC sealed original award and plan (not
        dated, surveyor John Sedgwick, whole township shown,
        buildings, 6 ch=1")
    iii CP Wakefield A96 late 19 cent. copy award

THWAITES (WR-WY) see Keighley

740 THWING AND OCTON (ER-H)   1769 : 1770
        Open fields, lands : 3763 acres awarded
        Commissioners John Raines, John Outram, Richard Cross
        Surveyor Peter Nevill
    i   ERRD AX/376/29 enrolled award and F2 copy plan made 1947
        (buildings, 16 ch=1")
    ii HCRO DDX/154/2 award
    iii HCRO IA two copies plan

741 TIBTHORPE (ER-H)　　　　　　　　　　　　　　　　　1794 : 1796
　　　　Open fields, pastures, commons, waste : 2810 acres
　　　　awarded
　　　　Commissioners William Hall, William Dawson, Samuel
　　　　Milbourn, John Hall
　　　　Surveyors Anthony Bower, Robert Atkinson
　　i　　ERRD BT/39/9 enrolled award
　　ii　 HUL DDSY/67/1 sealed original award and plan (1794,
　　　　buildings, 12 ch=1")
　　　　Related documents HCRO DDCV/164/1-3 commissioners'
　　　　papers

742 TICKHILL (WR-SY)　　　　　　　　　　　　　　　　1765 : 1766
　　　　Commons called the High and Low Commons in Tickhill, in
　　　　Yorks and Notts : 1700 acres estimated
　　　　Commissioners Thomas Judson, Samuel Brailsford, Thomas
　　　　Smith, Henson Kirkby, Joseph Pursglove
　　i　　NRA Report Lumley MSS copy award
　　ii　 Doncaster RO Enc.25 award and copy plan made 1877
　　iii　Doncaster RO P56/9/A1 award

　　　TIMBLE (WR-NY) see Knaresborough, Forest of

743 TICKTON (ER-H)　　　　　　　　　　　　　　　　　1790 : 1792
　　　　Carr or common : 234 acres awarded
　　　　Commissioners Peter Nevill, John Wood sen, Joseph
　　　　Dickinson, John Wood jun
　　　　Surveyor John Wood jun
　　i　　ERRD BG/329/47 enrolled award
　　ii　 HCRO IA sealed original award and plan (1/91, buildings,
　　　　shows township and carr, 4 ch=1")
　　ii　 Hull CL copy award and plan
　　　　Related documents to settle tithes exemption claims ERRD
　　　　BP/21/3, HCRO IA with plan, HCRO DDCV/165/2 with plan,
　　　　Hull CL

744 TOCKWITH (WR-NY)　　　　　　　　　　　　　　　　1792 : 1797
　　　　Open fields, ings, meadows, commons and wastes : 1020
　　　　acres awarded
　　　　Commissioners Richard Clark, William Dawson, Robert
　　　　Stockdale
　　i　　York City RO Vol G enrolled award
　　ii　 CP Wakefield A102 sealed original award and plan (1792,
　　　　unsigned, buildings, whole township shown, 6 ch=1")
　　iii　Parish council award and plan
　　iv　 YAS MD 110 award

　　　TODWICK (WR-SY) see North Anston

745 TOLLERTON (NR-NY)　　　　　　　　　　　　　　　1810 : 1817
　　　　Open field, ings and wastes : 736 acres awarded
　　　　Commissioner John Humphries
　　i　　NRRD DZ no.20 p138 enrolled award and plan (buildings, 6
　　　　ch=1")

746 TOPCLIFFE (NR-NY)   1761 : 1761
        By agreement. Common and and open field
     i   Hill-Walker archives formerly in NYCRO, withdrawn by
            1985
     ii York Minster Library U2(2)2, pre-enclosure plan (draft)

     TRANBY (ER-H) see Hessle. There is a pre-enclosure plan 1773
        HCRO DDX/202/65

     TRANMORE (WR-NY) see Eggborough

747 TRUMFLEET (WR-SY)   1865 : 1871
        Trumfleet Marsh and Ings : 140 acres awarded
        Commissioner William Paver
     i   CP Wakefield A73 sealed original award and plan (1869,
            surveyor J. Hindle, buildings, open field features, 2
            ch=1")
     ii PRO (MAF 1 595) award

748 TUNSTALL (ER-H)   1777 : 1779
        Open fields, meadows, pastures : 938 acres awarded
        Commissioners John Outram, Robert Dunn, Peter Nevill
        Surveyor Robert Atkinson
     i   ERRD BB/134/17 enrolled award and plan (1777, buildings,
            8 ch=1")
     ii   HCRO PE/42/11 sealed original award and plan
     iii HCRO DDCC/142/2,16, copy and draft award
     iv   HCRO DDCK/32/15 award and plan
     v   HCRO DDX/100/4 plan
     vi   HCRO IA plan
     vii HCRO DDHE/39/1 copy plan
          Related documents HCRO DDCK/32/15 schedule of ancient
            enclosures

749 TUNSTALL (near Catterick) (NR-NY)   1806 : 1813
        Moor and waste : 150 acres awarded
        Commissioner Alexander Calvert
     i   NRRD DT no. 69 p115 enrolled award and plan (buildings,
            3 ch=1")

750 UGGLEBARNBY AND ESKDALESIDE (NR-NY)   1760 : 1760
        Moor, common or waste : 1498 acres awarded
        Commissioners William Richardson, Michael Smith, George
        Duck, Isaac Scarth, George Pearson
    i   NRRD AG no.19 p149 enrolled award and plan (surveyor
        John Kirby, buildings, 4 ch=1")
    ii NYCRO PR/ESK copy plan

751 ULLESKELF (WR-NY)   1835 : 1853
        Open fields, ings, commonable lands : 659 acres awarded
        Commissioner James Bulmer
    i   CP Wakefield A9a sealed original award and 2 plans in
        volume (not dated, unsigned; (1) allotments on the
        common, buildings, 3 ch=1"; (2) Ulleskelf inclosure,
        buildings, open field names, 3 ch=1")
    ii Leeds RO original award and plan

752 ULLESKELF (WR-NY)   1853 : 1857
        Ulleskelf Mires : 137 acres awarded
        Commissioner William Paver
    i   CP Wakefield A38 sealed original award and plan (1856, 2
        ch=1")
    ii PRO (MAF 1 790) award

753 ULLEY (WR-SY)   1798 : 1800
        Common fields and waste : 358 acres awarded
        Commissioners Arthur Elliott, William Rodgers
    i   WRRD B20 pp188,299 enrolled award and plan Vol 4/10
        (1798, surveyor John Brown, whole township shown,
        buildings, open field features, scale not stated,
        decorated cartouche)
    ii Rotherham CL award and plan
    iii Sheffield CL E (295) 67 photocopy of plan

754 ULROME (ER-H)   1765 : 1767
        Open fields : 1200 acres estimated
        Commissioners John Dickinson, John Outram, John Raines
    i   ERRD AH/331/9 enrolled award
    ii HCRO DX/154/15 copy award
    iii HCRO DDCC(2)/G(13) copy plan (1787, surveyor Charles
        Tate sen, 12 ch=1")

755 UPPER DUNSFORTH WITH BRANTON GREEN (WR-NY)   1770 : 1776
        Common fields, meadow, common pastures, stinted pastures
        and common : 600 acres estimated
        Commissioners John Outram, John Graves, Joseph Butler
    i   WRRD B11 p79 enrolled award
    ii YAS DD/44 sealed original award and plan (parish award
        on deposit) (1770, surveyor ... Clark, whole township
        shown, buildings, 6 ch=1", worn)
    iii PRO DL/45/1 enrolled award

756 UPPER HELMSLEY (NR-NY)   1865 : 1868
         Common : 162 acres awarded
         Commissioner W.J. Ware
      i NYCRO QDD(I) no.22 enrolled award and plan (1866, W.J.
         Ware, 3 ch=1")
     ii PRO (MAF 1 740) award

UPPER MIDHOPE (WR-SY) see Midhope

UPPERTHONG (WR-WY) see Wooldale

UPTON (ER-H) see Dringhoe

WADDINGTON (WR-Lancs) see Grindleton

757 WADSLEY AND LOXLEY (WR-SY) 1784 : 1789
    Common or waste and open fields in Wadsley and Loxley Chase
    Commissioners John Kent, John Birks (died), Arthur Elliott, Joseph Outram
- i   WRRD B17 p161 enrolled award and plan Vol 2/8 (1789, surveyor William Fairbank, buildings, 10 ch=1")
- ii   Sheffield CL ACM 546 sealed original award and plan
- iii   Bradfield parish council award

758 WADWORTH (WR-SY) 1765 : 1767
    Open fields, undivided inclosures, commons and waste : 1962 acres awarded
    Commissioners John Arthur, Samuel Hallows Hamer, Thomas Loxley, Robert Dawson, Thomas Smith (died)
- i   WRRD B6 p52 enrolled award
- ii   Sheffield CL PR 13/71-74 award and plan
- iii   Doncaster RO P21 award and plan

WADWORTH (WR-SY) see Doncaster

759 WAKEFIELD, STANLEY, WRENTHORPE, ALVERTHORPE AND THORNES (WR-WY) 1793 : 1813
    Awards of 1805 and 1813. Open fields, ings, commons and waste : 2634 acres awarded
    Commissioners Richard Clark (refused), John Renshaw (died), John Sharp (died), William Whitelock, Thomas Gee, Samuel Cawthorp, John Dutton
- i   WRRD B23 p1 and B30 p39 enrolled award and 4 plans Vol 4/28 (1 & 2 1805, surveyor Jonathan Teal, parts of the parish of Wakefield, including part of the town of Wakefield, Wrenthorpe and Alverthorpe, buildings, open field names, 6 ch=1"; (3) not dated, surveyor Thomas Gee, part of the townships of Wakefield and Stanley at the time of enclosures, buildings, 6 ch=1"; (4) 1813, surveyor Samuel Gawthorp, estate of the late earl of Strafford in Wakefield, buildings, 5 ch=1")
- ii   YAS MD 225 award and 3 plans
- iii   Messrs Farrar & Co Oulton, certified copy award of 1805
- iv   Leeds RO plan by Thomas Gee of part of Wakefield and Stanley as above, 1805
- v   PRO (Chancery Lane) MPA A4 three enclosure plans showing estates of earl of Strafford in Wakefield and Sandal Magna; also PRO (Chancery Lane) J 90/324 copies
- vi   WYAS QD4 amended award and Strafford(s estates Z44/1; Z65 photocopy plan

760 WALDEN (NR-NY) 1806 : 1807
    By agreement. Stinted pastures : 90 acres awarded
    Commissioner Alexander Calvert
- i   Mr Johnson, solicitor, Hawes, had original award and plan in 1967
- ii   NRRD DG no.3 p4 enrolled award

WALES (WR-SY) see Aston cum Aughton

761 WALKINGTON (ER-H)   1794 : 1795
Supplementary award 1797. Open fields, meadows, pastures, commons : 2891 acres awarded
Commissioners Arthur Mowbray, John Levitt, Peter Nevill, Robert Carlile, William Hall, Joseph Dickinson
Surveyors Joseph Dickinson, John Wood
- i   ERRD BT/57/1 enrolled award and plan IA. Supplementary award ERRD BT/423/51
- ii   HCRO PC/5/54 sealed original award and plan (1795, 12 ch=1")
- iii   HCRO DDX/65/3 copy award and DDX/90/1 tracing and photograph of plan
- iv   Durham HCR sealed original award and plan
- v   HUL DDCV/168/4,5 copy award and plan

Related documents HUL DDBA/8/99-111; also HUL DDCV/168/3-13

WALLINGFEN (ER-H) see Everthorpe; Howden

762 WALMGATE (York)   1824 : 1828
Stray called Half Year Lands : 140 acres awarded
Commissioners William Ware, John Ayer. Umpire James Bulmer
- i   York City RO TC DP/1/7 sealed original award and plan (1828, unsigned, buildings, 4 ch=1")

WALTON (near Wetherby) (WR-WY) see Thorp Arch

WALTON (Wakefield) (WR-WY) see Sandal Magna

WANSFORD (ER-H) see Nafferton

763 WARLEY (WR-WY)   1848 : 1858
Moor and waste : 2000 acres awarded
Commissioner Thomas Bradley
- i   CP Wakefield A17 sealed original award (printed) and 3 plans (1855, 1A Harewood Well Moor, Sentry Edge, Tower Hill, Camp End; 2A Saltonstall Moor, both show buildings, both 3 ch=1"; B whole township shown, buildings, 6 ch=1")
- ii   Halifax TC award
- iii   YAS MD 225 sealed original award
- iii   Leeds RO printed award
- iv   PRO (MAF 1 177) award

764 WARTER (ER-H)   1794 : 1795
Allotting roads and improving lands : 7587 acres awarded
Commissioners Thomas Nicholson, Cuthbert Atkinson, Peter How
Surveyor Thomas Oxtoby
- i   ERRD BT/32/5 enrolled award

Related documents ERRD BG/455/74, CQ/212/14, CQ/315/17

765 WARTHILL (NR-NY) 1756 : 1757
Four common arable fields : 40 oxgangs
Commissioners Robert Bewlay, John Cleaver, Robert Bewlay jun
- i   NRRD AB no.18 p78 enrolled award
- ii NYCRO CR ONT 13/13 copy award

766 WARTHILL (NR-NY) 1812 : 1826
Open fields, commons, waste : 500 acres awarded
Commissioner and surveyor John Tuke
- i   NRRD no.6 sealed original award and plan (buildings, 6 ch=1")

767 WATH UPON DEARNE (WR-SY) 1810 : 1814
Open fields, mesne inclosures, meadows, ings, commons and waste
Commissioner Thomas Gee
- i   WRRD B30 p226 enrolled award
- ii   Rotherham CL award and plan
- iii Sheffield CL NBC 80 copy award

WATH UPON DEARNE (WR-SY) see Brampton Bierlow

WAULDBY (ER-H) see Elloughton

768 WEAVERTHORPE AND HELPERTHORPE (ER-NY) 1801 : 1804
Open fields, pastures, leys, commons, waste : 2873 acres in Weaverthorpe, 2512 acres in Helperthorpe awarded
Commissioners William Whitelock, John Hall, Isaac Leatham
Surveyor John Dalton
- i   ERRD CA/329/44 enrolled award and plan (not dated, buildings, 12 ch=1")
- ii   NYCRO ZDS copy award
- iii HCRO IA copy plan (1801)
Related documents HCRO IA notebook of surveyor; HUL DDSY/98/1

WEEL (ER-H) see Woodmansey

WEETON (ER-H) see Welwick

WEETON (WR-NY) see Dunkeswick

769 WELTON (ER-H) 1750 : 1752
By agreement of 1750, act 1751. Grassland : 350 acres estimated
Commissioner Joseph Thompson, Richard North, John Raines
- i   ERRD B/303/53 enrolled agreement; ERRD B/321/54 enrolled award
- ii   ERRD original agreement and award
- iii HCRO PR/3173 award
- iv   HCRO IA 19 cent copy plan (unsigned, buildings, 8 ch=1")

770 WELTON (ER-H) 1772 : 1775
      Open fields, waste : 1074 acres awarded
      Commissioners John Lund, John Outram, Robert Dunn
      Surveyor Peter Nevill
- i   ERRD AT/257/29 enrolled award
- ii   ERRD sealed original award and plan (1773, buildings, 8 ch=1")
- iii HCRO PE/106/34 award and plan
- iv   Durham HCR sealed original award and plan, also copy plan
- v   Leeds Brotherton Library MS 311/4 19 cent copy award
- vi   HCRO DDTH/68(ii) damaged copy plan
- vii Hull CL copy plan

771 WELWICK AND WEETON (ER-H) 1768 : 1771
      Open fields, lands, grounds : Welwick 994 acres, Weeton 557 acres awarded
      Commissioners Edward Cleaver, William Iveson, Thomas Carter
- i   ERRD AN/34/5 enrolled award
- ii   ERRD sealed original award and plan (1771, buildings, no scale)
- iii HCRO DDX/31/26 sealed original award
- iv   HCRO DDCC/142/10 copy award
- v   HCRO DDCK/32/10-11 copy award and DDCK/35/1(e) plan (old enclosures)
- vi   HCRO IA copy plan

772 WENSLEY AND REDMIRE (NR-NY) 1809 : 1809
      Common stinted pasture called Redmire Pasture, Redmire and Preston Moors and other waste : 2819 acres awarded
      Commissioner Alexander Calvert
      Surveyor W. Alderson
- i   NYCRO Bk O p31 enrolled award and plan QDD(D) (buildings, 8 ch=1")
- ii   NYCRO QDD(I) no.44 original award and plan
- iii NYCRO ZBD original award
- iv   NYCRO CR ONT 13/16 typed transcript award

WENTBRIDGE (WR-WY) see Darrington

773 WENTWORTH AND KIMBERWORTH (WR-SY) 1814 : 1821
      Open fields, undivided inclosures, commons and waste : 267 acres awarded
      Commissioner William Bingley
- i   WRRD B35 p214 enrolled award
- ii   Sheffield CL NBC 62 award and 2 plans (1814, (1) Wentworth Commons, buildings, 8ch=1"; (2) Thorpe fields, buildings, 8ch=1")
- iii Sheffield CL Fairbank Collection draft plans and surveys

774 WEST ARDSLEY OR WOODKIRK AND EAST ARDSLEY (WR-WY)   1826 : 1838
       Awards of 1829, 1838. Commons and waste : 579 acres awarded
       Commissioners Jonathan Taylor, George Hayward
- i   CP Wakefield A1 sealed original award of 1829 and 2 plans (not dated, surveyor Alfred Smith, (1) West Ardsley, whole township shown, buildings, 6 ch=1" ; (2) East Ardsley, whole township shown, buildings, 6 ch=1"); also CP Wakefield A76 sealed original award 1838, no plan
- ii Morley Public Library award
- iii Leeds RO draft plan of East Ardsley

775 WEST AYTON (NR-NY)   1779 : 1780
       By agreement. Moor
       Commissioners John Foord, Thomas Palliser
- i   NYCRO ZDS V 2/3/1 sealed original award and later copy plan (not dated, unsigned, scale not stated)

776 WEST AYTON AND HUTTON BUSCEL (NR-NY)   1790,1792 : 1797
       Amendment to award 1798. Open fields, meadow, pasture, common, waste : 2120 acres awarded
       Commissioners Isaac Leatham, Richard Clark, Timothy Parke
- i   NRRD CA no.56 p153 enrolled award and 6 plans (1795, surveyor Robert King, buildings, 8 ch=1")
- ii NRRD CS no.4 p5 enrolled amendment 1798
- iii NYCRO ZDS V 3/2 sealed original award and 6 plans

WEST BRADFORD (WR-Lancs) see Crindleton

777 WEST BURTON (NR-NY)   1804 : 1805
       Pasture : 1961 acres awarded
       Commissioners Alexander Calvert
- i   NRRD DB no.16 p31 enrolled award
- ii NYCRO ZMI 11 plan (1801, surveyor John Humphries, scale not stated)

778 WEST COTTINGWITH AND THORGANBY (ER-NY)　　　　　1810 : 1817
　　　　Open fields, ings, common pasture, commons, waste : 1194
　　　　acres awarded
　　　　Commissioners John Hall, Richard Clark
　　　　Surveyors Daniel Tuke, Robert Plummer Weddall
　i　　ERRD DA/44/3 enrolled award
　ii　　HUL DDJ/14/395 sealed original award and 2 plans (1
　　　　Thorganby, 1816, buildings, 6 ch=1"; 2 West Cottingwith,
　　　　not dated, buildings, 6 ch=1")
　　　　Related documents HUL DDJ/14/31-2,393 and DDJ/34/63

779 WEST ELLA, KIRK ELLA AND WILLERBY (ER-H)　　　　1796 : 1799
　　　　Open fields, meadows, pastures, commons : 1784 acres
　　　　awarded
　　　　Commissioners Peter Nevill, John Wood, John Hall
　　　　Surveyors Thomas Barrow, John Dalton
　i　　ERRD CA/6/3 enrolled award
　ii　　HCRO IA copy plan (1796, buildings, 12 ch=1")
　iii　 Hull CL copy award and plan
　iv　　HUL DSJ/64 copy award
　v　　 Hull City RO copy plan

WEST ELLA (ER-H) see North Ferriby

780 WESTERDALE (NR-NY)　　　　　　　　　　　　　　　1811 : 1812
　　　　Open field : 171 acres awarded
　　　　Commissioners William Merry, Leonard Holdstock
　i　　NRRD DO no.11 p65 enrolled award and plan (6 ch=1")

781 WEST HADDLESEY, CHAPEL HADDLESEY, EAST HADDLESEY AND TEMPLE
　　　　HIRST (WR-NY)　　　　　　　　　　　　　　　1789 : 1793
　　　　Open fields, ings, pastures, commons and waste : 868
　　　　acres awarded
　　　　Commissioners William Whitelock, Isaac Leatham, Richard
　　　　Clark
　i　　WRRD B19 p1, p123 enrolled award
　ii　　Borthwick Institute, York, PR C/HAD/15 plan (not dated, unsigned,
　　　　whole township shown, buildings, 2 cartouches, 10 ch=1"); also schedule

WEST HARDWICK (WR-WY) see Pontefract

782 WEST HESLERTON AND YEDINGHAM (ER-NY)　　　　　 1770 : 1774
　　　　Open fields, common pastures : 1753 acres awarded
　　　　Commissioners John Cleaver, Joseph Butler, Isaac
　　　　Milbourn
　　　　Surveyor Isaac Milbourn
　i　　ERRD AT/60/7 enrolled award
　ii　　NYCRO ZDS I 4/55 sealed original award
　iii　 NYCRO DC/NRR copy award

WEST LUTTON (ER-NY) see East Lutton

WEST NESS (NR-NY) see Stonegrave

WEST TANFIELD (NR-NY) see Thornborough

783 WEST WITTON (NR-NY) 1779 : 1781
Stinted pasture and moor : 1335 acres awarded
Commissioners George Jackson, Ingram Gill, William Head Gayles
- i NRRD ZKW I sealed original award and plan (buildings, 8 ch=1")
- ii NYCRO CR ONT 13/6 typed transcript award

784 WETWANG AND FIMBER (ER-H) 1803 : 1806
Open fields, common pastures, commons, waste : Wetwang 3207 acres, Fimber 1840 acres awarded
Commissioners Joseph Dickinson, Isaac Leatham, William Whitelock
Surveyors John Dalton, Robert Stickney
- i   ERRD CI/141/9 enrolled award and 2 plans, C5, D3 (1 Wetwang, not dated, buildings, 8 ch=1"; 2 Fimber, not dated, buildings, 8 ch=1")
- ii HCRO/PE 48/23 copy award
- iii HUL DDSY/72/3 sealed original award and 2 plans

Related document HUL DDSY/98/1

785 WHARRAM LE STREET (ER-NY) 1766 : 1768
Pastures, ings, meadows, common carrs, other fields : 1597 acres estimated
Commissioners John Cleaver, John Outram, Joseph Foord
- i ERRD AK/181/10 enrolled award
- ii Notts Univ. Lib. Middleton MSS Mi Da 165 plan

786 WHELDRAKE (ER-NY) 1769 : 1773
Open fields, meadow grounds, ings, moor, common, waste : 2045 acres awarded
Commissioners Robert Bewlay jun (refused), John Outram, John Dunnington, Miles Dawson
- i ERRD AT/3/2 enrolled award
- ii Borthwick Institute York PR WHEL/101 sealed original award; also 19 cent copy award and survey

Related document HUL DDFA/18/245

787 WHISTON (WR-H) 1816 : 1823
Commons and waste : 231 acres estimated
Commissioners Francis Raynes, Thomas Gee
- i   WRRD I C no.401 p424 memorial of award; copy part of plan Z
- ii Sheffield CL award damaged by fire
- iii Sheffield CL, 2 drafts of plans (1817, surveyor William Fairbank, whole township shown, buildings, scale not stated, very large)

788 WHITGIFT (WR-H) 1757 : 1757
By agreement dated 1756, confirmed by act. Pasture called Whitgift Pasture : 174 acres awarded
Commissioners Marmaduke Lawson, Samuel Milbourn
- i WRRD BS p11 enrolled award

789 WHITGIFT (WR-H) 1827 : 1833
　　　　By agreement. Moors
　　　　Commissioner William Pilkington
　i　WRRD B39 p324 and p326 enrolled award and plan Vol 4/15
　　　(not dated, unsigned, 6 ch=1")
　0　Sealed original award to be deposited in Whitgift church
　　　under the act. Not found

790 WHITLEY (Kirkburton) (WR-WY) 1821 : 1826
　　　　Common or moor called Grange Moor and other waste : 142
　　　　acres awarded
　　　　Commissioner William Pilkington
　i　WRRD B38 p180 enrolled award and plan Vol 4/14 (1821,
　　　surveyor Thomas Dinsley, whole manor shown, buildings, 6
　　　ch=1")
　ii　Kirklees RO　sealed original award and plan in volume
　　　(formerly in church)
　0　Award to be enrolled with manorial records under the
　　　act. Not found

WHITLEY (Osgoldcross) (WR-NY) see Pollington

WHITLEY THORPE (WR-NY) see Pollington

791 WHITWOOD (WR-WY) 1804 : 1807
　　　　Commons and wastes : 204 acres awarded
　　　　Commissioner William Whitelock
　i　WRRD B25 p116 enrolled award

792 WHIXLEY AND GREEN HAMMERTON (WR-NY) 1801 : 1806
　　　　Open fields, stinted pastures, commons, commonable lands
　　　　and waste : 959 acres awarded
　　　　Commissioner William Dawson
　i　WRRD Roll 16 sealed original award
　ii　Whixley parish council sealed original award and 2 plans
　　　(1805 (1) Whixley, not signed, whole township,
　　　buildings, open field names, 6 ch=1"; (2) Green
　　　Hammerton, whole township shown, buildings, open field
　　　names, 6 ch=1")
　iii　CP Wakefield A56a late 19 cent. copy award and copy
　　　plans
　iv　YAS MS 932 copy plan
　v　Leeds RO draft plan

793 WIBSEY SLACK AND LOW MOOR (WR-NY) 1881 : 1888
　　　　Wibsey Slack and Low Moor Commons : 400 acres awarded
　　　　Commissioner Joseph Smith
　i　WRRD Roll 19 plans on 8 sheets (not dated, surveyors
　　　Smith Gotthardt & Co, buildings, various scales)
　ii　CP Wakefield A83 printed award and plans
　iii　City of Bradford award and plans
　iv　Leeds RO printed award and plan
　v　PRO (MAF 1 583) award

794 WICKERSLEY (WR-SY) 1814 : 1817
        Open fields, commons and waste : 500 acres awarded
        Commissioner Thomas Gee
   i   WRRD B34 p1 enrolled award
   0   Sealed original award to be kept in parish church under the act. Not found

795 WIGGINTON (NR-NY) 1769 : 1771
        Common and waste : 396 acres awarded
        Commissioners Joseph Butler, John Graves
   i   NRRD AX no.43 p152 enrolled award and plan (buildings, 4 ch=1")

796 WIGTON (WR-WY) 1797 : 1797
        By agreement. Moor common or waste, Wigton Common : 500 acres estimated
        Commissioner Jonathan Teal
   i   WRRD B19 p302 enrolled award and plan Vol 4/11 (1797, surveyor Jonathan Teal, buildings, 7 ch=1")
   ii   Leeds RO (Harewood archives) sealed original award and plan

WILBERFOSS (ER-H) see Catton

797 WILFHOLME (ER-H) 1806 : 1814
        Common or waste : 532 acres awarded
        Commissioner Joseph Dickinson
        Surveyors William Rawson (John Dalton named in act)
   i   ERRD CQ/323/19 enrolled award and plan (1814, 4 and a half ch=1")
   ii   HCRO DDX/22 draft award
   iii HCRO DDBL/21/1 copy plan (8 ch=1")

WILLERBY (ER-H) see North Ferriby; West Ella

798 WILTON (NR-NY) 1773 : 1774
        Open fields lands and ground : 620 acres awarded
   i   NRRD AX nos 62-63 p223 enrolled award

799 WILTON, LAZENBY, LACKENBY AND WEST COATHAM (NR-Cleveland)
        1803 : 1810
        Common fields, pastures, moors and wastes : 1460 acres estimated
   i   NYCRO Bk N no.43 p217 enrolled award and plan
   ii   Cleveland County achives U/S/95 original award and plan
   iii NYCRO ZK 4279-80 copy award

WINKSLEY (WR-NY) see Sawley

WINSLEY (WR-NY) see Hartwith

800 WINTERBURN (FLASBY WITH WINTERBURN) (WR-NY)   1856 : 1858
        Winterburn Moor : 224 acres awarded
        Commissioner James Powell
    i   CP Wakefield A36 sealed original award and plan
        (buildings, 3 ch=1")
    ii PRO (MAF 1 721) award

801 WISEWOOD (WR-SY)   1815 : 1819
        Common : 100 acres awarded
        Commissioners Josiah Fairbank (refused), William Bingley
    i   WRRD B34 p203 enrolled award
    ii Sheffield Town Hall MS award and photostat of plan
    iii Sheffield CL Fairbank Ecc 187 copy plan (1815, unsigned,
        buildings)
    iv Sheffield CL SC 572 award and plan

WISTOW (WR-NY) see Cawood

WITHERNSEA (ER-H) see Hollym

802 WITHERNWICK (ER-H)   1802 : 1814
        Open fields, meadows, pastures, commons : 1535 acres
        awarded
        Commissioners John Hall, Joseph Dickinson
        Surveyors Robert Atkinson, Samuel Dickinson
        Arbitrators Robert Osborne, William Walton
    i   ERRD CQ/245/16 enrolled award and plan (1812, buildings,
        8 ch=1")
    ii Hull CL plan

803 WOLD NEWTON (ER-H)   1772 : 1776
        Open fields, commons, pastures : 2000 acres estimated
        Commissioners Calisthenes Marshall, Samuel Milbourn,
        John Outram
        Surveyor David Tate
    i   ERRD AT/354/37 enrolled award
    ii HCRO DDX/154/9,21 two copies of award
    iii HCRO IA copy plan (1772, buildings, 8 ch=1")
    iv HUL DDCV parcel 40 sealed original award

804 WOMBLETON (NR-NY)   1670
        Moor Field, Gildersdale and the Hollowe or Howle
        Commissioners Thomas Wayte, John Pibus, Robert Hunter
    i   NYCRO ZEW V 2/1

805 WOMBLETON (NR-NY) 1753 : 1754
By agreement.
Commissioners Thomas Robinson, Thomas Coomber, Charles Cooper
Surveyors Samuel Milbourn Joseph Foord
- i NYCRO ZEW V 3 original agreement
- ii NYCRO ZEW V 2/1 original award and plan

806 WOMBWELL (WR-SY) 1763 : 1767
Commons or waste : 700 acres awarded
Commissioners John Spencer, William Marsden, Francis Hall
- i WRRD B6 p142 enrolled award
- ii Sheffield CL NBC 81 copy award
- iii Wombwell UDC certified copy award

807 WOMERSLEY (WR-NY) 1800 : 1805
Open fields, ings, pastures, commons and waste : 625 acres awarded
Commissioners William Whitelock, William Shipton
- i WRRD B23 p255 enrolled award and plan Vol 4/12 (1805, surveyor Robert Lumb, whole township shown, buildings, open field features, 6 ch=1")
- ii HCRO DDCL/246 19 cent. copy award and plan
- iii Sealed original award to be kept in parish church under act. Not found 1962

WOODALL (WR-SY) see Harthill

WOODHALL (WR-NY) see Sicklinghall

WOODHOUSE (Normanton) (WR-WY) see Normanton

WOODKIRK (WR-WY) see West Ardsley

WOODLESFORD (WR-WY) see Rothwell

808 WOODMANSEY, THEARNE, WEEL AND SKIDBY (ER-H) 1785 : 1786,1788
Awards of 1786 (Weel Carr) and 1788. Lands, grounds, carrs, common pastures : 976 acres awarded
Commissioners John Wood, Joseph Dickinson, Jonathan Teal
Surveyor Joseph Dickinson
- i ERRD BG/95/5 (Weel) and BG/216/20 enrolled awards and plan (1788, Thearne Commons with Skidby Carr and Ings, buildings, 8 ch=1")
- ii HUL DDCV/176/1 Weel award and plan
- iii HUL DDMM/29/168 copy award
- iv HCRO IA plan (1801, Woodmansey and Thearne, signed S. Dickinson, 8 ch=1", possibly copy of enclosure plan)

809 WOOLDALE, FULSTONE, CARTWORTH, HEPWORTH, SCHOLES, AUSTONLEY, UPPERTHONG, HOLME (The Graveship of Holme townships) (WR-WY)   1828 : 1834
        Commons, waste and moors or heaths, common fields : 9335 acres awarded
        Commissioners Thomas Bradley, Frederick Robert Jones
    i   WRRD B43 printed award and 8 plans Roll 6 (1834, surveyor Christopher Lonsdale Bradley, buildings, 8 ch=1")
    ii YAS MD 225 printed award and plans
    iii Kirklees RO printed award and plans

810 WOOLLEY (WR-WY)   1768 : 1769
        By agreement. Common or waste called Woolley North Moor, Low Moor, or Haigh Moor
        Commissioners John Spencer (did not act), George Walker, Benjamin Micklethwaite
    i   WRRD B7 p259 enrolled award and plan B7 p264 (not dated, unsigned, buildings, scale not stated)
        Related papers YAS DD 200

811 WORSBOROUGH (WR-SY)   1817 : 1826
        Commons and waste : 300 acres awarded
        Commissioner Thomas Gee
    i   WRRD B37 p64 enrolled award
    ii Sheffield CL EM 639/2 copy award
    iii Sheffield CL NBC 63 award and 5 plans (buildings, scale not stated)
    iv Worsborouigh UDC copy extracts from award, and plans

812 WORTLEY (Leeds) (WR-WY)   1833 : 1847
        Commons or waste : 45 acres awarded
        Commissioner Thomas Newsam
    i   CP Wakefield A8 sealed original award and plan (not dated, not signed, buildings, 3 ch=1")
    ii Leeds Civic Hall sealed original award and plan
    iii YAS MS 1248 photocopy plan

813 WORTLEY (WR-SY)   1806 : 1810
        By agreement. Common or waste
        Commissioner Elias Wright
    i   WRRD B27 p359 enrolled award and deposited award 4/13
    ii Wharncliffe Estates, Wortley, award

    WRELTON (NR-NY) see Aislaby

    WRENTHORPE (WR-WY) see Wakefield

814 WYKE (Bradford) (WR-WY)   1813 : 1821
        Open commons, moors, waste, other commonable lands and grounds : 151 acres awarded
        Commissioner Thomas Buttle
    i   WRRD B50 sealed original award and plan (not dated, surveyor Samuel Swire, buildings, 4 ch=1")
    ii WYAS D81 sealed original award

815 WYKEHAM AND RUSTON (NR-NY)   1785 : 1787
         Commons and waste : 4261 acres awarded
         Commissioners Edward Cleaver, Samuel Milbourn, William
         Willmott
         Surveyor Isaac Milbourn
    i   NRRD CA no.2 p11 enrolled award
    ii   NYCRO ZDS V 3/1 original award and 3 plans; also ZDS V
         4/5-6 copy award
    iii PRO DL/45/7/2 enrolled extract of award

816 WYTON (ER-H)   1763 : 1763
         By agreement. Pasture called Wyton Holme : 70 acres
         estimated
         Commissioner John Dickinson
    i   ERRD AC/255/11 enrolled award

816 YAFFORTH, THRINTOFT, LITTLE LANGTON AND DANBY WISKE (NR-NY)
                                                          1788 : 1790
         Moor : 417 acres awarded
         Commissioner Richard Clark
    i   NRRD no.25 original award and plan (4 ch=1")
    ii   NYCRO ZBM 24 copy award

817 YAPHAM AND MELTONBY (ER-H)   1731 : 1733
         Open field, common : 1639 acres estimated
         Commissioners John Carr, Richard Yeward,   Thomas
         Armistead, Thomas Jackson, John Hotham
         Surveyor James West
    i   HCRO DDBD/56/1(c) bound copy award
    ii   Pocklington church 1970 copy award
    iii York City RO M20 p249 copy award

818 YEADON (WR-WY)   1803 : 1813
         Commons and waste : 321 acres awarded
         Commissioner William Dawson
    i   WRRD B30 p60 enrolled award and map Vol 4/16 (1806,
         surveyor John Humphries, buildings, 6 ch=1")
    ii   Aireborough UDC award

819 YEARSLEY (NR-NY)   1864 : 1867
         Moor : 249 acres awarded
         Commissioners Robert Wyse
    i   NYCRO QDD(I) 45 sealed award and plan (3 ch=1")
    ii   Borthwick Institute York PR Cox/32 original award and
         plan
    iii PRO (MAF 1 541) award

     YEDINGHAM (ER-NY) see West Heslerton

820 YOKEFLEET (ER-H)   1794 : 1794
         By agreement. Open fields : 275 acres estimated
         Commissioners William Dawson, Joseph Dickinson
    i   ERRD BG/420/66 enrolled award
    ii   HUL DRA/869 sealed original award

     YORK see Acomb; Clifton; Dringhouses; Walmgate

821 YOULTHORPE (ER-H)   1769 : 1777
         Open fields, common pastures : 666 acres awarded
         Commissioners Richard Cross, Joseph Butler, John Graves
         Surveyor Richard Clark
    i   ERRD BB/60/11 enrolled award

INDEX OF ENCLOSURE COMMISSIONERS AND SURVEYORS

by Jan Crowther

The numbers refer to the entries and not to the pages of the list. No distinction is made in the index between commissioners and surveyors, because so many men acted in both capacities. The index does not differentiate between those who acted, and others who either refused to act, or died in the course of their commission.

Abbey, John 310
Addinell, George 98,212,730
Ake, Michael 464
Alderson, Christopher 584
Alderson, George 62,63,387,435
Alderson, W. 772
Alexander, James 86,219,669
Allanson, John 660
Armistead, Thomas 101,817
Armitage, Joseph 269
Arthington, Robert 160
Arthur, John 758
Ascough, Thomas 729
Ash, Matthew 607
Ashbey, Francis 337
Askwith, John jun 305
Asquith, J. 689
Atkinson, Cuthbert 764
Atkinson, Robert 188,361,379,457,464,543,669,741,748,802
Ayer, John 140,762
Ayrton, Richard 701
Bainbridge, John 122,440,558,571,682,708
Bainbridge, Timothy 208,241,368,636
Barker, George 115
Barker, William 490
Barrow, Thomas 254,281,361,371,416,611,688,779
Battie, John 108
Baxby, John 233
Beckwith, M. 468,597
Beckwith, Richard 317,429
Beighton, John 78,414
Beilby, John 401
Bell, John 64,103,314,441
Bell, Robert 280,562,672,720
Benton, Robert 405
Bewlay, Robert 8,100,113,166,168,232,257,291,383,384,
    425,476,549,558,666,690,703,765
Bewlay, Robert sen 179,398,434,642
Bewlay, Robert jun 96,102,166,179,227,245,398,434,508,
    524,577,614,642,691,705,765,786
Bingley, William 69,115,124,211,212,213,259,553,567,643,
    686,731,735,738,773,801

Binns, John   120,169,734
Birks, John   74,218,247,456,757
Birks, Richard   202,466,570,646
Birkwood, Thomas   167,210
Bishop, Joseph   46,115
Bower, Anthony   201,645,741
Bower, John   6,41,80,212,272,342,403,417,475,506,641,674
Bradford, John   249,429,498,655
Bradley, Chrisopher Lonsdale   250,369,809
Bradley, James   128
Bradley, T.   494
Bradley, Thomas   1,41,42,57,155,187,198,264,322,391,
    486,491,678,694,695,763,809
Bradley, William   40,632
Brailsford, Samuel   130,246,307,489,664,742
Bramskel, Thomas   269
Brigham, Ralph   167
Broderick, Edward   59,344,716,728
Bromehead, Jonathan   218,535
Brooke, Charles   510
Brown, J.   192
Brown, John   210,753
Brown, Nicholas   61,76,132,208,259,342,461,480,516,683,
    708
Brown, William   40,50,167,210,288
Buckels, Robert   151
Buckley, John   215,501
Bulmer, James   171,226,277,324,364,389,501,542,627,692,
    750,762
Burgess, John   592
Burton, Ralph   184,242,283,528,552,688,718
Burton, William   701
Bushell, H.   137
Butler, John   622
Butler, Joseph   60,153,168,200,233,240,316,373,434,440,
    455,639,755,782,795,821
Buttle, Thomas   49,73,334,346,478,633,734,814
Byass, William   348
Calvert, -   500
Calvert, Alexander   29,55,56,141,163,176,301,320,321,
    343,381,391,415,451,490,529,693,715,749,760,772,777
Carlile, Robert   761
Carr, Francis   140,359,389,452
Carr, John   224,621,817
Carr, Thomas   257,632,771
Carter, John   696
Carter, Thomas   151
Chamberlain, Thomas   114,189
Chambers, Benjamin   116,327,411,591,682
Charlesworth, G.   461,516
Chippendale, Thomas   197,311,351
Chippendale, William   316,440
Clapham, John 566
Clapham, Richard   84,329,382,470,477,632,659
Clapham, Richard jun   172

Clapham, William 36,445
Clark, - 755
Clark, Richard 107,129,138,150,161,162,168,175,184,
    203,204,214,230,273,274,301,332,368,388,414,424,
    430,467,498,504,511,513,514,537,541,547,575,605,606,
    615,616,617,631,708,739,744,759,776,778,781,816,821
Clark, Richard jun 161,368,413,443
Clarkson, Anthony 519,529
Cleaver, Edward 26,52,131,149,253,268,295,385,422,433,
    508,523,528,622,677,696,704,771,815
Cleaver, John 4,11,100,252,377,384,385,523,559,639,
    640,666,697,702,703,765,782,785
Coates, George 16
Colbeck, J. 677
Colbeck, James 684
Colbeck, Joseph 30,34,136,167,209,651
Colbeck, Joseph sen 145
Collett, Cornelius 171,542
Conyers, John 89,167,210,224,227,548,663,703
Coomber, Thomas 805
Cooper, Charles 805
Cooper, James 257
Coopland, Thomas 660
Cordeaux, William 269
Cossins, William 621
Coulton, James 97
Coulton, Jeremiah 1
Coulton, Thomas 326
Crabtree, Richard 90
Crompton, William 597
Cross, Richard 8,65,92,102,239,263,740,821
Crossley, William 376
Crowder, John 75,275,575,676
Crowther, George 525
Cutts, Mordecai 330
Dalton, John 256,454,511,629,714,768,779,784,797
Danby, Francis 592
Danby, William 597
Danser, John 386
Darley, Richard 257
Dawson, John 465,577
Dawson, Miles 8,31,34,65,92,143,144,158,160,229,230,
    232,284,351,353A,365,420,439,463,467,499,504,508,
    513,539,545,577,590,639,680,704,708,719,786,792
Dawson, Robert 220,758
Dawson, Samuel Appleby 355
Dawson, William 18,26,37,38,39,71,75,92,102,138,
    161,165,230,241,267,276,284,304,308,323,342,
    349,354,368,372,403,410,413,424,437,447,448,463,
    466,482,483,499,506,513,540,545,555,552,589,
    609,625,635,643,644,656,676,687,698,708,714,
    741,744,818,820
Dealtry, John 548,568,572,691,704
Denison, Robert 592
Dickinson, Elihu 208,461

Dickinson, John 4,11,19,81,83,87,96,147,151,195,
   225,227,252,279,358,383,488,548,559,572,649,658,
   681,705,720,754,816
Dickinson, Joseph 4,43,87,93,102,131,149,161,188,196,
   242,254,278,281,283,290,313,372,373,379,386,
   396,422,430,457,469,471,479,483,495,506,511,
   543,545,608,610,611,645,653,669,670,679,688,
   713,743,761,784,797,802,808,820
Dickinson, Samuel 281,283,372,379,396,448,469,483,
   495,511,596,610,634,802
Dinsdale, George 40
Dinsley, Thomas 61,306,480,525,683,790
Dodsworth, John 27,28
Dodsworth, Thomas 458,531
Donkin, Edward 5
Donkin, Thomas 318
Downing, William 619
Dowthwaite, G. 321
Duck, George 759
Duffield, Peter 157
Dunn, James 233,371
Dunn, Robert 196,371,483,502,539,579,593,602,608,
   657,669,713,723,748,770
Dunnington, John 43,223,239,786
Durham, Makin 140,177,583
Dutton, John 759
Dyson, Thomas 136,154,267
Eamonson, William 160
Earnshaw, Leonard Brooks 287,318,527,542
Ebden, James 406
Eden, William 722
Elam, John 216
Elliott, Arthur 753,757
Ellershaw, Henry 84
Elliot(t), Arthur 134,247,327,423,615
Ellison, Henry 118
Ellison, Michael 570
Elstob, Edward 406
Eyre, Anthony 564
Fair, James 515
Fairbank, - 553
Fairbank, F. 317
Fairbank, J. 446
Fairbank, Josiah 46,333,801
Fairbank, W. 446,497
Fairbank, William 46,74,134,204,246,247,327,333,388,
   409,637,757,787
Fairbank, William jun 409,423
Farrer, John 132,661
Farthing, James 133
Featherstone, Ralph 548
Fillingham, William 584
Finley, Samuel 167
Fletcher, Ralph 215,613
Fletcher, Thomas 105,365,518

Flintoff, John 52,53,130,143,162,174,274,440,616,711,727
Flintoff, John jun 31
Foakes, John 283
Foord, J. 245
Foord, John 16,27,28,238,278,458,472,622,638,774
Foord, Joseph 16,266,299,303,521,785,805
Foord, Thomas 266
Foord, Timothy 137
Fordon, William 303,702
Forster, Edward 11,12,70,85,108,564,585,664
Forster, John 84
Foster, John 172,470,630
Foster, Richard 426
Foster, Robert 148,243,479
Fothergill, Alexander 40
Fothergill, William 97
Fournes, Francis 566
Fowler, Richard 421
Fox, John 67
Fox, Joseph 106
Frank, Richard 12,564
Fretwell, John 308
Furness, Thomas 440
Gainford, Francis 100,257
Garside, James 551
Garth, Francis 296,728
Garth, Richard 2,58,344,520
Garth, Richard jun 344,560
Gawthorp(e), Samuel 298,635,636,759
Gee, - 356
Gee, Thomas 24,51,61,124,135,157,217,259,289,364,378,
   397,446,533,557,563,581,615,624,652,675,683,
   686,731,735,736,759,767,787,794,811
Giles, J.C. 9
Gill, Ingram 50,139,297,459,783
Gore, Spencer 588
Goss, Thomas 84
Gotherlesse, John 326
Goulton, Thomas 406
Gouthwaite, Richard 462,474
Graham, Reginald 597
Graves, John 4,102,168,200,233,243,268,285,347,514,523,
   540,639,696,707,710,717,755,795,821
Gray, Ambrose 174,284,476,577,591,682
Gray, Benjamin 310
Gray, Edmund 692
Greaves, Charles 582
Greenwood, John 109,173,353,382,484
Haigh, Francis 543,669
Haignton, Richard 144
Hall, Francis 806
Hall, John 20,90,119,171,212,244,253,256,261,281,
   283,309,372,396,416,448,457,469,483,495,511,542,
   565,569,596,610,611,630,634,669,673,688,713,714,724,
   741,768,778,779,802

Hall, Joseph   501
Hall, William   239,255,263,268,361,457,471,489,539,
   571,608,669,707,713,741,761
Halliday, Thomas   41
Hamer, Samuel Hallows   758
Harding, William   303
Hardy, John   74
Hargreaves, James   189
Harper, William   319,355
Harrison, John   468,729
Harrison, Robert   257
Harrison, Thomas   189
Hartley, John   235,236
Hawkshead, Thomas   84,362
Hawkyard, Joel   613
Hay, John   517
Hayes, George   540
Haynes, Mark, jun   16
Hayward, George   350,774
Hayward, Richard Francis   335
Haywood, J.   342,646
Haywood, Joseph   71,437
Head, William   783
Headlam, Charles   257
Heaton, Joseph   641
Hebb, Edward   622
Hebden, George   384,402,638
Hebdin, James   401,680
Heelis, John   659
Hellard, Samuel   89
Hesslegrave, Joseph   613
Hildyard, William   539,602
Hill, William   7,31,60,74,121,218,246,295,308,386,420,
   512,535,573,607,639,680,719
Hindle, J.   747
Hirst, Joshua   689
Hobson, William   411
Hodgson, Marmaduke   99,660
Holdstock, Leonard   780
Holgate, Edward   128,568,649,705
Holgate, George   386
Holmes, Richard   633
Holt, Henry   339
Horsley, William   405
Hotham, John   817
Housman, John   570
How, Peter   764
Howgate, John   509,628
Howlett, Henry   228
Hoyle, Nathan   358
Hudson, Thomas   13,27,28,266,299
Hudson, William   326

Humphrey(s), Thomas 288,297
Humphries, - 500
Humphries, John 23,29,98,234,237,253,271,272,292,294,
    300,312,349,354,403,447,481,494,526,532,598,626,650,
    654,692,745,777,818
Hunter, Joseph 282
Hunter, Robert 804
Hutchcroft, Henry 442
Hutchinson, Thomas 405,465
Hutton, John 597
Ingham, Joshua 436
Ingle, John Benjamin 21,248
Ingleby, Sir John 597
Ingleby/Ingilby, Thomas 13,197,311,380,445,478,732
Ingman, George 450
Ingram, William Perrott 583
Ireland, John 561
Iveson, Robert 542
Iveson, William 151,240,705,771
Jackson, Benjamin Whitewood 367
Jackson, George 45,82,183,284,288,305,317,361,404,
    465,535,612,783
Jackson, John 182
Jackson, Peter 90,261,379,396,543
Jackson, Thomas 817
Jagger, Joseph 180,456,546
Jewitt, Joseph 386
Johnson, Edward 128,148,195,252,361,455
Johnson, John 175,501
Johnson, Peter 648
Jones, Frederick 306
Jones, Frederick Robert 501,637,809
Jopson, William 297
Jowett, Nathan 376,411,590,722
Judson, Thomas 742
Kay, John 105,121,535,607
Keighley, James 386
Keighly, Robert 412
Keld, Christopher 645
Kelk, George 34,104,105,218,275,518
Kelk, William 34,518
Kendall, John 25,285,531,648
Kent, John 134,247,456,757
(King, Margaret) see 3,20
King, Robert 231,458,472,531,571,776
King, Thomas Firbank 3
Kirby, John 750
Kirkby, Henson 7,45,48,104,121,125,450,573,584,604,742
Knowles, Stephen 632
Knowsley, Robert 402
Lambe, William 199
Lamplugh, William 83,85
Lane, Robert 114
Lang, Robert 84,566
Langdale, Thomas 592

Law, John   7
Lawson, Marmaduke   257,585,690,788
Lay, William   492
Lazenby, Richard   326
Lazenby, Thomas   67,225,559,649
Leach, Thomas   722
Leafe, -   500
Leake, William   330
Leatham, Isaac   25,249,273,278,281,422,443,495,496,
   513,615,634,651,688,707,768,776,781,784
Lee, John   171,256,379,506,569,611,673
Levitt, John   670,761
List, William   406
Lister, G.T.   21
Lister, Samuel   83
Lister, William   101,621
Lockwood, John   256
Lockwood, William   417
Lodge, Ralph   142,340,352,419,484
Lorrimar, Edward   602
Loxley, Thomas   220,758
Lumb, Robert   807
Lund, John   83,151,229,316,347,373,377,385,393,502,
   523,536,559,640,658,697,705,770
Lund, John sen   43
Lund, John jun   43,150,275,467,518,540,719
Lyth, Robert   458,531
Macdonald, Eneas   117
Macvicar, John Young   315
Marsden, William   337,497,604,806
Marsh, George   30
Marshall, Callisthenes   803
Martin, Samuel Dickinson   159,177,222
Mason, Richard   166,291
Mason, William   405
Mawe, James   592
Merry, Peter   231,430,552,648,668
Merry, William   292,780
Micklethwaite, Benjamin   810
Midgeley, Thomas   329,558
Milbank, John   597
Milbourn, Isaac   104,153,158,227,295,365,393,524,536,544,
   552,593,665,782,815
Milbourn, Samuel   100,137,139,144,280,291,295,420,425,
   489,544,571,572,593,638,642,663,690,697,723,741,788,
   803,805,815
Mills, Robert William Fenwick   127,359
Milner, James   208
Milner, Thomas   464
Mitchell, Benjamin   150,631
Mitchell, Thomas   100,137,207
Moiser, John   310,379,543
Moore, John   84
Moore, Robert   157,289,717
Moorsom, Constantine Richard   192,206

Mortimer, Timothy 353A
Morton, John 526
Mosey, William 457
Mould, Thomas 78,129,184,223,322,386,586
Mowbray, Arthur 441,761
Mowbray, John 498,718
Moyer, John 597
Musgrave, Thomas 140,177,673
Neck, Samuel 89
Nevill, Peter 47,65,81,83,96,113,131,133,148,151,
    188,195,196,225,240,243,254,263,279,285,313,336,
    361,371,373,383,385,396,404,420,469,471,499,522,
    524,562,568,579,596,602,608,614,645,657,658,670,
    679,681,705,720,740,743,748,761,770,779
Newman, Thomas 37
Newsam, Thomas 812
Newton, William 460,538
Nicholson, Thomas 764
Nicholson, William George 549,639,690,691
Norsdale, Edward 729
North, Richard 89,167,224,280,559,562,672,699,769
Norton, Fletcher 597
Norton, Gabatis 597
Oates, Edward 30,45,70,117,125,450,497,535
Oldham, Hugh 722
Osbaldeston, Richard 401
Osborne, Robert 379,802
Outram, Benjamin 448,665
Outram, John 8,19,25,43,60,65,67,81,83,87,92,96,102,
    113,128,130,131,133,143,148,149,153,195,225,229,240,
    245,252,255,279,307,313,316,336,347,383,385,393,404,
    479,488,499,502,508,512,522,524,536,545,549,579,608,
    614,639,640,645,649,658,665,666,702,705,710,727,740,
    748,754,755,770,785,786,803
Outram, Joseph 134,247,327,333,423,739,757
Overend, Peter Wilson 35
Oxtoby, Thomas 764
Page, Edward 68,126,171,190,261,314,318,426,673
Page, Gregory 318,487
Page, Richard 290,309
Palliser, Thomas 775
Parke, Alexander 210
Parke, Timothy 449,571,724,776
Parker, John 584
Parkinson, Richard 209
Pashley, George 117,220
Patchett, Benjamin 180,376,546
Paver, Christopher 10,146,177,185,267,304,359,474,620
Paver, William 177,700,747,752
Pearson, George 750
Peirson, George 17,182
Peirson, Matthew 16
Peirson, William 89
Pibus, John 804
Pickering, Christopher 82,727

Pilkington, William 6,95,140,152,157,212,306,342,357,
    428,507,561,567,599,624,628,641,674,686,725,789,790
Pinkney, George 207
Plaxton, John 257
Plummer, George 717
Pocklington, Roger 200
Porter, William 80,501
Potter, James 600
Powell, James 88,205,800
Preston, John 13,380,477,478
Preston, John sen 734
Preston, John jun 734
Preston, William 328,477
Pursglove, Joseph 48,70,517,604,742
Pursglove, Joseph sen 719
Raines, Henry 479,681
Raines, John 11,19,47,81,87,128,133,149,188,225,233,
    279,280,307,373,404,420,455,499,524,568,579,614,
    658,699,740,754,769
Raper, Thomas 729
Rawson, Thomas William 21,248
Rawson, William 287,542,797
Rawsthorne, William 353
Rayner, William 501
Raynes, Francis 135,157,158,185,201,294,684,787
Read, John 664
Reed, Anthony 110
Renshaw, John 105,246,759
Renshaw, Joseph 105
Reynard, William 35,99,660
Rhodes, Gregory 597
Richardson, Richard 82,122,144,316,317,440,465,
    521,573,591
Richardson, William 25,182,287,663,750
Roberts, William 480
Robinson, Joseph 203
Robinson, Thomas 137,619,805
Rodgers, Robert 154
Rodgers, William 209,327,333,553,753
Rodham, John 459,589,647
Roebuck, John Sybury 125
Rogers, William 401
Rutherford, James 32
Sands, Francis 429,619
Sands, William 99
Scarth, Isaac 750
Scarth, Richard 231,668
Scholefield, James 686
Scott, Henry 194,287,315,318,527,712
Scott, Thomas 23,68,90,237,287,389,400,582,623
Scott, Thomas jun 68
Seaton, Daniel 184,205
Sedgwick, John 739
Sharp, John 75,138,390,424,460,510,590,605,689,759
Sharpe, John 180,241,323,376,411,546,698,706

Shaw, Joseph 613
Shepherd, James 405
Sherwood, Robert 471
Shipton, William 18,22,71,119,129,145,157,161,178,
  290,332,368,370,396,413,438,443,456,467,482,
  541,576,674,807
Simpson, George Dyson 118,186,219
Simpson, Richard 571
Simpson, Thomas 464
Simpson, William 12,45,70,85,108,337,585,664,669
Singleton, John 290,360,569
Sisson, William 146
Skilbeck, John 257
Smeaton, John 220
Smith, Alfred 709,774
Smith, Edmund 588,729
Smith, John 566
Smith, Joseph 9,14,79,444,550,793
Smith, Joseph jun 408
Smith, Michael 182,750
Smith, Robert 314,485,583
Smith, Thomas 45,48,337,604,742,758
Smith, William 228,358
Smithson, Robert 167
Smyth, John 83
Sotheron, William 664
Spence, Michael 40
Spencer, John 30,806,810
Spofforth, Robert 543
Squire, John 189,612
Staines, Mark jun. 27,28
Stamper, Robert 228
Staplyton, Sir Miles 597
Staveley, Isaac 426
Stickney, Richard Allen 314
Stickney, Robert 374,416,483,565,611,634,713,784
Stickney, William 314,542,594
Stockdale, Robert 744
Storr, Richard 137
Stott, Elias 510
Stovin, Cornelius 385
Stovin, James 373
Strafford, George Henry 286,366
Strickland, Arthur 20
Stringer, George 282
Strutt, James 455
Sunderland, John 436
Sutcliffe, John 436
Swales, S.J. 519
Swire, Samuel 29
Swire, Samuel jun 701
Sykes, John 510
Talbot, William 109
Tate, Charles 96,128,131,151,195,233,243,252,455,502,
  522,536,562,579,649,720

Tate, Charles sen 754
Tate, David 252,614,803
Taylor, E. 446
Taylor, Jonathan 37,61,120,122,169,251,350,407,410,503,
    578,721,774
Taylor, Joseph 501
Taylor, Robert 371
Taylor, Robert jun 371
Teal, Henry 6,132,152,177,203,277,304,407,427,480,
    580,606,725
Teal, J. 189,574
Teal, Jonathan 6,78,98,120,164,201,202,203,208,230,241,
    323,399,407,414,427,431,461,480,538,575,580,606,619,625,
    646,652,657,687,706,759,796,808
Telford, John 729
Telford, Robert 598
Tennant, John 328
Thackray, Joseph 202,327
Thompson, Joseph 132,280,488,536,562,672,699,720,769
Thornton, Thomas 594
Thornton, William 338,340
Tilburn, Richard 437
Tofield, Thomas 104,220,308,512,665
Tomlinson, William 257
Tootell, Hugh 183
Townsend, George 517
Travis, George 504
Tuke, Daniel 38,119,226,270,364,391,482,555,730,778
Tuke, John 23,39,129,237,249,324,391,396,433,482,496,
    541,555,587,643,692,766
Tuke, Jonathan 39
Turner, Charles H. 605
Turner, Samuel 30,651
Vessey, Samuel 126,315
Waddington, Henry 35,40,50,160,172,311,329,331,362,445,
    470,612,632,732
Waddington, Robert 478
Walker, George 30,108,604,810
Walker, Thomas 133
Waller, Bryan 380
Walton, William 802
Ward, Robert 406
Ware, W.J. 756
Ware, William 261,314,627,762
Warner, Richard 330
Wastling, Timothy 621
Watford, Alexander 310
Watkinson, John 563
Watkinson, Thomas 189,659
Watson, Christopher 82
Watson, Thomas 405
Watterson, Edward 65,113,274,449,545,547,648,665
Wayte, Thomas 804
Webster, Crayston 112,302,341
Webster, Leonard 497

Weddall, John George 44,66,103,487
Weddall, Robert Plummer 90,244,778
Wells, Dymoke 623,668
Wentworth, Godfrey 108
West, James 269,817
Wharton, Anthony 220
Whitaker, John 220
Whitaker, Joseph 69,86,136
Whitelock, William 15,24,33,71,75,95,107,169,209,211,
    217,242,273,332,356,390,414,424,438,454,460,469,504,
    533,557,578,596,615,651,675,676,724,759,768,
    781,784,793,807
Whitle, Joseph 355
Whyman, Thomas 305
Wilkinson, Andrew 597
Wilkinson, Christopher 295,710
Wilkinson, Henry 30,108
Wilkinson, William 422
Williamson, William 280
Willmott, William 245,531,593,622,723,815
Wilson, Matthew 331
Wilson, Thomas 416,565
Wilson, William 348
Winder, John 228
Wings, John 278
Wise, Robert 601
Withers, William 379
Wood, John 188,196,263,278,361,374,457,545,586,657,
    670,679,761,779,808
Wood, John sen 743
Wood, John jun 188,196,457,743
Wood, William 468
Worsop, Richard 664
Wrathall, Henry 197,732
Wrather, William 468
Wright, Elias 813
Wright, Francis 101,269,621
Wright, James 30,108,497
Wrightson, W. 222
Wyse, Robert 819
Yarborough, Henry 257
Yarburgh, Thomas 664
Yorke, John 331
Young, Joseph 61,684
Yeward, Richard 817

A SELECTIVE BIBLIOGRAPHY OF YORKSHIRE ENCLOSURES

By Jan Crowther

I am grateful to Professor M.W. Beresford, Dr A. Harris and Professor B. Jennings for a number of references. The responsibility of selection remains of course my own. It is difficult to draw a distinction between works on enclosure and those on field systems before enclosure. In general the latter have been excluded but one or two works which seem to overlap are included in the list. General studies of individual parishes have not been included, despite the fact that they often contain sections on enclosure. Had they been listed the bibliography would have been far too lengthy. For those parts of Yorkshire covered by the Victoria County History volumes useful information on the enclosure of individual parishes can be found in the Economic History sections.

ANON. 'Allotments and awards under the Garforth enclosure act', Publications of the Thoresby Society, v.37, 1945 (=Thoresby Miscellany, v.11), pp.105-31.

ANON. 'Manor records: Saddleworth inclosure', Bulletin of the Saddleworth Historical Society, v.9, pts 1 and 2, 1979, pp.12-15 and 33-9.

ADDY, J. The agrarian revolution. London, 1972. - Chapters 3 and 5 include Yorkshire material.

AGERSKOW, M. 'The reclamation of waste in the Forest of Knaresborough: a study in settlement and enclosure'. M.A. thesis, University of Leeds, 1958.

ALLERSTON, P. 'Field and village in the Pickering district of North Yorkshire'. M.Sc. thesis, University of London, 1966.

ALLISON, K.J. 'Enclosure by agreement at Healaugh (W.R.)', Yorkshire Archaeological Journal, v.40, 1961, pp.382-91.

ALLISON, K.J. The making of the English landscape : East Riding of Yorkshire. London, 1976 - Especially Chapters 6-8.

BERESFORD, M.W. 'Glebe terriers and open-field Yorkshire', Yorkshire Archaeological Journal, v.37, 1950, pp.325-68. - Traces the history of enclosure through glebe terriers.

BERESFORD, M.W. 'Habitation versus improvement: the debate on enclosure by agreement', in Fisher, F.J., ed. Essays in the economic and social history of Tudor and Stuart England in honour of R.H. Tawney, Cambridge, 1961, pp.40-69.

BROWN, R. General view of the agriculture of the West Riding of Yorkshire.... London, 1799.

CHAPMAN, J. 'Changing agriculture and the moorland edge in the North York Moors, 1750 to 1960'. M.A. thesis, University of London, 1961.

CHAPMAN, J. 'Parliamentary enclosure in the uplands: the case of the North York Moors', Agricultural History Review, v.24, 1976, pp.1-17.

CHURLEY, P.A. 'The Yorkshire crop returns of 1801', Yorkshire Bulletin of Economic and Social Research, v.5, 1953, pp.179-97.

COWLING, G.C. The history of Easingwold and the Forest of Galtres. Huddersfield, 1968.

CROSSLEY, J.C. 'On the rural landscape of Middle Wharfedale'. M.A. thesis, University of Sheffield, 1955.

CROWTHER, J.E. 'Parliamentary enclosure in eastern Yorkshire, 1725-1860'. Ph.D. thesis, University of Hull, 1984.

DENT, J.G. 'Mechanics and effects of the parliamentary enclosure of common grazings: an example from north-west Yorkshire', Folk Life, v.21, 1983, pp.83-99.

DODD, E.E. 'Bingley enclosures', Bradford Antiquary, new series, v.7, pt.35, 1950, pp.293-302.

DODD, E.E. 'Two Bingley postscripts', Bradford Antiquary, new series, v.8, pt.39, 1958, pp.194-6.

ENGLISH, B.A. Handlist of West Riding enclosure awards. Leeds, 1965.

FIELDHOUSE, R.T. 'Agriculture in Wensleydale from 1600 to the present day', Northern History, v.16, 1980, pp.169-95.

FIELDHOUSE, R.T. and JENNINGS, B. A history of Richmond and Swaledale. Chichester, 1978. - Chapters 6,7 and 15.

FIELDHOUSE, R.T. 'Some evidence of surviving open fields in the seventeenth-century Pennine Dales, and the gradual elimination of communal agriculture', Yorkshire Archaeological Journal, v.54, 1982, pp.111-18.

FUSSELL, G.E. *Farming systems from Elizabethan to Victorian days in the North and East Ridings of Yorkshire.* York, 1946.

GLEAVE, M.B. 'Dispersed and nucleated settlements in the Yorkshire Wolds', *Transactions of the Institute of British Geographers*, v.30, 1962, pp.105-18. Reprinted in Mills, D.R., ed. *English rural communities: the impact of a specialised economy.* London 1973.

GLEAVE, M.B. 'The settlement pattern of the Yorkshire Wolds, 1770-1850'. M.A. thesis, University of Hull, 1960.

HAMMOND, B. 'Two towns' enclosures', *Economic History*, v.2, no.6, 1931, pp.258-66. - Sheffield and Lambeth.

HARRIS, A. 'The agriculture of the East Riding of Yorkshire before the parliamentary enclosures', *Yorkshire Archaeological Journal*, v.40, 1959, pp.119-28.

HARRIS, A. *The rural landscape of the East Riding of Yorkshire, 1700-1850: a study in historical geography.* Oxford, 1961, 2nd edition, Wakefield, 1969.

HARVEY, J.C. 'Common field land and enclosure in the Lower Dearne Valley: a case study', *Yorkshire Archaeological Journal*, v.46, 1974, pp.110-27

HASTINGS, R.P. *Rudby-in-Cleveland: the enclosed landscape, c.1600-1914.* Rudby, 1980.

HODGSON, R.I. 'Some aspects of enclosure in northern Ryedale, Yorkshire', *Journal of Durham University Geographical Society*, v.9, 1967, pp.56-74.

HOLLAND, D. *Changing landscapes in South Yorkshire.* Doncaster, 1980.

JENNINGS, B. ed. *A history of Harrogate and Knaresborough.* Huddersfield, 1970. - Chapters III(e), VI(b), XI, XIII(e).

JENNINGS, B. ed. *A history of Nidderdale.* 1st ed., Huddersfield, 1967; 2nd ed., York 1983. - Chapters Va, VI, VII and XIII.

KING, H. and HARRIS, A. eds. *A survey of the manor of Settrington.* Leeds, 1962. - Yorkshire Archaeological Society. Record series, v.126.

KIRK, M. 'Parliamentary enclosure in Bulmer wapentake'. M.A. thesis, University of Leeds, 1948.

KIRK, M. 'The Vale of York: the evolution of a landscape', *Geography*, v.40, 1955, pp.228-36.

LEATHAM, I. *General view of the agriculture of the East Riding....* London, 1794.

LONG, W.H. 'Some notes on the size of fields after enclosure', *Yorkshire Archaeological Journal*, v.54, 1982, pp.141-7.

LOUGHBROUGH, B. 'An account of a Yorkshire enclosure: Staxton, 1803', *Agricultural History Review*, v.13, 1965, pp.105-16.

LOUGHBROUGH, B. 'Some geographical aspects of the enclosure of the Vale of Pickering in the eighteenth and nineteenth centuries'. M.A. thesis, University of Hull, 1960.

MACMAHON, K.A. ed. *Acts of Parliament ... relating to the East Riding and Kingston upon Hull. 1529-1800.* Hull, 1961. - The majority of those for the eighteenth century are enclosure acts.

MARSHALL, W. *The rural economy of Yorkshire....* London, 1788. 2nd ed., London, 1796.

NEAVE, V. *A handlist of East Riding enclosure awards.* Beverley, 1971.

NEWMAN, P.R. 'Absentee landlords and the enclosure of the open fields: Hessay in the Ainsty of York', *York Historian*, v.3, 1980, pp.32-8.

NEWMAN, P.R. 'The Hessay enclosure of 1831: a study in the economic and social history of an Ainsty township in the nineteenth century', *Journal of the North Yorkshire County Record Office*, v.9, 1982, pp.89-165.

NEWMAN, P.R. *Moor Monkton and its people, 1600-1916: aspects of the social and economic history of a township in the Ainsty of York.* Moor Monkton, 1983.

PAULUS, C. *Unpublished pages relating to the manor and parish of Eccleshall, including the enclosure of the common and waste lands there.* Sheffield, 1927.

PETFORD, A.J. 'Documents relating to the Saddleworth enclosure act of 1810', *Bulletin of the Saddleworth Historical Society*, v.10, no.4, 1980, pp.68-77.

RAISTRICK, A. *The making of the English landscape: West Riding of Yorkshire.* London, 1970 - Especially Chapter 3.

RAISTRICK, A. 'Village effort 100 years ago', *Yorkshire Dalesman*, v.6, no.1, 1944, pp.5-8. - Long Preston enclosure.

REES, R.A. 'Aspects of social and economic change in the parish of Selby, North Yorkshire, 1752-1851'. M.Phil. thesis, University of Leeds, 1978.

RENNIE, G. *General view of the agriculture of the West Riding of Yorkshire* .... London, 1794.

RODGERS, W.S. 'Distribution of parliamentary enclosure in the West Riding'. M.Comm. thesis, University of Leeds, 1953.

RODGERS, W.S. 'West Riding commissioners of enclosure, 1729 - 1850', *Yorkshire Archaeological Journal*, v.40, 1962, pp.401-19.

RUSHTON, J.H. 'Landscape history at Brompton by Sawdon', *Transactions of the Scarborough and District Archaeological Society*, v.1, no.6, 1963, pp.24-5.

RUSTON, A.G. and WITNEY, D. *Hooton Pagnell: the agricultural evolution of a Yorkshire village*. London, 1934.

SHEPPARD, J.A. 'Field systems of Yorkshire', in: Baker, A.R.H. and Butlin, R.A. eds. *Studies of field systems in the British Isles*, Cambridge, 1973, chapter 4, pp.145-87.

SHEPPARD, J.A. 'Pre-enclosure field and settlement patterns in an English township: Wheldrake, near York', *Geografiska Annaler*, v.48B, no.2, 1966, pp.59-77.

SINGLETON, F. *Industrial revolution in Yorkshire*. Clapham, 1970 - Chapter 5.

STAMP, L. Dudley and HOSKINS, W.G. *The common lands of England and Wales*. London, 1963. - Contains a list of unenclosed commons, pp.337-50.

STRICKLAND, H.E. *General view of the agriculture of the East Riding of Yorkshire.* York, 1812.

TATE, W.E. *A domesday of English enclosure acts and awards*, edited and with an introduction by M.E. Turner. Reading, 1978. - See Yorkshire sections.

TUCKER, D.N. 'Linear parishes and farm structures in the Vale of Pickering', *Geography*, v.57, 1972, pp.105-19.

TUKE, J. *General view of the agriculture of the North Riding of Yorkshire*. 1st ed., London, 1794. 2nd ed., London, 1800.

WILKINSON, O. *The agricultural revolution in the East Riding of Yorkshire*. York, 1956. - East Yorkshire Local History Society. East Yorkshire local history series, no.5.

YELLING, J.A. *Common field and enclosure in England, 1450-1850.* London, 1977. - Includes a section on Wolds enclosures.

ADDENDA

Number in main list	Place	Dates Act : Award
132	BRIESTFIELD (WR-WY) Kirklees RO plan (1816) and valuation	1816 : 1849
195	COTTINGHAM (ER-H) Hull City RO copy award and tracing of plan	1766 : 1771
196	COTTINGHAM (ER-H) Hull City RO modern copy plan, no award	1791 : 1793
217	DEWSBURY (WR-WY) Kirklees RO, plan (1804, surveyor Jonathan Taylor) ; also microfilm of enclosure papers from originals at Dewsbury Library; other papers at Messrs Watts and Son, solicitors, Dewsbury	1803 : 1806
224	DRIFFIELD (ER-H) Hull City RO tracing of plan	1741 : 1742
254	ELLOUGHTON etc. (ER-H) Hull City RO tracing of plan of Wauldby only	1802 : 1810
374	HOLMPTON (ER-H) Hull City RO copy plan	1800 : 1807
416	KEYINGHAM (ER-H) Hull City RO copy plan	1802 : 1805
460	LINDLEY (WR-WY) Kirklees RO plan from Tolson Museum and copy award	1798 : 1798
469	LITTLE WEIGHTON (ER-H) Hull City RO tracing of plan	1801 : 1804
502	MELTON (ER-H) Hull City RO copy plan	1771 : 1773
525	NETHERTHONG (WR-WY) Kirklees RO commissioners' minutes and two plans (c.1826, land enclosed, other details)	1826 : 1829
568	PATRINGTON (ER-H) Hull City RO copy plan	1766 : 1768
579	PRESTON (ER-H) Hull City RO copy plan	1773 : 1777

596	RIPLINGHAM (ER-H) Hull City RO tracing of plan	1801 : 1803
611	RYHILL AND CAMERTON (ER-H) Hull City RO tracing of plan	1805 : 1810
614	SANCTON (ER-H) Hull City RO tracing of plan	1769 : 1771
636	SHELLEY (WR-WY) Kirklees RO additional plan (c.1807) with extra details	1803 : 1826
652	SKELMANTHORPE (WR-WY) Kirklees RO sealed original award and plan from Denby Dale UDC	1800 : 1802
665	SNAITH AND COWICK (WR-H) Doncaster RO plan	1773 : 1781
779	WEST ELLA etc. (ER-H) Hull City RO draft award and tracing of plan	1796 : 1799
790	WHITLEY (WR-WY) Kirklees RO additional plan with wider area	1821 : 1826